People, Places & Peabod

People, Places & Peabod

A Collection of Travel Stories

R.P. Taylor

Writers Club Press
San Jose New York Lincoln Shanghai

People, Places & Peabod
A Collection of Travel Stories

Writers Club Press
an imprint of iUniverse.com, Inc.

For information address:
iUniverse.com, Inc.
5220 S 16th, Ste. 200
Lincoln, NE 68512
www.iuniverse.com

ISBN: 0-595-18289-5

Printed in the United States of America

TO PRINCESS

who fills my days with sunshine,
and makes my travels through life the ultimate journey

CONTENTS

PREFACE

PEABOD'S TOP TEN QUOTES TO TRAVEL BY

DANIEL BOORSTIN:

"A traveler goes in search of people, of adventure, of experience. A tourist goes for sightseeing. Just like the question is more interesting than a statement, and a road more intriguing than a map, I aspired to be a traveler. Be brave. Go through open gates."

PAUL THEROUX:

"It is rare for two people to see the same qualities in a place."

C. S. LEWIS:

"One who has journeyed to a strange land, cannot return unchanged."

SIR FRANCIS BACON:

"When a traveler returneth home, let him not leave the countries where he hath traveled altogether behind him."

OSCAR WILDE:

"The true mystery of the world is the visible, not the invisible."

LAWRENCE DURRELL:

"Let the tourist be cushioned against misadventures; your true traveler will not feel that he has had his money's worth unless he brings back a few scars."

RUDYARD KIPLING:

"All things considered, there are two kinds of men in the world—those that stay at home and those that do not. The second are the most interesting."

TOAST BY ROBERT KINCAID

PLAYED BY CLINT EASTWOOD IN

THE BRIDGES OF MADISON COUNTY

"To ancient dreams and distant music."

PAUL THEROUX:

"All places, no matter where, no matter what, are worth visiting. But seldom-visited places where people were still living settled traditional lives seemed to me the most worthwhile, because they were the most coherent."

CHARLES KURALT:

"The reality of any place is what people remember of it."

THE SWAN AT LAVENHAM

When Beth Jacobsen hung up the phone she was floating on air. For more than six months, in her capacity as the first full-time travel editor of the *Winston-Salem Journal*, she had been contacting tourist boards and public relations people from every discipline of the hospitality industry with little or no success. She had written or telephoned just about every cruise line, airline, tour operator, incentive house, destination management company and anyone else she could think of in the business. Now, at last, the effort was paying off, and the result was beyond her wildest expectations.

The conversation began innocently enough. "Beth, this is Ian Lampley with British Airways. Do you have a moment?"

"Of course," she replied. Beth was thrilled to be talking with someone in the industry after so many queries, but she was not yet certain as to why Lampley had called her.

"I have a little press trip to England coming up in the next couple of weeks, and I was wondering if you'd like to join us."

Beth couldn't contain her excitement at her first official invitation to participate in a formal press junket. She knew, of course, that she had to be cautious in her acceptance, contingent upon having it cleared by management, but she didn't anticipate any difficulty. After all, she was the travel editor, and that's what travel editors do. They travel. "I'd love to go along, but I can't give you a firm commitment until I check with my supervisor. Can I get back with you tomorrow or the next day?"

"No problem. There's still some time before we go, but please let me know within a couple of days because our space is limited, and I need to find a replacement if you're not available?"

"Can you give me some details?" asked Beth. "Just so I'll have all the information and ammunition I need when I talk to the boss."

"Sure. We'll be visiting East Anglia," Lampley answered.

"East Anglia! Wow, that sounds great!" responded Beth enthusiastically, though, truthfully, she had never heard of the place.

Lampley continued, "It'll be a small group. Just four others and myself. I'll reserve a van for us in London and we'll take off through the country-side, if you can tolerate my driving. We'll stop in Cambridge and Norwich and a few other small villages in the region. Then we'll pop back to London for about a day and a half before we return home. Does that sound like something you'd be interested in?"

Did it ever! Beth was familiar with Cambridge, and she vaguely recalled reading something about Norwich, though she didn't know anything about it. Most of all, she was pleased by the fact that there would also be some time in London since she had never been there either.

The truth was, Beth had never really been anywhere. She had only traveled out of the country on one previous occasion. That was a trip to Spain with about 250 other people during a bank promotion when she was just out of college. It was a marketing gimmick by the bank to provide young graduates with special services in an effort to change their stuffy image and attract a more youthful clientele. The project was a tremendous success, and in the process Beth had become one of the organization's charter members, which ultimately resulted in a trip to the Costa del Sol in Spain.

Despite numerous logistical problems during that first international travel experience, the journey had unleashed an overwhelming wanderlust spirit within Beth that she never knew existed. The concept of totally immersing herself into a completely different culture had thoroughly captivated her. Adjusting to the language, the customs, the cuisine and the living history and traditions of another country provided a sense of place for her that she had never realized about her personality. By the end of the trip, she found herself spending most afternoons in Spain doing little more than sitting idly at tiny sidewalk cafes, observing the tableau of life that spread out before her, watching the fishing boats arrive from their marathon days at sea and drinking the local beer. Until that time in her life, Beth had never acquired much of a taste for beer, but the practice quickly became a daily ritual as a refreshing substitute for Spain's unpotable drinking water.

There had been a peacefulness watching those weather-beaten little boats. How many generations of fishermen had each family produced, Beth wondered. In their own way, they became a link to centuries past for her. These were uncomplicated people who appeared content with the ever-present rhythms of their daily lives. For most of them, the scope of their knowledge of the world probably didn't extend much beyond the next village, yet there was no outward sign that there was a need or urgency to know more than that. In some ways Beth felt sad that their boundaries were so limited, but she also took solace in the fact that there were still places in the world where man and nature were so intimately intertwined, and where so little had changed for hundreds of years.

The experience in Spain was the singular defining moment that led Beth to pursue a career in travel writing. It had filled a void in her soul and created an insatiable desire to explore the far corners of the earth and to tell others about her journeys. From the beginning she knew it was an idealistic undertaking. She also knew that most of her friends and relatives wouldn't take her seriously. After all, travel writing wasn't "real work". But for Beth it was. To her it was the equivalent of a paid education, as if she was now able to personally absorb the world through her pores and make it part of her. It had bred tolerance for other points of view within her. It had created understanding and awareness. It had opened her eyes to history and legend, fact and fiction, literature and music and art, and it had given her insights into nationalistic pride and the origins of words and languages that she would otherwise never have discovered.

Her big break came with the inauguration of nonstop international air service to London out of Charlotte, which was about 80 miles down the interstate. That's when the *Journal* decided to expand its lifestyle section by actively seeking a travel editor. Beth applied for the job thinking that her lack of travel experience didn't give her a realistic chance at the position. As it turned out, it was that limited background that resulted in her being hired for the job. That, and the fact that the paper could employ her at a lower salary than a veteran writer.

The way the paper viewed the travel editor's position was that someone with great desire, and little knowledge, would likely bring a fresh perspective to the challenges of the job. Most probably, they would also relate more closely to their demographics than a writer who had already been everywhere and done everything. Suddenly the world was becoming both larger and smaller at the same time. Larger because it was now an unlimited source of exploration, and smaller because each day that world was getting increasingly more accessible. Suddenly the paper had a motivation to discover that world. Suddenly Beth was being given the opportunity to become a foreign correspondent. And suddenly her dream had become an overnight reality.

Until Ian Lampley called, most of Beth's stories had been regional articles about places within a 100-mile radius of Winston-Salem. As time went on, her reporting had occasionally broadened to include some more eclectic and exotic pieces highlighting interesting people, as well as places. Now and then she had even been able to develop an article or two with a national emphasis. Best of all, since there was no precedent for anything she produced, Beth had almost total creativity in determining what to include in her section. It wasn't like writing for a paper in New York or Los Angeles, or even Atlanta, where every destination on the planet had been revisited dozens of times. No, for Beth this was one grand and glorious experiment to bring something new and vibrant about the world to her readers, and to allow them to explore that world through her eyes.

Ian continued with his background information. "If you can join us, we'll take the first Concorde flight out of Kennedy and..."

"Concorde?" interrupted Beth in a stunned voice. She pulled the phone away from her ear trying desperately to catch her breath, hoping not to sound unprofessional or inexperienced as she quickly tried to regain her composure. "Did I misunderstand or did you say the Concorde?"

"That's right. Why is anything wrong?" Lampley asked.

Upon hearing Ian's clarification, Beth's attempts at containing her excitement now failed miserably. "Oh no. I just didn't expect to be flying to England on the Concorde! I mean with all due respect, this East Anglia place sounds charming and wonderful and all, and I've always wanted to see London, but to go there on the Concorde, wow! I could do a story just on the flight alone."

"My company would appreciate that very much. That's why we invited you. All the better for British Airways," came an amused voice at the other end of the line. The conversation continued for several more minutes before Beth hung up. She was going to Great Britain come hell or high water. There was absolutely no doubt in her mind now. Approved or not, she was going to find a way to go to East Anglia. This was a once in a lifetime opportunity that was not to be missed. Beth Jacobsen, travel editor, was going to fly on the fastest commercial airplane in the world!

The Concorde lounge at Kennedy Airport in New York City was elegant, but it seemed surprisingly compact until Beth considered that at any given time the space only needed to accommodate 100 passengers. With that thought in mind, the room became considerably roomier and more stylish, though Beth couldn't figure out why such a little change in perspective would alter the ambience of the room so drastically in her mind.

An assortment of coffeecakes, doughnuts, cookies, soft drinks, coffees and mixed drinks spread out on a table along the wall at one end of the reception area. Another table offered a selection of international newspapers. In yet another corner, there were five fax machines and a copier, as well as several writing desks, which were arranged in such a way as to afford privacy. Along the opposite walls were two large banks of telephones, but for those who chose to remain in the comfort of their lounge chairs, there were also numerous phones conveniently placed around the room.

Beth stared out of the oversized windows at the sleek, needle-nosed bullet she would soon be encapsulated within, hurling at twice the speed of sound toward Great Britain. She pinched herself on the arm to see if she was awake, and if this really was happening to her. She had no idea what her fellow traveling companions looked like. All she knew was that other than Ian there was another man and three more women on the tour. Beth looked around the room trying to guess if any of the others had arrived. Then she decided to play a little game to see if she could determine who the other writers were. So far there was no one that seemed to fit Beth's imaginary profile of a travel writer. Then again, she had to admit that she wasn't entirely sure what that image was supposed to be either.

A wonderful sense of optimism came over Beth's as she observed her fellow passengers going about their duties as travelers of the globe. It was as if she had discovered some great secret before anyone else. While the rest of the world was attending to its daily drudgery, she would be flying off to England on a fabulous exotic adventure. On the Concorde no less. In her moments of reflection Beth remembered two quotes by the well-known traveler, Paul Theroux, who wrote in one of his early books *The Old Patagonian Express*, "The signs did not speak to me. These were local matters, but I was leaving this morning. And when you are leaving, the promises in advertisements are ineffectual." The other quote stated that, "All travelers are optimists. Travel itself is sort of an optimism in action." Now Beth understood what Theroux meant, because her own positive feelings were undeniable and uncontrollable. At long last she had attained one of her goals, and soon it would begin with lunch at nearly 1,500 miles an hour.

The timing for the trip couldn't have been better. After three years of dating Todd Harper, Beth had recently broken off her engagement. It wasn't so much that she was unhappy as it was that they just didn't seem to be going anywhere. In the end, the relationship was uneventful. The sex had been OK, but it lacked passion, and the prospect of facing a non-event for the rest of her life far outweighed the comfort of having a permanent companion. At least for now. She and Todd had been friendly enough, but ultimately that was the extent of it, a friendship. The early dreams faded quickly. Everything became routine. Matter of fact. Each of them had been searching for something without finding it, and their personal agendas never quite meshed. Somehow those individual goals and aspirations always drew them further apart rather than closer together. So this journey was also a test. A test of discovery and hope. Perhaps now Beth would know for certain if her love for travel was real or merely a desire to break from the boredom that had slowly crept into her life.

Careerwise Beth felt she had turned a significant corner. If there was any uncertainty in her life at the moment it was that time was passing her by. The world was changing rapidly and dramatically, and that bothered her. Beth wasn't quite sure she was changing with it. Still, at 35 she did feel good about herself. She was nearly 5 feet 7, about 115 pounds, depending upon the day. Her shoulder length auburn hair suited her skin tones and her classic features, and her green-blue eyes had a sparkle that gave the impression to others that there was always something more, maybe even a little devious, going on in her mind. Combined with a winning smile, and a quick tongue, Beth exuded a vibrancy that was difficult to ignore. While on the surface she could appear outwardly helpless, she was a pillar of strength and impossible to comprehend. She was beguiling and mysterious, flirtatious and coy, gracious and bewitching. She was the quintessential embodiment of one of the most complex creatures on the face of the earth, the southern woman. But vibrant and lovely as she was, it was the twinkle in her eyes that added spice to her entire personality.

In five more years she'd be 40. Not a happy thought. At the same time she was proud that, so far, she had physically managed to retard the ravages of time and the forces of gravity. Her breasts were not large, but they were ample enough, round and well shaped. They were also symmetrical, which pleased her greatly. And they still had the ripeness of youth. It felt good to go braless under a T-shirt with the same sensuality she had felt at 24, or 21, or even 19. Better yet she had legs that wouldn't quit, and she knew it. They were her best feature. At least in her mind they were. Well-toned, well-proportioned calves connecting with perfectly shaped thighs. They were the kind of legs that stirred masculine imaginations. The kind of legs that made men wonder about the mystery of where they came together. Not bad for 35. Pretty good reasons, in fact, to feel optimistic.

Beth was engrossed in her thoughts when a large woman in her mid to late 60s burst into the reception area. She was stylishly outfitted despite her considerable girth, and she was wearing an oversized wide-rimmed hat that was cocked to one side almost covering one eye. As the woman trudged across the room "Mae West Style," she caught the eye of someone she obviously knew. She waved enthusiastically to him and called out, "Burt Potter, how are you? Hello there, Burt, it's good to see you again."

In a room so small, every head turned toward the "Grand Dame" who was oblivious to everyone else except Burt. Burt was seated two chairs to the left of Beth, and had been quietly reading a paper when his boisterous acquaintance made her flamboyant entrance like a professional wrestler on the way to the ring.

Potter put his paper down, looked around sheepishly and rose to his feet. "Hello Doris," he said in a subdued tone, "I take it you're going to England with Ian Lampley."

"Wouldn't miss it for the world, darling. How have you been? Haven't seen you since we were in Paris together a couple of years ago. Been traveling much? I've been everywhere. Just came back from Thailand. Hardly had time to wash my clothes, and now here I go again. Gee, it's great to see you. Are you still writing for the Chicago newspaper?"

Every time Burt tried to respond, Doris spewed forth like *Old Faithful* with another question or statement. The game was half over for Beth. She now knew fifty percent of her traveling party, and from the looks of it, she was going to know a whole lot more about this pair than she wanted to know before the plane ever left the ground.

The two writers sat down and continued their mostly one-sided conversation. "Tell me Burt, do you know this Lampley chap? I've never met the fella. Only know him from phone conversations. Sounds delightful. When was the last time you were in England? I'll be glad to get to London again," said Doris in rapid-fire style.

Whenever Doris had to pause to take a breath, Burt would interject a brief comment, then she would charge ahead again with more of her running commentary. Sitting so close to the conversation, Beth couldn't help but overhear what they were saying. She didn't feel as though she was eavesdropping, however. After all, Doris and Burt were loud enough that anyone who wanted to could hear every word anyway. But more importantly, Beth felt it was a good chance to study these creatures Known as "travel writers." After all, she herself was doing an on-the-job apprenticeship to become one of these characters. Soon she would be a "virgin" no more, having advanced to the embryonic stages in the process of developing and refining her craft.

The more Beth listened, the more intimidated she became. These people were talking about Australia and Russia, or comparing Rome and Paris, or discussing the merits of one five star hotel over another as if they were everyday occurrences. For someone with no more traveling experience than a glorified fraternity party in Spain, Beth was beginning to wonder what she could possibly bring to a conversation during the coming week.

Gradually the intimidation began to fade, leaving Burt, and especially Doris, sounding pretentious and braggadocios about their worldly escapades. Beth kept trying to tell herself that these people were professionals who, by the looks of them, had been in the traveling game for decades, and who therefore carried resumes of destinations that read like a world atlas.

Burt was a mousy chap with a full, black mustache that appeared to be overtaking his upper lip. He had an affinity for cheap cigars and loud bow ties, but his personality was generally low-key until he found himself in the presence of the loquacious Ms. Doris.

Doris Blackstone, on the other hand was a 200-pound blob of energy. She had begun travel writing at the age of 60, and now eight years later she was determined to see every country in the world before she turned 70. As she later stated in a conversation with Beth, "I want to see every place once before I see any place twice." At first, Beth thought that was a marvelous philosophy for a writer to adopt, but as she became more experienced in her travels, she began to modify that proposition radically.

Beth had heard just about enough when a slender, well-dressed gentleman walked over to Burt and Doris and said, "Hello, I'm Ian Lampley. You must be Doris Blackstone and Burt Potter. I'm glad you could join us."

What a relief. Beth stood up and introduced herself to Lampley and the other two writers, and then, for the next several minutes the process of getting acquainted dominated the conversation.

"Who are you with, dear?" Doris asked Beth in her throaty voice.

Beth was surprised that Doris was going to allow her an opportunity to answer. "I'm the travel editor for the *Winston-Salem Journal* in Winston-Salem, North Carolina. I do three travel columns a week, and put together an extensive Sunday travel section."

"Oh. Maybe I've read your column. Are you syndicated? What's it called?" asked Doris.

At first Beth thought the question was sincere, but then she decided it had a snooty edge to it, as if to say, "I'm sure you've never written anything of any quality, but I'll ask anyway so that I can tell you all about my column later."

"No I'm not syndicated. I'm new to this business. I guess you'd classify me as a rookie. My full name is Elizabeth Peabody Jacobsen. Everyone calls me Beth, but back in my high school days I had some really close buddies who nicknamed me "Peabod." They thought it was cute. So I call my column *Travels with Peabod*. I figured it was distinctive and a little unique," said Beth with a reply that was considerably more detailed than she had intended.

While Beth got to know more about Doris, Ian Lampley went to the front desk to check on the other two members of the party. A few minutes later they arrived at the reception counter, and as they began to make inquiries, Lampley introduced himself and brought them over to where Beth, Doris and Burt were sitting.

"Folks, please meet Liz Cutler and Joyce Marchant. I'll let you all get to know one another while I make sure our reservations are in order," said Lampley.

And with that the awkward chitchat began all over again, as the countdown toward departure continued.

The flight was scheduled to leave at 8:30 a.m., but a mechanical problem forced cancellation. Fortunately, there was a second Concorde departure at 11:15, which the group was able to take. With a scheduled flight time of only three hours and fifteen minutes, the arrival time in London would be 7:30 in the evening, 2:30 in the afternoon New York time.

As she boarded the plane, Beth couldn't help thinking that she was a human specimen entering a gigantic syringe with wings. As with the waiting area, the interior of the Concorde was not spacious. In fact, by most standards it was a bit cramped. There were 25 rows of seats with two seats per row on each side of a single aisle, making the configuration such that every seat was either by a window or on an aisle.

As soon as everyone settled into their seats, a flight attendant came down the aisle with hot towels before offering a choice of champagne, orange juice or a mimosa, which was a refreshing combination of both. Soon after that, amenity kits were passed out to each passenger along with a pocket-sized hardcover book about British antiques and a selection of international newspapers.

Moments before takeoff Beth buckled her seat belt and glanced toward the flight deck where she noticed a small rectangular screen on the bulkhead which she had never seen on any other flight. Her curiosity now had the best of her. Beth leaned forward, tapping Ian on the shoulder and asked what it was.

"That's the Machmeter," Lampley replied. "Once we get airborne, it'll show the air speed, and it will let us know when we hit Mach Two, or twice the speed of sound. We have to get out over the water first, because of the sonic booms. By that time, we'll be at about 65,000 feet. At that height we are considered to be at the edge of space. When the time comes, I'll take your picture by the Machmeter, if you want."

"That's a picture I won't miss," said Beth.

There was no unusual sensation of increased ground speed during the takeoff, and once the anticipation of the experience of flying on the Concorde began to abate, the flight itself wasn't much different than any other. What was unique was that every passenger on this flight was essentially flying first-class. The service was structured in such a way that it basically amounted to an elegant, extended dining experience in the air, culminated by touching down at London's Heathrow airport in less time than it took to watch *Gone With the Wind* or a professional football game on TV.

Up ahead Beth could hear Doris droning on with her constant chatter, burning the ears of the person next to her. Thankfully, she couldn't make out what Doris was saying, but the gravelly voice carried far enough through the fuselage so that Beth had a perpetual reminder of her presence. The saving grace came when the meal service began and Doris ceased her steady discourse to inhale large quantities of food and drink.

During the course of the flight, Beth developed a diversionary tactic for herself by talking briefly with the flight attendant whenever he had an opportunity to break from his duties. It proved to be a productive exercise in which she learned that the Concorde actually expanded ten inches during flight. She was also informed that on her return, she would witness a double sunset because the plane would depart London as the sun was going down and they would actually arrive in New York an hour earlier than when they left.

"Amazing," thought Beth, "In a way this really is time travel. What would it be like to celebrate New Year's Eve in London, and then do it all over again in New York, and then once more in Los Angeles? I wonder if that's possible? Wow, what a concept!"

The Concorde landed at Heathrow precisely on schedule. There was a welcoming group dinner scheduled at 8:00 p.m., before everyone made feeble efforts at going to bed at what amounted to 4:30 or 5:00 in the afternoon according to their personal body clocks.

The next day dawned with a trip to *Champneys*, an exclusive health resort near the village of Tring. Doris spent most of her time en route detailing her exploits in Romania where she had done several articles about a woman who had supposedly discovered a means of slowing down the aging process.

In Cambridge, Doris provided a lengthy lecture about the tradition of "punting on the Cam," and another regarding the historical background of Henry VIII's involvement with the founding of Trinity College.

The tour of the east coast led to an exhaustive search for a mustard shop in Norwich, and a discussion of the merits of the crabs for which the town of Cromer was famous.

Then there was the sermon about the derivation of certain words. "Did you know, my good people, that many of the words we have in the U.S. came from right here in jolly old England? It stands to reason, of course," explained Doris. "Just take the word 'England' for example. The country used to be made up of Druids. Then the Jutes, the Danes and the Angles. Now put the word 'Angle' and the word 'land' together and say it quickly. 'Angle-land, Angle-land, Angle-land.' See! It sounds like 'England' doesn't it? Isn't that amazing? I wonder why they didn't call it 'Jute-land' or 'Dane-land?' Oh well, no matter. Now take the word 'Norfolk,' Now that's the area of the country we're in now. You know, like Norfolk, Virginia. All it means is that this is the region of 'the North folk,' Isn't that interesting? I think it is. Therefore, 'Suffolk' is the region of 'the South folk,' and correspondingly, I like that word 'correspondingly,' there's 'Essex.' Now that's the region of 'the East Saxons.' 'Wessex' stands for 'the West Saxons.' and 'Sussex' for 'the South Saxons.' I thought that was really neat when I first heard it. Maybe none of you do, but you know what I say to that? Well I say just what I heard on the radio this morning, 'Hard cheddar!' Isn't that a lovely expression? 'Hard cheddar.' I just thought that maybe you'd like to pass these things along to your readers. I mean if you want to, of course. You know I don't mind, just feel free to…"

Everyone just shook their heads. Beth smiled to herself and wondered where in the world Ian had found this woman.

At Thetford, Doris was informed that her room was haunted, which prompted a great deal of research into English ghosts, and of course, which resulted in a verbose narrative about the topic.

By the time the group reached Bury St. Edmunds, Beth was certain that Doris had exhausted every imaginable subject in her encyclopedic memory. She was wrong. Only Doris could possibly know of a tradition called "Morris dancing" where men dressed in women's clothing during certain times of the year and danced vigorously while carrying bells in their hands. On that occasion, all it took to trigger Doris was a small sign she had seen on a shopkeeper's door announcing Morris-dancing performances near Bury St. Edmunds.

In truth, despite all the tedium of the "Blackstone Diatribes," as they came to be known, Beth had learned an important lesson from Doris. She found that no matter where she went, there was almost always something unique and unusual to be discovered which she could add to her knowledge of the world. Sometimes it amounted to little more than mindless trivia, but more often, it resulted in some intriguing little gem of information that brought a destination to life and gave it a completely new personality.

Bury St. Edmunds was as good a place as any for Beth to really get her feet wet. After listening to Doris for several days now, she made a personal decision that she, too, was going to uncover whatever tidbits of information she could in this little known village near the eastern coast of England.

It didn't take Beth very long, and the results were fascinating. With a population of about 250,000, Bury St. Edmunds had been important to the region of East Anglia since medieval times. Part of that significance came from its abbey, which is now in ruins, but which was founded in 1020 upon the shrine of Edmund, the last king of the East Angles.

It was at the Abbey of Bury St. Edmunds, in November of 1214, that 25 barons swore on the high altar to force King John to sign the Magna Carta. The king ratified that document at Runnymede in the spring of the following year, and in the process, established the basis for what we know today in the United States as the Bill of Rights.

Beth thought to herself, "Imagine, in this little spot that nobody has ever heard of, an event took place that had major significance for two of the most powerful countries in the world. Something that happened almost 800 years ago, in a remote, out of the way village that affects the lives of every single American today. What a wonderful little factoid."

Beth wasn't finished. The more she explored, the more she learned. Just up the street about three blocks, around the corner to the right, she came upon what was reported to be the smallest pub in Great Britain. The building was so tiny that there was only room enough for the bar and per-haps three or four people to drink at any one time. As a result, most folks took their pints of bitters out to the street for consumption, giving new definition to the words "Happy Hour," and creating a marvelous little street party every day after work.

Even the hotel where the group had lunch proved to be an unexpected source of revelation. The *Angel Hotel* had hosted Charles Dickens on two occasions in the mid-19th century, during which time he gave readings of *David Copperfield*. To this day, room #15 remains exactly as it was in 1859 and 1861 when Dickens referred to his "fine room" in later writings about his accommodations.

Dickens, like George Washington in the colonies, must have slept in just about every town on the island of Great Britain. Had Washington spent the night in every place for which he is credited, it's little wonder that he's called "the Father of his country." By the same token, Beth reasoned, Dickens must surely have been "the Father of England."

Despite her annoying personality, Doris truly had been an inspiration. For all of her "diarrhea of the mouth." she had inadvertently taught Beth to seek and discover, to look beneath the surface and to peel away the layers that everyone else sees, to become a "traveler" rather than a "tourist."

Beth couldn't wait to get to the next stop on the itinerary. For the entire week everyone had been saying that Lavenham would be the highlight of the trip. Located just a few miles down the road from Bury, Beth was not only eager to experience this quaint little burg, but she was also ready to test her newly enhanced curiosity one more time.

What Beth discovered when the group arrived in Lavenham was a storybook village with a "Pied Piper" quality about it. The timber-framed houses dating to the 15th century were so old that time had caused most of them to go askew, leaning forward and sideways in all manner of odd little angles, creating the illusion that they were holding each other up. Many of the streets literally emptied into lush farmland, virtually making the town an oasis of medieval cottages nestled in the heart of the green expanse of the Suffolk countryside.

It had been wool that made Lavenham prosper. By 1524, it was the 14th richest town in all of England. By contrast, today it nestles peacefully in a landscape of rolling hills and meandering hedgerows, 65 miles northeast of London, where only occasionally is it afforded the distinction of even being located upon a map.

The group was registered at *The Swan Hotel*, itself a 15th century landmark, on the prominent corner of High Street and Water Street. Once it had most probably been three different houses, but now *The Swan* had been combined into a single dwelling and converted into a popular hostelry.

The story of *The Swan* was the story of most English inns—one of constant adaptation to meet the needs of the people and the times they served. In olden days, the street was little more than a dirt tract where men and women who filled the inn came on horseback or by carriage, splashed with mud in winter and covered with dust in the summer. By the middle of the 19th century, the property had primarily become a posting inn, catering to travelers who were in a hurry and merely sought a place for a change of horses.

Beth loved it! *The Swan* was like no place she had ever been before. The main lounge was divided into four areas, which exuded an inviting, homey quality that was enhanced by the soft illumination of natural light from several large windows. Notable among the furnishings were three grandfather clocks plus an antique sideboard with a display of soft blue print china, all of which were dominated by a large open-hearth fireplace.

In many places on the first floor of the main building, guests were forced to duck to keep from bumping their heads on the unusually low beams, which were permanent reminders of the height, or lack of it, of those who lived hundreds of years ago. Rather than posting signs, the only warning to guests about the menacing timbers were large exclamation points strategically placed above each exit.

Beth's room was on the second floor at the far end of the building facing Water Street. With every step she took the floor creaked and moaned from centuries of continuous use. Upon reflection, Beth surmised that despite the romantic ambience of this wonderful little hotel, it would a horrible place for an intimate rendezvous because every thrust and parry would resonate throughout the building, along the corridors and above the parlors.

On the way to her room, Beth could see the Wool Hall down below. While it had been in existence for hundreds of years, the Wool Hall had only been incorporated into the property in recent times, and Beth later learned that it was originally built by the Guild of Our Lady in the 15th century. It was often assumed that these guilds were solely craft guilds when, in fact, many were also religious institutions. When all religious guilds were suppressed during the Reformation, the Wool Hall in Lavenham became the center for the buying and selling of raw wool. Today it serves as the primary meeting room for the hotel.

Dinner was set for 7:30 with cocktails in the Old Bar at 7:00. It was 5:30 when Beth began the usual reconnaissance of her room, checking first, as standard operating procedure, the bathroom. If that facility passed her inspection, there was a good chance that she'd write about a property in one of her columns. In the case of *The Swan*, the bathroom was a moot point because she planned to write about the inn anyway.

Not only was the bathroom spacious, complete with a built-in hair dryer, it also boasted a deep, claw-footed European-style bathtub, which was invitation enough for Beth. She couldn't get out of her clothes fast enough. In minutes, she was soaking in a steaming porcelain lake full of bubbles with a book in one hand and a glass of wine from the mini-bar sitting on the small table beside the tub.

After her luxurious soaking bath, Beth dressed for dinner and went down to the Old Bar early to scout around. She was glad the pub was empty when she arrived, allowing her the freedom to explore before the others came down. Moving around the room, Beth could feel an eerie presence throughout the chamber, though she was certain the place was vacant. It was a sensation she couldn't quite put her finger on. She continued her self-guided tour slowly browsing around the room, when the bartender came in and introduced himself in a raspy British voice. He was a wrinkled and salty old coot, with wispy strands of thinning gray hair and a three-day-old beard. He walked with a slouch that forced him to shuffle his feet with every step that he took. In addition, his neck was rigid as if connecting his head to his shoulders with a board, so that when he turned from side to side, his entire upper body moved in tandem.

"Name's Sean," he said, "Welcome to the Old Bar at *The Swan*."

"Thank you Sean. I'm Beth. I love the inn. It's got such a wonderful history."

"Indeed it does, madam. 'Tis quite a place this. This 'ere pub is most 'istoric, as well. Would ya like for me ta tell ya 'bout it?"

"I'd like that very much," replied Beth.

"Well, I'll begin with these 'ere bells above the bar," the bartender answered, obviously pleased that Beth wanted to hear his story. "Ya likely saw the church up there on the 'ill at some time or other. Though Lav'n'am is a wee small, 'twas once a prosp'rous 'amlet she was, and 'cause o' that, our minster is much grander than most other towns o' the same size in England. Durin' them years when the church was being' bilt, there were no place ta put the bells, so they used this 'ere room 'til the bildin' were done, and the bell ringers come down 'ere fer re'earsals, they did. When the church were finished, them bells were moved back up the 'ill. So in a gesture of gratitude, the congregation gave them bells that were fer re'earsin' to *The Swan*. Them bells been 'angin' over this 'ere bar ever since, and ta this day, them bell ringers still 'ave practices now and agin right 'ere in this lil pub. The tenor bell was made by a fella name o' Miles Graye in 1625. Some say 'tis the finest toned bell in all of England, prob'ly e'en the world. Right 'ere in Lav'n'am 'tis."

"What a lovely story," said Beth.

"Yep, but ya know, e'en though most of the 'istry in this 'ere town and 'otel goes back 'undreds o' years, there's lotsa stories in this 'ere pub ain't so old atall," Sean replied.

"Really? What do you mean? Tell me more."

Sean walked across the room to the end of the bar and moved to a corner where a large knee-length glass boot stood gathering dust on a shelf. He reached up and took the boot from its resting-place. "Durin' the war this 'ere Old Bar in Lav'n'am was a fav'rite waterin' 'ole fer yore American flyers who was stationed near 'ere afore they would leave fer combat on the cont'nent. This 'ere were their glass boot. Them soldiers would fill it up with lager, and then they'd make bets 'bout who could drink the boot dry the quickest. If ya look o'er 'ere on the wall, ya can still see the marks of the names of them chappies whene'er a new record were 'stablished. As ya mighta figgered, this were a rowdy place in them days."

Beth was beginning to get an understanding of what that eerie feeling was. Though she'd never given much thought to the idea of ghosts, she could clearly sense the presence of those who had been there during the war. Their spirit was alive in the room. Beth could hear their voices and their laughter, and she could visualize the raucous atmosphere when it would have been filled with smoke and jammed with flyboys heading off to battle.

Sean gingerly made his way over to another corner of the room. "Over 'ere madam," he said. "I've som'thin' else ta show to ya. 'Tis the medals. Afore they left, the boys put their medals up 'ere on the wall. 'Twas a r'minder of the good times they 'ad while they was 'ere, and a promise ta return. We put'em all behind that there glass ta preserve'm."

The wall was covered with all manner of medals and decorations. It made Beth feel good to be standing there. The war was only a page in the history books for her, but she was close enough to the fringes of it to appreciate the deeply felt commitment to country and to friends by those who had participated in it. The ghosts Beth felt were not unhappy spirits. Not at all. No, these were the apparitions of youth and pride and dedication, and they reminded her of a quote by H. V. Morton when he wrote, "The ghosts of the past are no strangers at this banquet, rather they sit at the head of the table." The ghosts were most certainly in that room. Beth knew it. She had felt their presence the minute she entered the pub, and now she also knew that they had been faithful to their promise, for indeed they had returned.

By now the rest of the group had entered the pub. Cocktails went as planned, and then everyone moved along to the dining room. The banquet hall had a wonderful medieval flavor to it that blended perfectly with the rest of the hotel. Everyone was disappointed to learn that it had been constructed in 1965, but they were equally astonished at the loving care and craftsmanship of the reproduction, which was so exquisitely executed that only an expert could tell it wasn't authentic.

About two days into the trip, each member of the group had begun playing a subtle little game of "Musical Chairs," the purpose of which was to avoid sitting next to Doris. On this particular night Beth lost, so she attempted to delay the onslaught of verbiage by pretending to engross herself in the menu.

The dinner began with a half of honeydew melon with port wine, followed by filet of Dover sole which was rolled in spinach, poached in white wine and coated with cream cheese sauce. There was also a selection of freshly cooked vegetables. Dessert was home made apple pie with farmhouse cream followed by coffee or tea and after dinner drinks. Doris made several short speeches on food preparation, how to make sauces, cooking with wine and the virtues of English tea, most of which Beth ignored or simply gave credence to by nodding her head in agreement.

"You know this town depended heavily upon the wool trade," said Doris between bites. "It was the original cottage industry."

"I didn't know that," said Beth with sarcasm in her voice. "Were you out talking to the sheep this afternoon?"

"Talking to the sheep? Good heavens no, dear. But I did do some reading." Beth's sarcasm had completely escaped Doris. "You'll never guess what I found out. You see the locals took up this wool business right in their own homes. The whole family would be involved with the men handling the heavy stuff, and the women doing the spinning, you know. Well guess what? This became the origin of the word 'spinster.' Sure enough right here in this little town. You see, it was a family business, and a young woman would be at home spending most of her days spinning. So they didn't get out much, and if a young girl never married, well all she had to tend to for the rest of her life was working with the wool. Hence the word 'spinster.' Isn't that fascinating?"

"Yes, Doris" mumbled Beth. Actually, she did think it was interesting, but she didn't want to encourage her.

"But wait, there's more," exclaimed Doris enthusiastically.

"I'm sure we're going to find out. What else did you learn today?" asked Beth.

"Well, you see this is Suffolk. Remember I told you about Norfolk and Suffolk? Anyway, this is Suffolk, which based its industry on making woolens, while over in Norfolk, they were specializing in worsteds. Well woolens are made from short-fibered wool, which is spun to give it an open, springy type of yarn. Then the yarn was washed and dyed. The wool from Suffolk was famous for its blue color, created by the use of woad and later indigo. And most of this wool from Suffolk was actually "dyed in the wool," which gives us the expression we have today when we're referring to someone who has a certain loyalty and character through and through. Isn't that great? Don't you just love it? I think it's a marvelous little story."

Doris ran on and on for several minutes, and then, as she was lifting a fork to her mouth, Beth spoke up, "I have a story you might like to hear," she said.

"Well I'm sure I would. What is it?" queried Doris with confidence that Beth couldn't possibly know something she didn't.

"Well, this is about a man name Isaac Taylor and his family. They came to Lavenham in the latter part of the 18th century. Even though the town was small, he made several moves while he was here, living first in Cook's House, then later in Arundel House and finally on Schilling Street. Eventually there was one last move around 1780, when what is now *The Swan* became his home. Taylor was an engraver by trade, and also an artist, and he had two daughters. The daughters were named Anne and Jane. Coming from such a creative background, they also had talent, which was writing children's poems, mostly for personal pleasure. Anne, however, became quite prolific, and soon she began to have some of her work published. It made her sister, Jane, a little jealous that she wasn't as successful as Anne. But then one day, in this very house, Jane also wrote something that she managed to get published, and ever since it has been known throughout the world for more than 200 years. Even though Jane Taylor herself is largely forgotten, the poem lives on as one of the most famous nursery rhymes ever written."

Beth knew she had scored a direct hit. Doris dropped her fork and had actually stopped eating. She couldn't believe the story she was hearing, and more importantly, she was stunned that this information had somehow passed her scrutiny. She finally concluded that Beth was concocting the entire episode. Doris decided to call her bluff.

"And so this poem that became so famous, my dear, what was it called? Have I ever heard of it?"

"Oh I think so," said Beth. "It begins like this, 'Twinkle, twinkle, little star, How I wonder what you are.' And then it goes on from there. You've heard that one, haven't you?" she asked Doris with a huge smile on her face.

Doris was speechless, choosing to complete the remainder of the meal in silence.

When dinner was over, as Beth moved toward the stairs to go up to bed, she caught a glimpse of Doris standing at the front desk. She could hear her talking with the receptionist who was saying, "Oh yes, that is quite true. The poem *Twinkle, Twinkle Little Star* was indeed written by Jane Taylor right here at *The Swan*.

When Beth got to her room she put the musty little book entitled *A Brief History of Lavenham and The Swan* back where she had found it in the drawer of the antique dresser. She had stumbled upon the dusty old volume while researching her room. It was the very book she had decided to read while taking her bath before cocktails and dinner.

Two months passed following the trip, then one afternoon Beth received a phone call at the newspaper. When she answered, a voice at the other end said, "Beth, this is Robert Silvers. I'm with a public relations firm representing Puerto Rico. A friend of yours, Doris Blackstone, suggested I give you a call. I have a press trip coming up, and she couldn't go because she'll be in Jordan. She told me that you'd make a wonderful replacement. Would you like to go?"

"I accept," said Beth, "But I'll need more details. When is the trip? How long is it? What do I...."

Wherever Doris was at that moment, Beth knew she was still talking about something. She might even be solving all the problems in the Middle East just by staying there long enough to wear them down. But in her heart Beth thanked Doris for the referral, because now she was certain that she had, at long last, earned the respect of her peers.

HANNIBAL CROSSES THE ALPS

The company apartment was located on the 25th floor of an upper east-side building overlooking the East River in Manhattan. It was a large two-bedroom, two-bathroom facility that could easily accommodate six or seven adults when the sofas in the living room were converted into beds, and the rollaway bed was used in another small room.

It was a great employee benefit for Beth Jacobsen because it not only saved the expense of a hotel, but more importantly, it was like having a home away from home whenever she was in New York.

The house rules were simple. The apartment was available to employees of the *Winston-Salem Journal* and their guests when accompanied by an employee. It could be scheduled on a first-come-first-served basis with the stipulation that business use took precedence over pleasure regardless of when a booking was made. In most instances however, there were few conflicts, even when last minute business arrangements arose.

Beth had reserved the apartment for five people, including herself, for two nights prior to leaving for Switzerland for ten days of vacation. Her group was actually leaving from Philadelphia, but they had all decided to spend a couple of days in New York before taking the train to Pennsylvania for the overnight flight to Geneva.

It was an odd assortment of traveling companions to say the least, primarily because they were not close friends by any means. At least not at the outset. It was the occasion of the 70th birthday of one Lawrence

Frederick Jacobsen, Jr., who was less formally known as Beth's father, that had prompted the excursion to the alpine splendor of Europe.

For his age, Lawrence was a spry, old gentleman whom everyone agreed had been born a century too late. As far as he was concerned, computers, television and VCRs were the work of subversive forces that had developed covert methods of destroying intellectual curiosity through a gradual process that would ultimately eliminate any human desire for books. He refused to dignify the modern propensity for casual attire, especially that of blue jeans and tee shirts. As he put it, "I don't believe in wearing clothes that you must read." Rather, he had preferred to indulge in the finer things throughout his life, including afternoon naps, a daily read in one of several biographies, which would be in various stages of completion and, which were always accompanied by a glass of wine, dressing for dinner and prying into other people's affairs, especially those of his family. It was his penchant for snooping that instilled his love affair with biographies because they allowed him the freedom to delve into the personal affairs of the rich, famous and notorious, though he would never admit to such an analysis of his personality.

With thinning white hair and a slender frame, Lawrence Frederick Jacobsen, Jr. was a man of tremendous pride and vanity. He had been a model of dignity in every aspect of his personal life, part of which derived from the genuine goodness of his heart and, to a lesser degree, partly from a deep-rooted fear of what others would say about him behind his back if he ever stepped out of line.

Lawrence was also a man of boundless energy. He was a volunteer at local hospitals, an avid historian, an elder in his church, a civic leader, an artist, an eloquent writer and frequently, a pain in the ass. He also possessed a hypnotic, "Rasputin-like" charisma coupled with great personal charm, which he notoriously used to his advantage. This enthusiasm and energy for living, particularly when surrounded by family and close friends, allowed him the luxury of being able to con anyone into doing just about anything for him. As a result he had the ability to make a project such as "whitewashing the fence" become "whitewashing the Great Wall of China", if he so desired, though everyone always knew precisely what he was up to. Yet, he was forever the epitome of decorum, and readily available to offer a helping hand to anyone in need. It was this combination of qualities which, not only kept him younger and more vigorous than his years, but also had an infectious influence on those around him, and endeared him to nearly everyone.

Still, he was unquestionably a product of another era. Any invention that postdated the telephone was not only bewildering to him, but a clear indication that technology had the world at the brink of Armageddon. As a result, he was a white-knuckle flier of the first order, and only his curiosity for knowledge, along with the status of traveling to Europe, were enough to overcome his fear. That, and some magic pills he had brought with him to further calm his anxieties.

Another member of the traveling party was Beth's older brother, Willis. Most people just called him "Jake." He was towheaded and skinny to the point of appearing gaunt at times, and he was nothing like his father. In fact, the two couldn't have been further apart in their outlook on the world. From earliest childhood, Jake had been extremely competitive and sports oriented. Lawrence, on the other hand, couldn't distinguish a golf tee from a kicking tee. If questioned on the subject, he would likely make some comparison between Orange Pekoe or Earl Grey, since those were the only teas he knew anything about with any semblance of expertise.

Perhaps because he felt the need to distinguish himself, Jake preferred individual sports, such as track and field and wrestling, to team sports. He was also an outdoorsman with a fondness for killing, capturing, hooking and stuffing things, all the while maintaining his devotion to Mother Nature and the environment.

While Lawrence was able to focus his energies in a reserved manner, by contrast, Jake was a bundle of nerves. He was constantly in motion to the extent that he could make everyone in his vicinity edgy if they were around him for any length of time. Now, with four other people heading to Switzerland with him, facing the prospect of sharing a rental car for nine days, the trip had all the makings of a disaster before the plane ever taxied down the runway.

The fourth person in the quintet was a doctor's wife whom Beth had met at a travel trade show several months earlier. Francine Mosely was in her early 40s, and she, too, was constantly on the go. Up to now, most of her travels had been on cruise ships, which were the result of restlessness and boredom more than any great desire to explore the world. One thing she did enjoy, however, was a good party, particularly if she could be the belle of the ball, and cruising was the perfect venue for that particular activity.

Fran could be described as having a "spunky" personality. She was taller than she looked, probably because her physique made her appear tiny. From the waist up, she was slender and petite with perky breasts that rested high upon her chest. But from the waist down she had a stocky quality with bulky, unflattering legs, as well as an oversized behind. During her high school days her barrel-shaped buttocks had earned her the nickname "Whale Tail." but in later years, friends returned to civility by just calling her Fran.

Her ravishing, midnight black hair was cut short to reveal a model's face, though she was seemingly unaware of her beauty. Or at least if she was aware of it, she was certainly not narcissistic about it. Being from eastern North Carolina, Fran had a thick southern drawl that magnified her moods and served to enhance her outgoing nature. She was the only member of the group who was bilingual, speaking English and also being fluent in profanity, though no one knew it as yet. So rich, colorful and extensive was her vocabulary that she could easily have been the author of *The Sailor's Dictionary*. Fran knew words no one else had ever heard before, boasting of a few that could have set world records for their number of letters.

There was one other distinguishing characteristic about Fran that was impossible to ignore. Her laugh. It was a piercing, high pitched, screeching noise that could permeate an entire room and, at the same time, call every canine within a 500-yard radius. It was a sound that the group would come to know intimately in the coming days of the trip.

Though she gave the outward appearance of brimming with confidence, Fran was basically insecure, but she was also the type of person who would be first in line to help a friend in trouble. She thrived on misfortune and the need to be needed, but when a crisis was over, the letdown often led to depression, soul-searching and, sometimes, self-pity.

Money had never been a problem for Fran. She had plenty of that. What she constantly required was attention, affection and a series of small projects to keep her overactive mind occupied. When those things weren't present, she became frustrated and bored because she had no hobbies and few outside interests, other than socializing. Still, she was good people, and no one who ever knew her could deny that when trouble came knocking, Fran would be the first person to call.

The final member of the cast was Sally Mae Kurtz, who was another acquaintance of Beth's from an earlier assignment. Sally Mae wasn't even as close a friend as Francine, but when Beth had mentioned the trip during a casual conversation, she pleaded to tag along. Beth was naturally delighted to have Sally Mae join the little traveling party because she could help defray some of the costs of the rental car and gasoline. She could also be a roommate for Francine.

Simply put, Sally Mae was huge. At just over 6 feet tall, and roughly 180 pounds, she was also extremely round. So much so that she could have been the model for the Michelin tire character. Her hulking size resulted in such severe awkwardness that, by omparison, the expression "a bull in a china shop" could be regarded as a reference to the *Bolshoi Ballet*. Despite her terminal clumsiness however, she had a most agreeable personality, she was exceptionally flexible and up for anything the group wanted to do.

To participate in the trip, Sally Mae had quit her job as a junior high school teacher after 21 years in the profession. As she saw it, this was a once in a lifetime opportunity, and something she was determined to do, so when her school refused to grant a brief leave of absence, she quit. A decision that wasn't as drastic as it appeared on the surface. For Sally Mae it was time for a change anyway, teachers were in short supply, and with all her years of experience, there would be little difficulty in acquiring a new assignment the following year. Nevertheless it was gutsy strategy at the very least.

To say that this was an eclectic collection of personalities was an understatement. For the next ten days, the continent of Europe was about to be terrorized by a group of inexperienced nomads that included a neophyte travel writer, a 20th century Victorian, a part-time predator, a pint-sized, profane beauty queen and a gigantic, bumbling, unemployed educator, the combination of which made the D-Day invasion look like a beach party.

Day one belonged entirely to the Jacobsen's. Fran and Sally Mae would arrive the following morning. Though Beth and Lawrence had been to New York on numerous occasions, Jake was unfamiliar with the city, so much of the time was spent showing him the sights and doing the usual first timer's list of touristy things. The convenience and location of the apartment allowed the opportunity to walk to most of the main attractions and still be able to return for short rest periods before venturing out again.

Since Jake was not the type to appreciate the subtleties of an elegant Manhattan restaurant for dinner, Beth remembered that the apartment was near a popular Irish pub known as *P.J. Clarke's*. The setting was perfect for Beth's less than sophisticated sibling, the price was right and everyone enjoyed the simple pleasures of a meal consisting of New England clam chowder and the house specialty, a bacon cheeseburger, all washed down with a couple of beers. Nothing sensational, but the atmosphere was typically New York, and it was a fun place to spend some time. Even Lawrence had to admit that he enjoyed temporarily being caught up in the hustle and bustle of the Big Apple.

When Fran and Sally Mae showed up the next day, the rpm of the group went up several notches. The women took off on an afternoon

shopping spree, while Lawrence and Jake headed out to a couple of museums. Lawrence was thrilled at the idea of having leisure time that was free
of obligation, allowing him the freedom to peruse some of his favorite
exhibitions. Jake could have cared less. Realizing that he had to compromise or suffer the consequences of a major revolt by his son, Lawrence
spent a couple of hours at the *Metropolitan Museum of Art*, before relin-
quishing the remainder of the time to the *Museum of Natural History*
where Jake could view the dinosaurs. It proved to be a diplomatic coup for
Lawrence who was also able to immerse himself in some of the other
anthropological displays during the visit.

Everyone had agreed to meet back at the apartment by four o'clock,
which would allow plenty of time to clean up before setting out once
more. By 5:30, the traveling quintet was sipping cocktails at *Top O'The
Sixes*, followed by dinner at *Sardi's* and later, a performance of *CATS*. After
the show, the group decided to amble back to the apartment at a casual
pace, stopping off for a nightcap at a neighborhood bar along the way.

Since they would not be leaving for Philadelphia until two o'clock the
next day when they would catch a train from Grand Central Station,
everyone chose to sleep later than usual. After a long train ride, and a cab
to the airport, the tedious process of the airport check-in and the transat-
lantic flight would follow, so everyone did their best to conserve as much
energy as possible. The orientation process of getting to know each other
continued throughout the day and was still in progress late in the morning
as everyone busied themselves with the tasks of re-packing their suitcases
and making last minute preparations for the trip.

Lawrence was always organized, and completed his personal chores
long before the others. In the remaining time prior to departure he sat
quietly in the living room reading the *New York Times* as the others frantically scurried around him.

"Daddy, have you got everything?" asked Beth after she had completed
her packing and placed her luggage by the door ready to go. She had long

ago learned to always double-check with her father because, though he was usually punctual and prepared, he was frequently absent-minded, or uncertain about the whereabouts of particular items.

"I think so, dear," he replied. All my documents are right here in my coat pocket. I have everything I need."

"Plane ticket. You've got your plane ticket?"

"Yes, see it's right here," Lawrence said cheerfully holding up the envelope.

"How about your pills, do you have them?" Beth asked.

"Lawrence, darlin' you make sure you've got everything. We don't wanta be losin' you in Philadelphia," shouted Fran from another room.

"OK, sweetheart," replied Lawrence. "I know you'll take care of me."

"What about your pills, Daddy? Do you have them?" asked Beth again.

"Ahhh, yes. In my side pocket, see."

"And your passport, where is that?" came another question from Beth.

"That's in my passport folder inside my coat," said Lawrence confidently.

"Let me see it. I just want to make sure you have everything."

Lawrence reached for his sport coat and went to the inside right pocket where he always carried his passport case. He fumbled with the coat for a few seconds before realizing the case was not there. "I don't have it. It must have fallen out on the floor somewhere. I'm glad we checked, but it has to be here, I just saw it last night. We'll find it," he said confidently.

Within seconds the entire apartment was in an uproar. Everyone was tearing the place apart trying to locate the missing passport, but it was nowhere to be found. They were rapidly running out of places to look. "Daddy, think," said Beth in a panic, "When was the last time you saw your passport case?"

The old man was confused now. At first, he was sure that he had seen it the previous night, but now he was beginning to doubt his memory, and the longer the search continued the more vague he became.

"Don't worry, darlin'," yelled Fran in a cheery voice, "We'll find it. You just sit on the sofa and let us look for it."

"I wuz fixin' to say," chimed in Sally Mae, "We've still got some time yet. Don't you fret. It'll turn up." Sally Mae was plodding around the apartment with lead footsteps that made the floor shake as she bumped into chairs and knocked over lamps in her search.

"I knew we shoulda left you home old man," said Jake. "Can't take you anywhere. Are you sure you brought that thing with you?"

"Yes. Definitely. I know I did. Your mother wouldn't allow me to leave without something as important as that," answered Lawrence in a frustrated, meek tone of voice. He was becoming tense, ringing his hands together and beginning to get overly nervous. The anxiety was visibly bothering him now as each passing minute made him increasingly fretful.

Fran had taken to flinging sheets and blankets everywhere. Sally Mae was looking in the bathrooms and closets. Beth checked under the beds and all around the luggage, and Jake was going through the motions of searching the living room without accomplishing much other than muttering to himself.

"If we don't find it soon, I won't be able to go. What am I going to do?" came a frantic question from Lawrence. His hands were shaking, the blood had drained from his face, leaving his complexion an ashy white. Disruptions such as these were so rare in his life, that when they did happen they became magnified tenfold by his all too vivid imagination.

While everyone else rushed around the apartment, Fran came in and sat down next to Lawrence trying to console him by putting her arm around his shoulder. "Don't worry, sweetheart, we'll find it. We just haven't looked in the right spot yet. Listen, I've got somethin' that'll make you relax. I always carry some magic potions with me, just in case. You didn't know this about me but I'm a witch. I'll have you fixed up in no time. Let me see, where is this stuff?"

When Fran opened her purse, it looked like a self-contained pharmacy. Lawrence was stunned by what he saw. The woman had just about every legal pill and drug known to mankind, and who could tell, maybe even a few illegal items as well. In her search for something to settle Lawrence's nerves, Fran was unaware that he had brought his own prescription medication with him, and amid the present turmoil, confusion, frustration and disarray he failed to mention its existence.

When Fran located the medication she was looking for, she went into the kitchen, ran a glass of tap water and returned to where the old man was sitting. Lawrence desperately took the pills in his hand, popped them into his mouth and swallowed them with a large single gulp. It was at that same moment that he became excited by a sudden burst of memory that he may have placed his passport folder in the bottom of his luggage, just to be certain he wouldn't lose it. "Beth," he called out, "Look in my suitcase and see if I packed it underneath my sweaters somewhere."

Beth picked up Lawrence's bag and put it on the bed. She opened it quickly and began rifling through the clothing to see if her father had indeed packed his passport case in the luggage before they left North Carolina and somehow forgotten that he did it. Sure enough, the folder was lying between a couple of sweaters. "Here it is," she shouted with great relief. "I found it!"

Lawrence let out a huge sigh and slumped down on the sofa as if someone had just given him a reprieve from the electric chair. Fran and Sally Mae set about the task of remaking the beds and restoring order to the apartment to its usual appearance. Meanwhile, Jake continued muttering about the entire incident under his breath.

Beth came into the living room and handed Lawrence his documents. "Daddy, this has been really upsetting for you. I think I'm going to give you a couple of your pills early so you'll be calm and ready to sleep when we get on the plane."

Lawrence had been so caught up in the discovery of his papers, that he didn't think about what Beth had just said, nor did he remember at that particular moment having taken the pills from Fran just a few minutes earlier. When Beth returned to the room, she handed her father a glass of water and took two capsules from the bottle in his coat pocket. "Here, take these and you'll feel a lot better," she said.

Lawrence looked up at Beth with a sheepish grin and said, "Thank you, dear. You're all so good to me." Then he consumed a second dose of medication, this time his own, with another big drink of water, and resumed his vigil of sitting quietly and reading until it was time to leave for Philadelphia.

When Beth's group arrived at the Philadelphia airport, Lawrence was a zombie. He had slept through most of the train ride, and couldn't remember the taxi from the railway station to the airport. He barely had enough energy to stand in line to check in for the flight, and once that task was complete, Beth and Fran had to ease him to a chair in the departure lounge where he remained in his comatose state. As yet, neither woman was aware that the other had separately administered large doses of medicine to their senior companion.

The tour was being coordinated through Dickinson College in Carlisle, Pennsylvania. In addition to the three Jacobsen's and their two partners, other members of the group at large were also arriving at the same time, forming a total traveling party of close to 50 people. By now it was 5:35 in the afternoon with a scheduled flight time of 6:20.

Pre-trip anticipation was in high gear as tiny clusters of adventurers gathered to ask questions and share information. Only a few of the participants had ever been to Switzerland before, and the prospect of spending ten days in the magnificent splendor of the Alps was beguiling. Headquarters for the program was a new ski resort just outside the village of Sion in the French speaking region of the country. Officially the resort was closed since skiing season was over, but the property had continued to operate in order to generate revenues from groups like the Dickinson tour that had an interest purely in sightseeing. Each day would provide organized side excursions for which the participants could pay an additional fee. Beth had been all through that drill during her trip to Spain, and she quickly learned that the extra junkets often came at a premium price and frequently left something to be desired.

The problem was that unless a person was intimately familiar with a destination, which most tourists were not, they could never quite figure out which tours offered the best value for the money. Frequently the trips would include a visit to some kind of factory or souvenir shop where the tour guide collected a profitable kickback for bringing the group.

Another difficulty in traveling with large packaged tour groups was the frequent need for pit stops. If one member of the entourage decided it was time to use the restroom, it was guaranteed that everyone else would follow, and what should have been a five-minute break would slowly deteriorate into a 45-minute waste of time.

After learning the routine in Spain, Beth decided that the thing for her crowd to do was to take advantage of the group rate for the air, hotel and meals that were included, and then leave the tour as soon as possible. Once safely in Switzerland, she would rent a car and her group could travel around by themselves at their leisure. It would have been a brilliant scheme except that Beth was still a neophyte at the nuances of the travel game. She would soon discover, in sometimes unceremonious and often awkward fashion, that there was a much larger learning curve to overcome than she had previously considered.

As the flight announcements began to sound over the public address system, Lawrence awoke momentarily and realized it was time to leave. Through the haze of his drowsy stupor he determined that if he could get to the men's room to splash some water on his face, he would be freshened up enough for the flight. He looked at Beth and the others, excused himself and staggered off to the bathroom. Beth gave Jake a concerned look and told him to make certain that Lawrence was all right, since it was highly likely that he might fail to return within a reasonable amount of time.

When Lawrence reached the restroom, he took out his comb and ran it through his snowy white hair. Then he straightened his clothing, and washed his face and hands. At that moment, in the murky haze of his subconscious, he reminded himself that he needed to take some pills to settle himself down during the flight. So with no memory of his previous double dose of medication, Lawrence downed two more capsules and returned to his traveling mates.

Under normal circumstances, Lawrence would have been conversing with fellow passengers as if they had been lifelong friends. On this occasion however, the daze of too much medicine left him uncharacteristically silent. As far as he was concerned, one moment he had been in a New York apartment looking for his passport, and in the next, he was in Geneva, Switzerland with no earthly idea of how he got there. He never ate dinner, never read the paper, never saw the movie, never took the hot towel service, never visited duty free, never had breakfast, just *POOF*, and he was magically transformed through the fog of some mystical technological time machine to Switzerland.

After everyone gathered their luggage in the baggage claim area, they moved outside to a double-decked motorcoach. Beth and Fran took Lawrence by each arm and guided him on to the bus while Sally Mae and Jake handled the suitcases. Since there were five of them, they worked their way to the rear of the coach where they would have more room to spread out. It was also a good place to shield Lawrence from the curious gazes of the others.

Lawrence sat slumped in the back of the bus, his head heavy with sleep, first falling forward on his chest, then ponderously sagging like a dead weight from one side to the other. The rest of the passengers were becoming concerned that there was something seriously wrong with the old man. As yet no one had dared to ask. Now and then Lawrence would let out a low moan when he lapsed into deep moments of slumber, and during those especially heavy stages of his deathlike sleep, he would drool on his shirt and tie. An experience that would have been totally abhorrent to him had he any knowledge of what was happening.

The silence of the other passengers was short-lived. Beth and her friends knew that it couldn't last forever, that it was only a matter of time before curiosity overcame tact. Shortly after the bus pulled away from the Geneva airport, one lady turned around in her seat and spoke to Jake, "Is that poor gentleman ill? Is there anything we can do for him?"

All his life Jake had watched his father conduct himself as a model of propriety, and now he decided to have some fun. "Oh no, don't worry about him, he's fine. We were trying to keep it a secret, and we didn't want anyone to notice. You see, he's an alcoholic. We brought him to Switzerland hoping to dry him out a little by spending some quality time with his family and friends. Trouble is, he had a bottle of bourbon hidden away that we didn't know about. Then those free drinks on the plane, and well, you know. He's just sleeping it off right now, but he'll be all right. He's really quite lovable when he's sober. I hope you'll have a chance to see him that way. It's been a terrible burden for us."

The woman was flabbergasted. The idea of spending a week touring Switzerland with a drunken old man was intolerable to her. After all, she and her husband had been planning their trip of a lifetime for nine months, and now she stood the chance of having it spoiled or, at the very least, being inconvenienced by traveling in the presence of some inebriated old fossil.

The whispers spread through the motorcoach like wildfire. Before long, Lawrence was the only topic of discussion amid a steady stream of glaring eyes and frowns of pity and disgust from up front. Recognizing that they were now the object of mounting scorn, thanks to Jake's little practical joke, Beth continued to make valiant attempts at reviving her father. Even though she was certain there was no way to ever return to the good graces of the other tourists, she still had hopes that Lawrence could awaken long enough to get a view of the breathtaking scenery along the shores of Lake Geneva.

"Daddy, look at the mountains. Aren't they gorgeous? It doesn't even seem real, does it? Look over there Daddy, look."

Every so often, after a few shakes, Lawrence would raise his head quickly, as if he had been poked with a cattle prod, give a momentary glance out the window just before making some obscure comment, then fall back into his wonderland of unconsciousness. "Uh huh. Ahh yes. Lovely. Mountains. Beautiful. Are we in Switzerland now?" Once again asleep, his head would crash forward onto his chest, and his body would go limp in the seat.

For the next two hours the motorcoach drove along the northern shore of Lake Geneva. The lake is a crescent shaped body of water. Geneva is tucked into the far western corner of the country near the border of France, and Montreux is the last major town in the east. The north coast borders Switzerland, while the southern side belongs to France. Since Montreux was the approximate halfway point of the journey, the bus made a short stop at a roadside facility overlooking the lake to allow people time for stretching their legs and using the restroom.

In textbook tourist fashion everyone got off the bus and immediately began snapping photographs, making the usual obligatory observations about how beautiful everything was and how immaculate the Swiss kept their country. Meanwhile, Beth and Fran busied themselves wrestling with Lawrence, trying to rouse him enough to move outside and get some fresh air. At long last they got him in motion and were able to shuffle their way down the aisle to the door and eventually step out of the coach.

Lawrence was still oblivious to anything that was happening around him. He was barely mobile. Beth knew that she had to find a way to get him circulating if he was ever going to overcome the effects of his medicine.

"Daddy, can you walk? Let's go to that little shop over there and see if we can get some ice cream. You love ice cream," said Beth. "Do you think you can walk by yourself?"

"Lovely. Just lovely. When will we be in Switzerland?" Lawrence replied.

Beth and Fran slowly edged their senior traveling partner toward the line for ice cream hoping that the coolness of his favorite treat would bring him around. While they were inching their way ever so slowly forward, the two women commenced a discussion with each other that lingered on for several minutes. When Beth interrupted the conversation to turn and ask her father what flavor he wanted, she was horrified to discover that he was no longer behind her. Worse yet, he was nowhere in sight.

"He's gone!" Beth shouted at Fran. "Where could he have gone? He was just here a minute ago."

"I don't know, but we better find him. He hasn't been himself since I gave him those pills, but I swear I didn't think they were that strong."

"Pills? You gave him some pills?" asked Beth in a disbelieving voice. "No wonder he's been out of it. I gave him some, too!"

"Well darlin', we've got to find him now. We've overdosed him, but the damage is already done, and there's no tellin' where he's wandered off to," screamed Fran. "If you see Jake and Sally Mae, tell them to help us look for him! Hurry!"

The two women split up and began scouring the area for Beth's missing father. They knew he couldn't have gone far because he didn't have enough energy to go anywhere, but they were afraid that in his present state of mind, he might accidentally hurt himself in some way.

Beth went back to the bus. Fran looked around inside the souvenir shop. They were moving quickly, asking everyone if they had seen any sign of Lawrence. It wasn't so much a matter of urgency, as it was a concern for his well being. By now, Jake and Sally Mae had also taken up the search without success. Sally Mae even went so far as to check under the bus.

When Fran couldn't locate Lawrence inside the shop, she went out the back door to see if perhaps he had walked behind the building. There was no sign of him on the long, sprawling terrace leading down to a vineyard that terminated at the shore of the lake. He wasn't at any of the picnic tables either, and she didn't see him at a smaller souvenir stand about 20 yards away. As Fran looked out toward the expanse of the lake, she wondered if Lawrence might have wandered in that direction for some reason. There were several large trees scattered about the terrace, but the missing Lawrence was nowhere to be seen. Fortunately, she just happened to be looking at one large tree in particular when she caught a glimpse of an arm as it suddenly appeared from behind the trunk and flopped out on to the ground.

Fran raced to the spot as rapidly as her short, chubby legs could get her there. Sure enough, Lawrence had found himself a cool, refreshing place in front of the tree, plopped down and returned to his realm of stupefied bliss. When Fran arrived, Lawrence had his eyes open slightly, staring blankly at the Castle of Chillon below, with the Alps rising loftily to the heavens in the background.

"This must be Switzerland," he said. "New York doesn't have mountains like this does it? Wonderful. Magnificent. Aren't they spectacular?"

Fran had to laugh. "You're a sight, darlin'," she said. "We've gotta sober you up, but how am I gonna get you back to the bus?"

She didn't want to leave him for fear that Lawrence might roam to some other unknown location. Or, God forbid, he might even straggle to the lake and drown before anyone knew it. As a precaution Fran decided to remain where she was, electing to call out to Jake for assistance.

In the struggle of getting Lawrence back to the coach, Jake continued his charade by seizing the opportunity to scold his father within earshot of other passengers so that they could clearly hear his mock admonitions. "Daddy, I told you not to take any more drinks. Where did you have that bottle hidden anyway? If you keep this up, we're not going to let you have any meals with us. We'll just leave you in your room with your booze and let you drink your way through Switzerland. My goodness, we came all this way to this beautiful country, and you embarrass us like this!"

The trio boarded the bus and made their way to the rear where Beth and Sally Mae were waiting. It was another hour to Sion, and Lawrence slept all the way. Meanwhile, the other travelers pretended to ignore the situation by staring out the windows at the passing panoramas. For the remainder of the journey they rode along in paralyzed silence.

It was mid-afternoon as the bus neared Sion. When it reached the center of town, the coach came to an intersection where it was supposed to make a 90-degree turn to the right for the drive up into the mountains. Before making the turn however, the driver pulled his vehicle over to the side of the road and came to a halt to let the five North Carolinians get off. During the search for Lawrence in Montreux, Beth had requested the stop so that her group could pick up their rental car in town without having to return later. The driver had agreed, and was now in the process of unloading the bags for the tiny band of Tarheel renegades. In the process, everyone else pressed their faces to the windows wondering what the latest delay was all about. Despite their obvious perplexity by yet another twist in the program, when the reason was made clear, the departure of the North Carolina contingent was greeted with rousing enthusiasm.

Beth and her party of vagabonds, were finally on their own, making their way through unfamiliar territory with luggage in hand. The first order of business was to locate the rental office. The temperature began to fall as the five explorers ambled their way through town in their quest for unlimited mobility. The cooler weather combined with the necessity of dealing with his two bags was enough to temporarily perk Lawrence up, because he was no longer afforded the opportunity of falling back to sleep. Though he was now semi-conscious, he was still battling the effects of the fatigue resulting from his multiple dosage of medication and jet-lag.

The town of Sion is over 2,000 years old, nestled in a valley in the canton of Valais. Switzerland has 26 such cantons, which are roughly equivalent to the states in the USA. The distinguishing features of Sion are two outcroppings of rock jutting from the floor of the valley and crowned by fortresses that immediately conjure a sense of history. Beth and her friends were walking along the Rue de Chateau, through the Old Town, toward the hill known as Valere. According to the instructions, the car rental company was located near the end of the street on the left.

After walking for a little more than five minutes, Lawrence suddenly erupted in an uncharacteristic surge of energy similar to the phenomenon when a chicken runs around the barnyard after its head has been severed from its body. The little cluster of travelers came to a halt. They were standing on the sidewalk when, for no apparent reason, Lawrence stopped dead in his tracks. After gazing around for a few seconds, he adamantly dropped his bags to the street, pointed to the majestic, snowcapped alpine peaks in the distance and in a voice of indignant frustration asked, "Just where the FUCK are we?"

His four traveling partners were dumbstruck. Their mouths dropped, looking at each other in bewildered silence before bursting into guffaws of hysterical laughter. What no one realized at that defining moment however, was that Lawrence had just opened Pandora's Box by establishing newfound verbal freedom for Fran's lucid vocabulary.

After securing the car, the group began the ascent to the hotel. The route up the mountain to the ski resort was breathtaking. Jake was at the wheel after demanding that he be appointed as designated driver. As the car made its way along its serpentine incline, Sion gradually receded into the landscape becoming increasingly miniaturized with each bend in the road. During the ascent, Jake was shifting gears to negotiate a hairpin curve when he spotted a long, narrow landing strip far below in the valley.

"Wow, look down there? What's that? That's really neat! Must be some kind of military facility or something."

Except for Lawrence, who was oblivious to anything by virtue of his ongoing tour of the twilight zone, the others were becoming increasingly nervous with Jake's enthusiasm for sightseeing as he drove up the mountain. When the car slipped off the edge of the road onto the shoulder, Beth spoke up. "Brother, you wanted to drive, so drive. If you want to look out the windows, we'll find someone else to get us around, but I don't feel like plummeting to my death this afternoon."

"I wuz fixin' to say," chimed in Sally Mae from the middle seat in the rear of the car, "I'd like to see where I'm stayin' before we take a shortcut down the mountain."

Fran was a nervous passenger anyway, and the idea of going up and down this narrow little road every day did not appeal to her at all. The incident in town with Lawrence had removed any semblance of decorum for the remainder of the trip. The gloves were off as she spewed forth a string of vulgarities that left no doubt about the way she felt. "Listen you little fucker," she said, "You get us to the top of this goddamned hill or I'll rip your balls off!"

Jake laughed to himself, ignoring the steady barrage of complaints. With renewed vigor he continued his quest for the summit. What he had seen below was indeed a military training ground. They could now see planes taking off and flying down through the valley. It was an awesome feeling to be so high in the mountains that they were actually looking down on planes in flight while riding in an automobile. It was an unexpected sensation, which Beth found difficult to define, a powerful feeling of omnipotence that was simultaneously humbling as well.

The rental car was a mid-range dark blue Renault that would have been relatively comfortable for five normal sized people, but with Sally Mae's added girth, it was cramped. Fortunately, Fran was smaller than most people so that allowed some compensation. Ultimately it was determined that whatever passenger configuration was chosen for a given day, it should be dictated by the basic premise that Sally Mae would ride in the middle of the back seat so as to create ballast for the upcoming long hauls.

One of Beth's hobbies was assigning nicknames to things, so after the rental car was secured in Sion, she informed the others that they needed to come up with a clever moniker for their vehicle. There was no lack of suggestions, everything from "Herbie" to "Rene" to "Van Go," "Bluebell," "Heidi," "Einstein," "The Blue Bomb" and "Jetlag" among others. Eventually, they took a vote and settled upon "Hannibal" since the car was going to take them over, under, around and through the Alps.

Though it was early May, the snow had not melted much at the higher elevations. Jake guided the car upward into the Alps as the drifts became steadily deeper, piling up to six or seven feet over their heads at the summit. Because of the twisting, turning climb to the top, it had been a good 25-minute drive from the valley to the hotel.

The accommodations were comfortable, but Spartan. Everyone else had already been checked in for an hour before the stragglers arrived. By now, those who were not overcome by the effects of the long day of travel following the overnight flight, had already made an orientation tour of the property. The rest of the group had settled in to their rooms to freshen up for the welcome party and dinner that evening. The respite proved a blessing for Lawrence, who was now able to lie down in a proper bed for a couple hours of sleep.

By dinnertime, Lawrence had recuperated enough to be partially coherent and aware of his surroundings. He was still groggy however, and would require an uninterrupted night of sleep to fully recover. The festivities called for casual attire, but for Lawrence that meant merely the absence of a tie. In every other respect he was the most formally dressed person in the room.

While in the process of mingling with his fellow passengers, he noticed a distinct hostility from many of them as he made great efforts to exude his customary charm. The unwelcome response was not a situation to which he was accustomed, leaving him quite taken aback by it all. "Are these people all snobs?" he thought to himself while making the rounds of the room.

Lawrence was grateful when the cocktail hour concluded and the meal service commenced allowing him to sequester himself with allies, sitting between Jake and Sally Mae and across from Beth and Fran during dinner. "These folks aren't very friendly," he commented to the group. "Everyone gave me the cold shoulder."

"Oh I think you're just imagining things," said Beth, "I met several people who were just delightful.

Francine had another take. "What'd you expect you old shit. You ignored them all the way over here and now you're tryin' to be Mr. Congeniality."

"Look we'll just have a nice dinner, and then we'll get plenty of sleep, and everything will be perfect in the morning," added Sally Mae. "By the way, how are you feeling now?"

"Weeell, I'm all right," Lawrence said without much conviction. His eyes were still heavy with the after-effects of the drugs, and everyone could tell that he was fighting to keep them open. He was trying his damnedest to be cordial, pleasant and his usual jovial self, but his eyelids might as well have had ten ton weights attached to them.

The dinner conversation continued among the other members of the group, but Lawrence was abnormally silent throughout. He was nearly halfway through the salad course when Beth looked over at him and asked, "Daddy we're having veal for dinner tonight. It's in a cream sauce with mushrooms and potatoes on the side. Do you like veal?"

"Oh, of course, dear. It's one of my favorites." Lawrence poked at his salad with his fork and then started to take another bite. Everyone continued to talk, failing to notice that he never finished his task. Lawrence had once again fallen asleep, only this time with his food halfway to his mouth. He was still sitting upright with his right forearm leaning against the table and his fork extended. Fran noticed it first, and elbowed Beth in the side. The conversation ceased as everyone stared at Lawrence with unbelieving eyes for a long silent moment. It wasn't long after that his body was forced to yield, and that's when the foundation of the human statue crumbled. Without warning, Lawrence's head and torso made a short backward motion before arcing forward and plunging face first into his lettuce with vinaigrette dressing and croutons. Day one in Europe had come crashing to an end.

The next day spilled forth with brilliant sunshine splashing across the snow-covered crest of the Alps. Without sunglasses the refraction of light off the snow was intense, severe to such a degree as to be blinding, but the warmth of its rays made the temperature comfortable enough to require only a light sweater.

Everyone was refreshed after a full night of sleep, eager to venture forth in the exploration of Switzerland. They all met at 8:30 for breakfast except for Lawrence. Though he was very much a morning person, Lawrence had decided to take his time preparing for the excursion, and asked Beth to bring him some coffee, juice and a roll.

"He's really fine now," said Beth to the others. "Just a bit of a headache and a touch of nausea, but I think he'll be OK when he's had a little something to eat and drink. He just wanted to have some quiet time to himself before we go."

"I've got just the thing to fix him up," chimed in Fran with enthusiasm. She was eager to help and, now that the worst was over, she was certain she had the perfect solution to finish off the recovery process. "Best stuff in the world. I'll go back to the room with you, and we'll have that old fart dancin' on tables in no time."

In the interim while Beth and Fran assisted Lawrence, Jake and Sally Mae also returned to their rooms to brush their teeth and pack a few items to take along for the day.

Fran burst into Lawrence's room with her usual flair. "Darlin' we're gonna' make you right! I've got some magic that'll have you back on your feet in no time."

"But I feel much better today. I don't know what happened to me yesterday. I just couldn't keep my eyes open. For some reason when I took my pills at the airport they just seemed to put me out," said Lawrence. Beth and Fran did a double take, then Fran let out one of her screeching bursts of laughter. "You mean you took your pills at the airport after we already gave you something?" asked Fran in surprise.

"That means you took a TRIPLE dose of medicine!" said Beth in astonishment. "It's a wonder you're still alive!"

"Well take this now and you'll be 100 percent." Fran reached down into her purse, pulled out a suppository and handed it to Lawrence.

Lawrence took the medicine and looked at Beth, "Would you get me a glass of water so I can take this, sweetheart?"

"Daddy, that's not oral medication," she answered with incredulity that he was unfamiliar about using such an item.

Fran wasn't so delicate. "You don't put it in that end, darlin'. All you do is stick it up your ass."

"My word," said Lawrence in a shocked voice. "That's disgusting."

"It may be, you old turd, but I guarantee you'll feel better when you do it. So either you get in there and shove that puppy into your butthole, or Beth and I will hold you down and do it for you."

Lawrence moved reluctantly to the bathroom and closed the door. When he came back a few minutes later, he had a strange look on his face. "Are you sure this is going to work? It's really uncomfortable, kind of scratchy and rough."

Fran and Beth looked at each other again, followed by more high-pitched laughter. "Scratchy and rough," said Fran. "It shouldn't feel like anything. It should be smooth. Wait a minute. Did you take the foil wrapper off that thing?" she asked.

"Well, no. I didn't know there was a wrapper on it. You didn't say anything about a wrapper. You mean I did it wrong?"

Fran let out a whine that could have caused an avalanche. "I guess you did do something wrong you dumb shit. Now look, I'm gonna give you one more chance. Go in there, take the other one out and throw it away. Then be sure to remove the foil from this one before you use it. If you do it right you'll feel better in about a half an hour." Lawrence had a boyish expression on his face, which was now red with embarrassment, as he lowered his head and shuffled back to the bathroom to make the proper adjustments.

For the next two days the five companions traveled through Switzerland and Italy with only minor mishaps. Sally Mae did manage to sit down on her camera once while getting into the back seat, thereby crushing it beyond recognition. She also broke the strap of her purse so that she was now either lugging it around under one of her gigantic arms, or letting it dangle at her side from the lone remaining strand of leather. At one point she even tied it into a knot under her belt so she wouldn't have to schlep it around any more. Lawrence, meanwhile, had not only become rather adept at inserting his rectal medicine, he had also become quite enamored with it, and kept begging Fran for more of her "silver bullets", but to no avail. As might be expected, there were also a few strained moments between Beth and Fran and Jake regarding map reading skills whenever Beth and Fran were in charge of the navigational chores.

"I'm sorry brother dear, but that turn wasn't marked clearly on the map. It's no big deal. We'll just turn around and go back," was a typical response from Beth.

Fran took another approach by incorporating her usual stream of obscenities into her distinctive style of communication. "Listen dickbird, if you can read it better than me, then I'll drive and you try to understand all this French and Italian shit. You're un-fuckin-believable you know it. Besides you drive like you're shiftin' with your prick. You men are all alike. We've got three pussys in this car and every one of us could drive better than you, so if you don't like the way I read a map then shove it up your ass and shit your own directions. Or else just keep quiet."

"My word," said Lawrence. "You know there are plenty of perfectly good synonyms you could be using when you go into one of your tirades. You really don't have to be so vulgar you know. I think we should work on your vocabulary, don't you?"

"Shut the fuck up, you old shit. I'll work on your vocabulary if you don't leave me alone. Don't forget I've got the medicine, so if you want to survive this trip don't cross my ass."

"Lord knows it would take a month to do that. We could cross the Alps faster," responded Jake sarcastically.

And so it went, though most of the time everything was spoken, and taken, in the context of good-natured fun.

On the first day out the plan was to make an attempt at going to Zermatt to see the Matterhorn. Beth had done some reading and knew that cars were not allowed in the village, but she figured they could get close enough to take another form of transportation for the final leg of the journey.

The first stop was the town of Brig. After a quick look around, they moved on to Visp, and then drove as far as possible toward Zermatt to a place called St. Niklaus. Everyone piled out of the car and went up to the postage stamp-sized railway station to see when the next train would be coming through, but the building was deserted. There was no sign that anyone might be returning any time soon either. Jake made a search to see if he could locate anyone who might be able to help, while Beth and Fran did their best to interpret the train schedule posted on the exterior wall. In later years, Beth would become well versed in reading and understanding train schedules, and using the rail system of Switzerland, but at this point she was a novice, and the timetable made no sense to her whatsoever. Sally Mae took off on a scouting mission for some snacks, managing to knock over a trash can and nearly falling down the stairs in the process, while Lawrence made use of the time by sitting on a platform bench and reading a biography of Benito Mussolini.

After twenty minutes with no trace of a train or the stationmaster, and without knowing how long it would be before either would appear, the group decided not to waste any more precious time and headed back to Sion in a different direction than the one in which they came.

The second excursion was a short trip into Italy to the resort village of Stresa. Since they were only going for the day, the five adventurers pooled their money and converted a minimal number of dollars to lira to cover things like sandwiches and drinks. They agreed that if anyone wanted to shop, they could exchange money as necessary on an individual basis, or use a credit card.

Stresa is a small resort at the base of Mt. Mottarone along the shores of Lake Maggiore. It is a popular year-round destination because of its mild climate, exceptionally beautiful parks and its proximity to the Borromean Isles, which are famous for their gardens, fountains, palaces and picturesque little houses.

Once more turmoil centered around Lawrence, who had always found considerable difficulty when dealing with foreign currencies. In this instance, he had purchased a cup of coffee for which the price was 3,000 lira. The sheer size of the number befuddled him, and though the actual cost of his drink was only about $2.00, he became overly flustered and confused by the transaction before being rescued, yet again, by his guardian angels.

It would have been impossible trying to explain to Lawrence what had happened in a manner that would be understandable to him, so on the way back to Sion everyone just let him ramble on about it, paying little attention to his muttering. "Can you believe 3,000 lira for a cup of coffee? That's ridiculous. Don't these people have any scruples at all? I certainly didn't leave a tip, I'll tell you that. Next time I'm just drinking water. That'll show'em. Thank goodness I didn't order a whole meal. We'd all be washing dishes now. How absurd."

"Listen everybody, I've got an idea," Jake interrupted while also trying to change the subject. "Whaddya think about driving down to Florence tomorrow, and then maybe going over to Monte Carlo the next day? I've been looking at the map, and it doesn't look all that far."

"Sounds grand," said Lawrence, who was delighted that his son wanted to pursue something cultural. He was keen on the idea, having been to Florence briefly once before. The artistic pursuits very much appealed to him, though he had no concept about the logistics of the journey. Neither did anyone else for that matter, placing their trust solely on the basis of Jake's research.

"Sounds good to me. I'd love to see Florence. Especially the David. I've always wanted to see that," said Beth.

"I wuz fixin' to say, David sounds good. Besides isn't Florence where *Room With a View* took place? I liked that movie. Let's go there," added Sally Mae.

Fran completed the unanimous vote in her usual blunt style. "Yeah shit, I don't give a fuck where we go, as long as you keep your ass on the highway, you son of a bitch. I would like to see Monte Carlo though. Maybe some rich prince will take us out on his yacht."

The next day was Saturday. Everyone packed a small bag with just enough clothes for a couple of days of touring, and off they went to Tuscany. Beth should have known better than to embark on a weekend excursion without first changing some money, but she figured it would be a fairly easy process somewhere near the border after crossing into Italy. Getting through customs just north of Aosta was not a problem, but there was no place at all to convert funds, and at the time, no one gave it a second thought as to being a potential cause for trouble later on.

Torino was the next major city en route. Normally, everything could have been taken care of there. The plan was to stop in Torino for a quick lunch, change money and then continue on to Florence. Unfortunately, they arrived at 1:15 in the afternoon. Siesta! Everything was closed. Torino was a ghost town.

The hungry road warriors piled back into Hannibal with Sally Mae now riding up front in the unfamiliar shotgun position, while Lawrence sat in the back, reading about Mussolini between Beth and Fran.

"We'll take the autostrada," said Jake with authority, "That's the fastest way. It's supposed to be like an interstate highway, but I'm gonna need to stop for gas pretty soon. I'm starting to get a little low, so keep your eyes open for a station."

Lunch was a haphazard affair consisting of the cookies, crackers and chips they had all brought along for snacks. The temperature was getting warmer now. Since the car had no air conditioning, everyone rolled down the windows for ventilation. While the strategy created plenty of circulation, the turbulence of the hot air blasting through the openings of the windows also had a tiring effect, especially on Jake who was feeling the added burden of the intense concentration of driving so long in unfamiliar conditions.

Cars whizzed along the superhighway at what seemed to be incredibly high rates of speed. It was Jake's first time driving in Italy and his inexperience with the protocol of the road, plus the strain of trying to interpret road signs in another language, combined with the oppressive heat was taking its toll. At one point, he found himself cruising along in the passing lane at better than 120 kilometers an hour when the car behind began blinking its lights. Jake quickly understood that he needed to move to the right to allow the faster traffic to get by. That's when he learned that in Europe, the left hand lane is for passing only, otherwise, be prepared to get run over.

Jake eased his way to the right, making room for the trailing vehicle to move on past, but as it went by, he was astonished to see that it was a hearse that was overtaking him. His traveling mates were equally surprised, except for Lawrence who calmly looked up from his book and asked matter of factly, "What's his hurry?" After that, nothing more needed to be said.

It was twenty miles further down the autostrada when the trouble really began, and the lack of preparation hit full force. That's when Hannibal and its five passengers encountered the first of several toll booths. Nobody had any Italian money, nor did anyone remotely speak or understand Italian. All hell was about to break loose.

The guard was polite enough. For a while. He just didn't speak any English. There was a lot of hand waving and gesturing mingled with rapid fire dialogue that ended mostly in vowels, but there was very little, if any, communication. Traffic was quickly stacking up behind the little blue Renault as Jake and Sally Mae attempted valiantly to make an arrangement for paying the officer. Nothing seemed to work, and it was becoming increasingly flustering in the heat of the Italian afternoon to deal with the language barrier, monetary conversion and the confusion. The only person who remained subdued throughout the incident was Lawrence, who was completely engrossed in Mussolini and totally unaware that any turmoil was even taking place.

At last the guard realized the plight of his ignorant customers from the United States and understood their predicament, or at least, he pretended that he did. He began making a gesture by brushing his thumb over the first two fingers of his right hand. Jake knew the guard was telling him to pay up in some form of hard currency. All the toll official wanted was to get Jake and his entourage out of the way so he could reduce the growing line of cars that now seemed to stretch all the way back to Switzerland.

Jake reached into his pocket and pulled out a wad of dollar bills. The guard leaned down and supposedly took the proper amount for the toll. But who could tell whether it was correct or not? At that point, it didn't matter. Jake only wanted to move beyond the barrier and drive on down the road, because he was now facing the prospects of another catastrophe. He was desperately in need of gas.

The guard signaled to Jake to move along and then made another gesture in the process. Though no one in the car grasped the meaning of his sign language, everyone knew it was something rude. Even Fran had the good sense to hold her tongue until the mini-crisis was over, however.

Once they were well away from the tollbooth, Fran spoke up, "I'll bet that WOP bastard spoke English! He was just trying to take advantage of us dumb Americans. They all speak English over here, those little fuckers. I'd like to pull their peckers right back through their assholes and give'm a tail."

"Look, we've got another problem," said Jake with mounting apprehension. "We need to find some gas soon or we're gonna be spending the night on the side of this autostrada."

They drove along for several more kilometers with no luck until Beth finally spotted a sign. "Look there's an "Esso". Isn't that what "Exxon" used to be called? I've got an Exxon card. Maybe we can use that."

The filling station was only a few more kilometers away. Less than five minutes later. Jake pulled in and drove alongside the pumps thinking his troubles were finally over. In truth, they were about to get worse. Not only would the station not accept the Exxon card, they wouldn't take any credit card except Esso, and the cash situation at this point wasn't even worth discussing. Jake was disheartened as he crawled back into the car and asked, "Now what'll we do?"

Beth's mind raced for a solution. "Well I think we should get off this autostrada as soon as possible," she suggested. "Then we'll stop at the first town we come to and see if we can get gas there. At least we'll be able to get near some type of civilization, instead of being stranded out here, and maybe we can eventually find someone who speaks a little English."

"Good fuckin' idea," said Fran.

"I wuz fixin' to say," added Sally Mae.

It was still the middle of siesta, and Hannibal was barely gasping on a few remaining fumes of fuel when Jake pulled up to a lone desolate looking gasoline pump somewhere well off the superhighway. Beth and Fran got out and went over to the garage, which was closed. Beth knew it would be better if the women went begging instead of the men. That was one lesson she had learned early in her career. If she made the right connection, a woman could always do better at the pity game than her male counterparts.

"What are we doing here?" asked Lawrence looking up from his book.

"We're trying to get some gas," said Jake. "Shut up and just keep reading your book, OK."

It was a remote setting, but it was the best possibility they had seen, and besides, there just weren't any other options. The garage connected to a weathered old house, which showed even fewer signs of life than the service facility. After several minutes of loud banging, a middle aged Italian woman finally came to the door.

Beth looked at her with forlorn eyes, giving an Academy Award performance as an American refugee, and said, "English, speaka da English?"

The woman stared back at her and shook her head no.

Beth pointed to the car sitting by the pump and said, "Petrol. We needa da petrol. Fuelo? Gasolina? Is OK? You pump for us?"

The woman understood what Beth wanted, and without speaking she communicated with a series of short gestures. Putting the palms of her hands together, she then rested them beside her head, tilting it slightly to one side and closing her eyes.

"Ah siesta. Si, si, si." said Beth. Then it was her turn to create some impromptu sign language of her own. Using the knowledge that Italy was predominantly Catholic, Beth first crossed herself, then she put her hands together and raised them in front of her face as if she was praying. Or pleading. Or both.

Whichever message came through, the Italian woman finally took compassion for their predicament and gave in. Holding up her forefinger she said, "Momento," and then disappeared for several minutes.

When the woman returned, she was walking quickly and pointing back to her left in the direction from which she had come. Moments later, a grotesque looking man emerged from the darkness, pulling his suspenders up over his slumped shoulders. It was difficult to tell whether he had been sleeping or not, but it didn't really matter because either way, he could have been a cast member from any one of a dozen slasher movies.

His matted black hair sprouted in wild clusters that went in every conceivable direction. Only one of his eyes functioned properly, the other was partially closed and drooping to the side with a severe scar running from the corner down to the middle of his left cheek. His mouth was also disfigured, and his body slouched as he moved forward on a stiff right leg that dragged behind the other. There was no need to worry about speaking Italian, or any other language, because the only sounds that emanated from this matinee monster were low guttural grunts and groans emerging from somewhere deep within the recesses of his throat.

Beth and Fran followed behind the oversized troll as he shuffled toward the pump. In a way, Beth felt guilty for thinking to herself that this man made Quasimodo look like a homecoming queen, but there was no denying that he was ugly with a capital "U". They had already created havoc in this poor Italian's life by disrupting his daily routine, and now here she was being overly analytical about his appearance. After all, he was in fact coming to their assistance at a time when there had been no other possibilities available.

Jake walked over to the two women. He had a huge smile on his face. "Sis, you're a genius. How in the world did you do it? How did you get this guy to fill up our tank when we don't have money," he said boisterously.

Both Beth and Fran turned in tandem, simultaneously shooting a glare at Jake as if they had been pistol-whipped. "Will you shut up," answered Fran between gritted teeth. Then she spoke in a hushed voice, "Let him give us the gas first, then we'll worry about how to pay for it later."

"Oh great," whispered Jake. "Look at this guy, he probably ate two babies for lunch. Who do ya' think he's gonna take it out on when we tell'em we haven't got any cash? From the looks of it, he hasn't smiled since before Vesuvius erupted. Matter of fact, from the looks of things he coulda been at the base of the volcano catching lava."

Beth kept motioning to Jake to lower his voice. "Keep it down will you, or he'll know something's wrong. Just smile and be polite, and we'll figure something out."

By now, Sally Mae had joined the rest of the group, yapping away with her usual jovial high-spirited personality. "Guess it won't be long now, and we'll be back on the road to "Davidville." What'd you offer to pay the gasoline phantom with, green stamps? Vino? Pasta?"

"Shhhh," came the immediate response from the other three onlookers.

In a scolding voice Beth said, "Be quiet will you. We don't know how much he understands."

It wouldn't be much longer before they found out. The pump stopped. The tank was once again full, and the Italian man replaced the gas cap. He turned to the pump and pointed to the price window, which no one could read because of the multiple zeroes. The four Americans stood there with impish, apologetic grins on their faces, looking alternately guilty and foolish, shuffling the dirt in arced motions with the toes of their shoes and generally resembling characters in a Looney Tunes cartoon. The attendant was not amused. He grunted, and pointed to the pump again, pressing his forefinger hard against the glass.

Jake took his hands out of his pockets and turned them palms up with his arms pressed close to his side and bent at the elbows as if to say, "Sorry." He flashed a silly embarrassed smile, which only served to aggravate the surly Italian further. It was clear the attendant was losing what little remaining patience he might have had. Once again, he looked at the pump, only this time he banged it sharply with his fist and snarled menacingly.

Beth was getting scared. She reached into her purse and took out some American money.

"No dollar. Lira. Italia," snarled the Italian who was now moving forward, dragging his right leg and holding his hands out as if he was going to strangle the first person he could reach. From out of nowhere, with a sudden burst of bravado, Sally Mae, who had been standing behind her three companions, pushed the others aside and took two giant steps forward. Sucking air into her lungs with one powerful breath, her breasts inflated to the size of what seemed like a pair of Goodyear blimps, and her entire body swelled up like a hot air balloon. Sally Mae spread her tree-like legs, standing flatfooted with her balled fists planted firmly against her abundant hips. Then she scowled at the Italian, "If you want my friends, you gotta come through me first."

It was shaping up as an encounter that would be considered a dream match for the World Wrestling Federation, but instead the ogre-man surprised everyone by suddenly stopping dead in his tracks. With his slouch, he must have been a foot or more shorter than Sally Mae, and as he looked up at her angry red face, he realized that one good pop on the top of his head might either drive him into the ground, or permanently crush his one good leg into a thousand pieces. Compromise was now in order.

"Is OK," the Italian said meekly. Moving toward the garage, he waved his left arm signaling the others to follow. When the danger had passed, Sally Mae exhaled a forceful gasp of relief from holding her breath for an extended period of time. Her heart was pounding like a riveting machine from the anxiety of her newly discovered courage, though she had to admit that she also felt tremendous exhilaration at her ability to respond in a crisis.

Trying to calm herself, Sally Mae leaned against a barrel beside the gasoline pump while attempting to sit down. In the process, she somehow managed to miss the rim of the barrel and crashed to the ground in a heap, all the while dabbing at her face with a handkerchief. Rolling around in a huge glob of embarrassment, with nothing hurt other than her pride, she waddled to her feet, thankful the others were preoccupied with more important matters and had not witnessed her misfortune.

Meanwhile, there were intense negotiations underway at the garage. The situation was finally resolved when the Italian woman made a phone call to find out the current exchange rate between lire and dollars. After much finagling and computing, it was agreed that the bill should be $30. Everyone chipped in a ten spot, leaving the extra $10 as a tip for all the trouble they had caused. Then the four wanderers loaded back into the car, and resumed their journey.

There were two additional toll booth incidents along the way to Florence, but this time Jake anticipated those eventualities, and though they were still maddening, they were nothing to compare with the first encounter back up the road. At long last, shortly before 4 p.m., Hannibal, and its harried band of travelers, rolled into Italy's artistic centerpiece on the Arno River.

The next hurdle was finding a hotel. No easy task under the best of conditions, but now further complicated by the cumulative effects of the heat, the haggling and the physical exertion of driving through Switzerland and Italy. In particular Jake was ready to stop anywhere in the middle of the first piazza he came to and surrender.

Since Lawrence was the only member of the group who had ever been to Florence, and now because he was also the most rested, he was given the task of locating the accommodations for the night. He had already mentioned to

Beth that he thought he knew of a good hotel, and felt he could remember where it was, once he recognized a familiar landmark. What Lawrence failed to realize was that he had been on a walking excursion during his previous visit, not driving, which radically altered his perception of the destination. At first that little difference didn't seem like much, but ultimately the maze of one-way streets, combined with the Italian signs and the hordes of visitors made it impossible for Lawrence to get any sort of accurate bearings.

"That looks like it. Oh no, I'm sorry. Turn left here. No, no I mean right."

"Can't turn right, it's one-way," said Jake who was becoming increasingly testy and frazzled.

"Well go straight then. Yes, that's right. I remember now. This looks familiar. I think it's just around the corner. Oops. No, it was back there. Sorry." Lawrence was getting more and more confused, and Jake was getting angrier with every turn, stop, whoops and reversal.

Jake's patience finally ran out when he passed the same piazza for the third time, and for the third time Lawrence said, "Yes, that's it. Now I know where we are."

The car came to a sudden, violent, screeching halt. Jake screamed an obscenity that even made Fran cower in the seat. Then he drove to the first side street he could find, pulled up beside a building and parked Hannibal Italian-style in the middle of the sidewalk. He got out of the car, slamming the door furiously. "Wait here. I'm gonna find a fuckin' hotel if it's the last thing I do. Just wait. I'll be back as soon as I can."

The others stood forlornly in the street as Jake stormed off in a blaze of fury, not realizing at the time how fortunate he had been in his choice of parking places. There was a small hotel directly in front of him, just two blocks away. When he saw the sign which read *Hotel de la Ville*, he might as well have found an oasis after a week in the desert. He ran as fast as he could to the revolving door and up to the front desk, praying that there were a couple of rooms available.

Not only were there two vacancies, they were only $100 a night. "I'll take'm," Jake shouted with glee. "Momento, momento. We'll be right back."

Jake had been gone less than ten minutes when he returned to the others. "Listen," he said excitedly, "I've found a place. They've got two rooms for a hundred bucks a night each. Let's take everything with us. We'll lock up the car and leave it right here, and wherever we go tonight, we'll just walk. We need some exercise anyway."

The little gang of road weary travelers couldn't unload the car fast enough. "Don't leave anything in the car," said Beth. "We don't have that much stuff anyway, but take it all."

Sally Mae chimed in with, "I wuz fixin' to say," and Fran added, "I can't wait to get my tired butt into a hot bath."

"That porcelain will be screamin' when it sees your ass bearin' down on it," laughed Jake.

"Shut the fuck up before I stick my shoe so far up your behind they'll have to give you bypass surgery to get it out," Fran shouted back.

Lawrence was silent. He was not accustomed to being yelled at for any reason, and his dignity had clearly been damaged for the moment. Fortunately, by the time everyone had checked in, and had an opportunity to freshen up and relax, apologies were made and hard feelings were put aside. While Jake was in the bathroom cleaning up, Beth took a few minutes to have a heart to heart chat with her father about the events of the day. When Lawrence was informed about all the difficulties, many of which had escaped him because of his involvement with his book, he understood the source of Jake's frustration, and he became his usual debonair self again.

Considering the many mishaps of the day, dinner turned out to be delightful. The evening was gentle and warm, and the ancient buildings in the Piazza della Signoria were bathed in an amber glow that washed away the rough edges of the peeling layers of history. The night air was filled with romantic softness that can only be found in Italy. Piazzas large and small were filled with music and the gaiety of life. Lovers strolled through the streets holding hands. All around were the same ambient sounds of living that have remained unchanged for hundreds of years; kitchen conversations, dishes being stacked on top of each other, violins at sidewalk cafes, the clip-clopping of horses pulling carriages over uneven streets.

The five explorers found a sidewalk cafe and sat down. Instantly, they were surrounded by Florence's love affair with the pageantry of life and all its medieval charms that were transposed into the 20th century. Not far away, across the street in front of a large hotel, musicians serenaded under the stars. A waist-high fence separated the hotel property from the street just 20 feet beyond where Beth's group was sitting. The fence was all that prevented them from paying for the very same music they were now listening to for free. It was a soothing, comfortable atmosphere that mellowed the frustrations of the day, pushing them far into the past as if they, too, had happened centuries ago.

The next day was spent doing the usual tourist sights of Michelangelo's hometown. In order to stay ahead of the crowds, Beth suggested that they go to the *Accademia* first to view the David.

Michelangelo believed the figures he sculpted existed within the material he was working on, and that his task was to release those forms from the marble through the divine gifts with which he had been born. He lived a full and productive, though troubled, life. While in his early 20's, he sculpted the magnificent Pieta, which can be viewed at *St. Peter's* in Rome, yet he designed the cupola for that basilica after he was 80 years old. He died in Rome at the age of 89, and was initially buried there, but his body was later smuggled out of the city by merchants who wanted to return the remains to the church in his old neighborhood. Today, he lies in the *Basilica of Santa Croce* in Florence.

In addition to being a sculptor and a painter, Michelangelo was also an architect as well as an accomplished poet. The great artist even wrote his own epitaph with a marvelous economy of words which simply say, "I

commit my body to the earth, my soul to God and all my worldly possessions to my family."

Besides the precision of his chisel, the genius of Michelangelo lies
within the subtleties of his work, which contain both symbolism and passion in his message that transcends the completed sculptures and paintings. For example, closer inspection of the Pieta shows that it was created
in the shape of a triangle representing the trinity of the Father, the Son
and the Holy Ghost. Similarly, the direction of David's glance had political significance based upon the artist's knowledge of where the statue was
to be placed in the Piazza della Signoria. It was Michelangelo's intent to
make a statement about Rome and the Medici family during his lifetime.
Beyond that were the intricacies of his techniques combined with a powerful, innate sense of perspective in relationship to the space in which his
works were to be viewed. Michelangelo believed his Moses would be witnessed from below, and therefore, the right side of the sculpture is not pro-
portional to the rest of the piece because he anticipated the point of view
to be from a totally different angle than the one that is seen today. Visitors
to the *Church of St. Peter in Chains* in Rome, where the Moses is presently
displayed, observe the sculpture at eye level rather than looking upward at
it, which alters the scale, but at the same time, further emphasizes the
incredible talent and proficiency of Michelangelo.

Walking through the *Accademia* leading toward the David, there are
several unfinished pieces by the artist where visitors can view examples of
figures that appear trapped within the raw material, as if trying desperately
to free themselves from the stone. By displaying these works first, the
magnificence of the masterpiece of the David is reinforced and enhanced
by allowing patrons to make comparisons.

"Stunning," was all that Lawrence could say as he moved toward the
classic sculpture with reverence in his stride.

Even Jake had to admit it was the most imposing work of art he had
ever seen. Confined to the indoor space where it now stood, the sculpture
looked even larger than the copy outside in the Piazza della Signoria. For

nearly 400 years, the David had withstood the elements in the piazza until it was brought inside at the end of the 19th century. The crowds were gathered all around the statue taking pictures from every angle, even though photographs were supposedly forbidden.

Beth was awe-struck. The craftsmanship and detail were beyond anything she had imagined. Sally Mae, Fran and Jake were equally taken by the magnitude of the piece. To see the work in person was to subliminally feel the presence of the man who had left the genius of his legacy permanently etched into the world of art and the very fabric of Florentine history.

This was a towering accomplishment that even the most cynical of art critics could not ignore, for it took no great understanding or expertise to be completely enthralled by the skill of its creator. This was perfection personified.

"I've done a little reading about this particular work," said Lawrence, "Would you like me to tell you more about it?"

"Sure," answered Beth enthusiastically.

"Well, it stands more than 14 feet high, although I think it looks taller than that myself. Besides the beauty of the finished sculpture itself, there are two other facts that make the end result even more remarkable. The first is that the original block of marble was abandoned by another artist who had begun the sculpture and couldn't make it work, so he quit. When Michelangelo took over, the David was therefore already in progress, and he had to overcome the errors of the previous sculptor."

"And what's the second fact?" asked Sally Mae.

"Well, that's even more interesting. You see, the marble wasn't very thick. It was just a long, narrow, rectangular slab that nobody thought had any practical use. It presented Michelangelo with the problem of depth, and whether or not he could produce an entire, three-dimensional figure. Obviously, he solved the problem."

"Look at the veins in his hands and the muscle tone in his chest and legs. What else do you know, you old fart," asked Fran.

"If you look at his right hand, David is still holding the stones. He's preparing for battle, and he has his sling over his left shoulder. For whatever reason, Michelangelo chose to depict his hero just before he killed Goliath, not the aftermath when he would have been celebrating the glory of his victory. In this way, the artist has captured not only the innocence and the youth of his figure, but also that moment of apprehension just before his triumph."

"There's another wonderful little bit of trivia about the David that not many people know. Michelangelo dearly loved the quarries of Carrara where he obtained his marble, and he sometimes spent days, even weeks, there looking for just the right piece of marble for his sculptures. You can't see it, but on the top of the David there is still one small portion of uncut stone, which experts say was intentionally left that way in order to maintain Michelangelo's connection with the place from which it came."

"When Michelangelo first unveiled this sculpture, the people threw fruit and vegetables at it. There's a dispute today among scholars as to whether they were upset by the political statement Michelangelo was making, or by the nudity of the male figure."

Everyone knew what was coming next. It was only a matter of time before Fran let out some of her more poignant observations. "Well darlin', let me tell you, he's got one hellacious ass," she said. Then she looked over at Jake and added, "And how'd you like to have your pecker get a hard-on like that one. Permanent. Never goes down."

"You don't know what you're talkin' about," said Jake. "I could have been the model for that thing."

"Model my ass. Shit, Michelangelo didn't have a chisel small enough for your dick. If you'da been the model he'd have spent most of his time lookin' for a piece of marble the size of a matchbox. Talk about proportion, we'd all be standin' here with magnifying glasses lookin' for that thing. Hell, we might even mistake him for a woman."

"Let me tell you somethin', if Michelangelo had been sculpting your ass, there ain't a piece of marble in all of Italy big enough. He could have started chiselin' your butt in the Middle Ages and wouldn't have finished until the Renaissance was over. The Alps aren't that big," replied Jake.

The fivesome spent the remainder of the day visiting other sights in Florence such as *Santa Croce* where the tombs of Michelangelo, Dante, Machiavelli and Galileo are located, among others. Afterwards they went to the *Duomo* and then over to the world famous *Uffizi Gallery* to view even more art.

Later, after lunch, they shopped along the Ponte Vecchio, the famed bridge across the Arno River, which is another landmark in the city. Sally Mae persisted in saying that she was visiting the Ponte Vecchio Bridge, which Beth tried to explain was the same thing as referring to it as "the old bridge bridge" since the word "ponte" means "bridge" and the word "vecchio" means "old". Somehow it never registered however, and Beth finally gave up.

By early evening, the three women had weaned themselves completely off art and were making a rapid transition to shopping mode. Lawrence took his map and made his way on foot to the Brancacci Chapel, across the river, to view the frescoes by Masaccio and Filippino Lippi, which had a major influence on Michelangelo's early life. Jake, who had no interest in either scenario, found himself a quiet sidewalk cafe and immersed himself in the biggest beer in Florence.

Upon departing Florence the next morning, there was another surprise awaiting the snake-bitten travelers. Hannibal had been vandalized. The driver's side window was completely smashed in, leaving thousands of tiny shards of glass scattered throughout the interior of the car. The thieves had apparently spotted the sticker identifying the car as a rental, and had taken the opportunity to relieve Hannibal of a window and any excess cargo. Fortunately, despite their fatigue on the day of their arrival, the group had the foresight to take all of their personal belongings with them to the hotel. The extent of the damage was nothing more than unwanted permanent air conditioning, and a benign laceration on Sally Mae's rear end when she accidentally sat down on a piece of broken glass.

It was a gorgeous day for an excursion. Billowy clouds puffed into a cobalt blue sky that became a brilliant backdrop for the outlines of white that etched their patterns into the rich blue curtain. The sun was warm, and the air was freshened by the lack of humidity. Everyone was rested and alert from the tortures of the journey into Italy from Switzerland, and this time they had taken precautions against any further surprises that might arise.

The first stop en route to Monte Carlo was Pisa, just so everyone could say they had seen the *Leaning Tower*. Afterwards, Jake decided to take the coastal road from Italy into France, figuring the views would be a stunning mixture of mountains plunging into the sea, quaint coastal villages and European charm in its most rustic sense. Sadly it turned out to be another monumental miscalculation.

There was nothing rustic or charming about the congestion and traffic along the way, and rarely was there ever a glimpse of scenery that was even remotely memorable. Somewhere in Jake's subconscious he had envisioned a breathtaking ride along a corniche reminiscent of the road Grace Kelly drove with Cary Grant in Alfred Hitchcock's classic thriller *To Catch a Thief*. Instead, the end result resembled outtakes from an Inspector Clouseau movie. At one point, there were so many people, automobiles and motor scooters to the left of their vehicle that Jake was forced to the right, where he sideswiped a jagged piece of rock jutting from the mountain leaving a two foot scratch and dent along the passenger's door. Hannibal was beginning to look like a survivor from a demolition derby. By the time they made their way through Genoa, Jake had had enough and chose to return to the autostrada.

Since the main road hugged the coast to some degree, the terrain presented a new phenomenon that had not been encountered during the inland adventures. Tunnels. At first, the tunnels fascinated Lawrence because each was so distinctive with a variety of sizes, shapes and lengths. As a way of passing some time, he decided to make a precise calculation as to the exact number by counting all the tunnels between Genoa and

Monte Carlo. He was well past two hundred, and begging for one of Fran's silver bullets, when Jake finally steered Hannibal down the winding road that led to the diminutive Principality of Monaco.

This time there was no scouring town for a place to stay. When Jake spotted the *Loew's* hotel down along the waterfront, he immediately drove in that direction. Within fifteen minutes, the group had checked in and was comfortably nestled in their rooms. It was now early evening. The clouds had succumbed to a glorious black canopy sequined with stars. The moon cast a silver path across the inky sea, highlighted by thousands of fireflies of light dancing upon the crests of the gently lapping waves. When everyone had changed for dinner, Jake drove to the top of the hill where they strolled through the world famous casino, fantasizing that they were spies on a secret mission to infiltrate some powerful international crime syndicate. Dinner consisted of sampling several types of crepes, washed down with a couple of bottles of the local wine. By 10:30, everyone was in bed.

Being an early riser, Beth was up with the sun the next morning. Choosing to take advantage of the coolness of the hour, she decided to explore her new environs on foot before meeting the others for breakfast. It was only a couple of weeks until the running of the world famous Grand Prix of Monaco which takes place at the end of May every year. Already the grandstands and viewing areas had been set up. Part of the track ran along the waterfront past the hotel, so Beth figured it would be an ideal way to see the layout first hand. She knew the course would eventually bring her back to the hotel and by following its path, she could not only learn the nuances of what the drivers had to endure, she would also get an excellent overall orientation of Monte Carlo itself.

By the time she got back to the hotel, about an hour later, the others were just coming down to the breakfast room. "How was your walk?" asked Sally Mae as Beth arrived at the table.

"Invigorating. This is a beautiful little place with all the yachts down by the harbor and the casino and the castle. I guess Grace Kelly was no dummy," answered Beth.

"Well you know what," said Fran, "After breakfast I'm goin' out by that pool and put my ass out in that gorgeous Mediterranean sun."

"Oooh, that sounds like fun," said Beth. "It's really getting nice out there now. What about you, Sally Mae, wanta join us?"

"I wuz fixin' to say. You know I never lay out back home, but what the hell you only get to Monte Carlo once. Ain't that right?"

"Well, I'll just take my book out by the pool and read while you ladies bake yourselves," said Lawrence.

When breakfast concluded, Lawrence excused himself to return to his room to pick up his biography. The women went to change into their swimsuits, and Jake sauntered out to the pool while waiting for the others to return.

Already the sun worshippers had arrived to soak in the golden rays of the Cote d'Azur. Though Jake knew in the back of his mind that he was in France, like so many Americans the first time they experience a European summer, he was still unprepared for the multitude of glistening mounds pointing to the sun in all their naked glory. At first he wasn't quite sure that his initial surveillance was accurate. Once he realized that his assessment was correct, and that he was indeed staring at a plethora of bare breasts, his attitude quickly changed from that of casual observer to one of all-consuming interest. Try as he may to camouflage his voyeurism, Jake's nonchalance was even more transparent than the swimwear. "What a great country," he thought as he plunked down on a lounge chair surrounded by his newly discovered oasis of flesh.

Moments later Lawrence arrived at the pool. He spotted Jake and walked over to him. Up to this point, the environment had not registered with him until Jake said, "Daddy, look at all these topless women!"

Lawrence stopped and stared, astounded by what he saw. His mouth dropped, and he began turning in circles. First one direction, then another. "My word! They're all naked! How could they do this? How shameful. I'm shocked."

"Yeah, ain't it great," said Jake with satisfaction. "This is my kind of place."

Despite the fact that Lawrence had been abroad on several occasions previously, he had never before encountered topless sunbathing, and his reaction, therefore, was virtually no different than Jake's. Father and son were now completely immersed in a near terminal case of "breast whiplash", craning their necks left and right as if they were mid-court at a tennis match. "I've never seen anything like this," said Lawrence. "My goodness, where is their modesty? Have these women no pride?"

"Screw the modesty, from what I can see, they should all be damned proud," replied Jake.

While Lawrence went on with his continuous commentary about what he was witnessing, Jake kept on smiling, yet neither of them moved from their seats. But it was only the beginning, for it was merely a scene setter for their three female traveling mates who were now making their way to the pool.

When Beth, Fran and Sally Mae walked up to Lawrence, he immediately brought their attention to the fact that most of the women at poolside were topless. "So they are," remarked Fran, "That's the way they do it here in Europe. I should think you'd be delighted. Look at all those boobs. Have you ever seen anything like it?"

"Delighted? What about their dignity?" answered Lawrence.

Beth was beginning to get the devilish twinkle in her eyes that meant she was up to something. "You know what, girls, I think we should experience this for ourselves. What do you say we go native?"

Fran looked over at Sally Mae and then back to Beth with a smile of approval. "Sounds good to me," she said.

"I was just fixin' to say," said Sally Mae. "These babies need to breathe in some of the French Riviera."

Lawrence was horrified, though he didn't really believe his partners would go through with their threat. He was even more shocked when

Beth pulled over a lounge chair, laid out her towel and proceeded to remove the bra of her bathing suit, exposing her breasts to the sun, sea and sky. Fran wasn't far behind, followed by Sally Mae who unleashed an avalanche of flesh that seemed to erupt from their source in slow motion. Her breasts surged together like two epidermal tidal waves crashing into each other from opposite sides of her body before bouncing upon her belly like overfilled water balloons. Sally Mae's bosoms were perpetually in motion, like human lava lamps that never stopped moving in one direction or another. Mammarys that could be described as resembling twin Hindenburgs. If Sally Mae was a metaphor for the Alps, then by comparison, Beth and Fran looked like foothills beside her.

The three women lay down on their chairs, snickering to themselves at how naughty they were being so far from home. The freedom was not only liberating, but exhilarating as well. It was unlike anything they had ever experienced.

"What's the matter, Lawrence darlin', ain't you ever seen titties before?" asked Fran.

Lawrence didn't know how to respond. "Well not yours and certainly not my own daughter's. This is terrible. Aren't you embarrassed? Don't you realize what you're doing? Goodness gracious, how would you like it if I just sat down and dangled my testicles in front of you?"

"Go ahead," said Fran smiling. "Wouldn't bother us. We'd like to see'm, wouldn't we ladies? Besides, if Jake had any balls at all, he'd show us Jake, Jr. As I recall, he claimed to be the prototype for the David didn't he? Now we can find out for sure."

Jake didn't answer. He was speechless. He had been defeated on the verbal battlefield, and he knew it. Neither he nor Lawrence now knew quite where to look as the three women busily oiled themselves with layers of sunblock. At any other time, in any other place, with any other women, the scene might have been a dream come true for Jake, but watching his sister, her close friend and the winner of the Andre the Giant look-alike contest grease up for a day in the sun was more than he could take.

Sally Mae was so large that at certain angles she occasionally blocked Beth and Fran from the sun, putting them momentarily into a shadow. The act of coating her plentiful endowment in coconut oil was a time consuming process. It was not unlike massaging a pair of freshly picked watermelons. For several minutes she slathered every inch of her massive chest. Flesh oozed out of the palms of her hands and between her fingers, from top to bottom, between her cleavage and all around her equally ample nipples. "Don't wanta miss anyplace. It'd be a helluva burn, you know. These puppies ain't ever been in the sun before," said Sally Mae matter of factly.

Lawrence had had enough. "Jake and I have some shopping to do, so we'll meet you later, OK," he said.

"Yeah, that's right," added Jake, "There's a couple of museums I've been wantin' to see too. With that the two men left the pool area, and did not return until dinnertime.

The following day, everyone checked out of the hotel early for the drive back to Sion.

"Never had an all over tan before," said Fran snickering happily from the back seat as the little traveling party drove back to Switzerland. "Would either of you gents like to see?"

"No thanks," replied Jake staring straight ahead at the highway.

"We've seen quite enough, thank you," answered Lawrence returning to his biography.

The women laughed and giggled while the men rode along mostly in silence as Hannibal strained its way back through the Alps. The grand experiment into Italy and France had, at long last, come to a merciful conclusion.

With only a few days of the tour remaining, the gang decided they wanted to use the time that was left to explore more of Switzerland. Beth had read much about the major alpine passes in the country, so they elected to drive over the mountains through the St. Gotthard Pass into another region. Officially this was the day of Lawrence's 70th birthday, and Beth was determined to find a quaint village somewhere during the drive where they could have a small but memorable celebration for her father. Since it was only anticipated to be a one day outing, no one packed additional clothing or supplies for the journey, other than a few snacks to nibble along the way.

Approximately two hours out of Sion, Jake reached the last town before entering the twisting, turning road up into the Gotthard. As Hannibal passed a small railway station at the edge of town, Beth noticed a sign with a picture of an automobile sitting on a flatbed railway car being pulled by a train. She laughed to herself at what an odd little symbol it was, but she didn't think anything of it until she later noticed a long line of motor vehicles actually being driven on to a train. "What a silly idea," she thought to herself. "Imagine taking your car on the train."

Beth was lost in her thoughts when Jake said, "It's just a few kilometers to the entrance to the Gotthard, does anybody need anything? Food, pit stop, drinks, anything?"

"I could stand to use the restroom," answered Lawrence, "But I suppose I can wait for now."

"All right then, here we go," said Jake. With that, Hannibal sped onward toward the St. Gotthard Pass with all of its promise for breathtaking alpine vistas and stunning panoramas.

With a full compliment of people, Hannibal had to work doubly hard in order to make its way up into the mountains. Jake was busy shifting gears and concentrating on the ascent, which might have been the reason he didn't notice a sign showing that the pass was closed. On the other hand, it could have been that he just didn't understand the sign. Or, perhaps he was simply ignoring it. Whatever the reason, neither Jake, nor anyone else, took heed of its message, and about a third of the way into the climb, the snowdrifts were gradually becoming thicker and higher.

It was late May. The weather was clear and sunny with temperatures in the 60s at the lower elevations. Still, Jake never gave it a second thought that the pass might remain covered with snow so late in the year. Not even when the drifts at the side of the road began to narrow and were now rising dramatically higher, inching ever closer to the car. For some unexplained reason, Jake apparently believed that if he continued onward, he would eventually round a bend and the road would be magically clear, as if Moses had come through and parted the snow. Jake never found Moses, nor did the snow disappear. Soon he had to once again accept the fact that he was wrong. In no time at all Hannibal was encapsulated by an igloo of snow and ice with nowhere to go except to return in the direction from which it had come.

Jake brought Hannibal to a stop. With a wall of ice directly in front of him, he had no other choice. Everyone got out of the car and began looking around for any other possible way to go. The sixty-degree temperatures were now closer to the mid-30s, and the increased chill factor had intensified Lawrence's need for a bathroom. While the others scouted for ways to get down from the mountain, Lawrence searched for a location of momentary refuge where he could relieve himself. Under normal circumstances, the concept of urinating outdoors would never have been given one moment of consideration, but desperation was yielding to drastic measures. Lawrence quickly made his way to the most private spot he could find and began to empty his bladder. Dr. Jekyll had relinquished his dignity to Mr. Hyde.

At an extreme altitude where the air is thin, a thick blanket of snow insulates everything beneath it and muffles the ambient noises down below. At the same time, it transmits other sounds across its surface. As a result, sound waves have a tendency to carry, becoming louder than normal. When Lawrence started peeing on a solid sheet of ice, it reverberated across the surrounding landscape with the resonance of a small cascading waterfall, causing the others to stop what they were doing and immediately begin looking for him.

Lawrence's task was still in progress when the group rounded the corner and located him. Fran was the first to speak after bursting into her now all too familiar screech of laughter. "Darlin' there ain't no way you can melt all this stuff, so you might as well quit trying," she said with glee.

"Oh god," moaned Lawrence in despair. "Is there no end to this lunacy? My life used to be so proper. What is happening to me?"

"Daddy, why are you peeing in the snow?" asked Beth trying to control her amusement.

Lawrence was standing with his back to the group. There was a short awkward pause, then he answered tersely, "Because I can! Now, is there anything else you'd like to know?"

"I guess not," said Beth giggling.

Jake had a comment of his own. "Good show old man. Now you know what it's like to be an outdoorsman. We do it that way all the time when we're hunting."

"Well you can tell your Neanderthal friends that I will never reduce myself to the level of a cave man again."

"Save a little for your signature. You always have to sign your name when you tee-tee in the snow," said Fran.

"Will you all pulleese go away and allow me some privacy. I've been doing this on my own for 70 years, and I can assure you I don't need an audience. So leave. It's the least you could do on my birthday."

The four Peeping Toms returned to the car laughing. Lawrence finished his business, and joined them, all the while unsuccessfully attempting to maintain a small degree of grace.

The consensus among the group was that they should return to the last town they had passed and then try to figure a way to go back to Sion without having to retrace their original route. That's when a light bulb of inspiration clicked on in Beth's head as she recalled the line of cars she had seen driving on to the train. She explained it to the others, and suggested they check that possibility as a means of making their way through the pass.

The idea was greeted with unanimous enthusiasm, but the first order of business now was to somehow maneuver the car into a forward position in the direction of the village. Jake inched Hannibal backward down the tricky incline while Sally Mae stood at the rear and gave hand signals. The road wasn't icy, but the lack of depth perception with all the surrounding snow made it treacherous. All Jake wanted to do was to find a space wide enough to allow him the room to go backward and forward three or four times, turning the wheel a little further each time. Eventually he would manage to have Hannibal heading back down the mountain. After much backing, shifting, turning, shifting, braking, shifting, cursing and more shifting, Jake managed to turn around. As the temperatures continued to drop even further, he was now secretly happy that the pass had been closed because the gaping hole in the driver's side window would not have been a pleasant experience while traveling along the crest of the mountain.

Beth's hunch about the car/train was correct. During the heavy snows of winter when passes are closed, the Swiss have ingeniously designed a system where people can literally drive their cars onto trains and tunnel from one side of a mountain to the other. The idea is so efficient, the Swiss also utilize it during summer months because the car/train is significantly faster than the tedious drive over the mountains. In effect, the mountain roads have become more of a scenic route and a tourist attraction than a practical means of crossing the Alps.

Unlike Italy, Switzerland generally does not present serious language problems for Americans, even in remote areas. Since the country has four languages, Swiss German, Italian, French and Romansh, nearly everyone has to be multilingual, and English is commonly used. Therefore, getting information about the car/train was not a difficulty, and soon, Hannibal was waiting in line with its five passengers, ready to roll its way on to a train. Another adventure was about to unfold.

"Don't know where we're goin', but I guess we'll find out when we get there," said Jake.

The car eased its way onto the flatbed between two other cars. Jake shut down the engine, and then everyone sat back and waited to see what was going to happen next. The tunnel was only about two hundred yards from the loading area. When Beth had made her inquiries, she was told that the ride through the tunnel would take approximately fifteen minutes. Nobody got out. Everybody remained in their cars.

There was hardly any sensation of movement when the train began to move. No jerking forward or rocking back and forth, and there was no sound of the wheels clicking along the tracks. One minute they had been stationary, and in the next, they were moving. Slowly at first, then gradually increasing in speed.

"Ooohh, this is fun," said Beth. "I like this idea."

The words were barely out of her mouth when the car plunged into a tomb-like darkness that would get no brighter even after their eyes adjusted to it. Fran wasn't about to sit still for fifteen minutes in a cocoon of darkness without stirring up a ruckus. She reached into her purse and fumbled around for her camera.

"Hey you little fuckers, we need to take some pictures!" she shouted.

Suddenly there was a split-second explosion of light. Then another. And another. The strobes lit up the cramped confines of the car like a discotheque. Fran had no idea what she was shooting. In the darkness there was no possible way to line up a shot through the viewfinder, but that didn't matter anyway. She was busy amusing herself, and succeeding marvelously at it. After the first flash everyone had double, triple and quadruple yellow moons in their vision, and each successive burst only exaggerated the situation. The reflections of the flash off the windows further intensified the brilliance of the light, blinding the passengers even more. Fran continued to click away for several more minutes, piercing everyone's ear drums with her raucous laughter and impairing their vision at the same time.

After being surrounded by a shroud of black for a quarter of an hour, the daylight was a welcome, but harsh relief when the train emerged from the tunnel. Just as Beth had been told, it came to a halt at the opposite end of the mountain fifteen minutes later. Beth now understood the convenience and wisdom of the system. When the pass was clear it took an hour and a half to navigate the terrain by going over it. This way the whole journey took a little more than a quarter of an hour. The car/train had reduced the traveling time by some 75 minutes.

Under normal circumstances, sitting inside of a car, in absolute darkness for 15 minutes, might have seemed like an eternity but thanks to Fran's playful ingenuity, the time had passed rather quickly.

"Where are we now?" asked Jake as he drove Hannibal off the train.

It was Beth's turn to navigate. She was trying to locate their position on the map. "It looks like we're in Andermatt," she said.

At that same moment, Jake noticed a road sign confirming Beth's reading. "You're right, Sis, we're coming into Andermatt. How far is it back to Sion from here?"

"I don't know, but my guess is that it's a pretty long drive," she answered.

Like so many places in Switzerland, Andermatt is a picturesque town that resembles a postcard brought to life. During winter months it is a popular skiing village, relying on tourism the rest of the year as its primary source of revenue. Winter is the key season however, because Andermatt is not along the beaten path for the throngs of visitors that other, more popular, destinations receive.

Without realizing it, the group had inadvertently made their way into the heart of the St. Gotthard Massif. At an altitude of nearly 5,000 feet, Andermatt nestles in the beautiful Urseren Valley at the junction of three of the major passes in Switzerland; the Gotthard, the Furka and the Oberalp. The Swiss enjoy the area for skiing because the convergence of three passes offers easy access, yet it doesn't attract the hoards of foreign skiers like many other areas, so it is usually less crowded.

For the five newcomers, Andermatt was a gem. One of those undiscovered treasures travelers so often find when they venture forth into unknown territory. Andermatt had a storybook ambience, a charm that captivated every member of the group. Though there was only a single, narrow main street running through town, that feature alone gave it a friendly, inviting quality, and the chalets and brightly colored flower boxes made it seem as though Christmas was a year-round celebration.

The day would soon be drawing to a close. There was growing enthusiasm among the contingent to park the car and explore the tiny hamlet on foot. Jake looked down at his fuel gauge and saw that there was no way to make it back to Sion without refilling the tank. Another consideration was the fact that driving all the way back would mean a late arrival in Sion, with nearly half the journey at night when it would be impossible to see anything. Jake also knew that Beth still very much wanted to have a special place to celebrate Lawrence's birthday, so it didn't take him long to conclude that perhaps they should consider spending the night in Andermatt.

"I've got an idea," suggested Jake. "What do you say we find a hotel and stay the night here? We'll walk around for a while, see if there's a good place to have dinner where we can celebrate Daddy's birthday, and then we can drive back to Sion in daylight tomorrow. Whaddya think?"

"Sounds good to me. Sometimes you're a pretty smart little shit, you know," said Fran.

"I like it," added Beth.

Sally Mae chimed in with her standard, "I was fixin' to say."

Only Lawrence had any doubts. "But we don't have any clothes. And what about our toilet amenities? Razors, tooth brush, combs?"

"Oh shut the hell up, you old fart. One day at 70 and already you're senile. We'll go to the store and get enough crap to last us one night. Besides, what the fuck else have you got to do," scolded Fran.

For the next 18 hours or so, the five travelers would call *Drei Konige & Post* their home. It was a tranquil, cozy, family-run establishment perfectly suited to their needs. It was neat and clean with down comforters on the beds, modern facilities that still had an antique flair, and the ever-present Swiss charm that practically guaranteed there was no possibility of making a mistake when looking for a good place to stay. It was the kind of place that made them feel that they belonged there from the moment they took refuge.

Within an hour, everyone had settled in and made a survival run to a nearby pharmacy for a night's worth of necessities.

There was a restaurant in the hotel, but whenever possible, Beth shunned eating in the same place she was staying. Switzerland has a tradition of providing "half-board" accommodations, which means that a hotel serves breakfast and lunch or dinner as part of a package price. Even so, Beth wanted to walk through town to find a different location for dinner. It was part of her travel writer's instinct to seek out as many places as possible and to observe as much as she could.

At a normal walking pace it would have taken only about five minutes to go from one end of Andermatt to the other. Maybe less. The streets were just beginning to glow with the soft amber halos of light that were overtaking the darkening remains of the day. There was no traffic to speak of, which made the walk even more pleasant and unhurried, as if there was no need to rush to be anywhere other than where they were going. Wherever that was. A casual stroll of fifteen minutes or so, led the little cluster of pioneers to a downstairs pub at the opposite end of the street.

Dinner was a cheery affair, filled with plenty of good wishes and many toasts. Lawrence opened his gifts, and everyone laughed and teased about all the events that had taken place during the previous days of their travels. It was obvious to the restaurant staff that a celebration was in progress, which caused them to join in the merriment, making the atmosphere even more joyful, as though everyone wanted to share in the fun. The festivities concluded with a pair of musicians coming to the table to sing several songs in honor of Lawrence's landmark birthday.

The evening was a most satisfying occasion. Walking back to the hotel, everyone was in a lighthearted mood from the combination of music, laughter and good food, as well as several glasses of wine. When the happy group entered the hotel and started up the stairs, they heard singing coming from another part of the building. It was well after 10. The restaurant was closed, but off to one side was a small bar. At first glance, it didn't appear that anyone was there, but the sounds were definitely coming from the pub. Beth pulled open the door and walked in as the others followed behind her. When she came around the corner, turning to the right, she found the source of the music. Back in the far corner of the room was a Swiss family sitting at a large table. From the size of the group, it appeared there were four generations of the clan gathered around singing and drinking beer.

The rest of her group caught up to Beth, and stood watching the family sing. All told there were fifteen people united in song, plus two infants, who were wide awake in their cradles, but obviously too small to participate. There was no interruption in the music even with the presence of the five visitors. If anything, it prompted the Swiss to sing louder now that they had an audience. One by one they each smiled and nodded their heads to acknowledge the presence of their guests and to signal a welcoming greeting.

Besides the babies, there were six adults, most likely the parents, and what appeared to be four grandparents. There were also five children ranging in ages from about 4 to 13. There was no mistaking who was in charge, however. The oldest gentleman at the table was clearly the leader of the group, and everyone followed his directions about what to sing and when. From his appearance, he must have been close to 90 years old, but he was full of himself, and completely in control of the situation. As the songs continued, he was the first to begin yodeling, and seconds later, the other members of his clan joined in.

Folkloric shows in Switzerland use yodeling as a mainstay of their performances so as to appeal to tourists who have come to expect it as part of the stereotype of the country. The same is true of Flamenco dancing in Spain, or belly dancing in Egypt or medieval banquets in England. To be sure, yodeling is a significant aspect of Swiss culture and tradition, but too often travelers make the mistake of interpreting that heritage as a country living only in its past. They regard the traditions as quaint, when in fact, such events are no more commonplace in modern Swiss society than square dancing would be in the United States today. As a result tourists often come away from other cultures with misconceptions, and invalid ideas, about the true meanings of many traditions.

In this case, on this night however, the music was genuine. It was sincere. Unpretentious. Natural. Traditions had been handed down from generation to generation, and this was a family gathering that had come together in celebration of that heritage.

When the music concluded with its sweet mournful tones penetrating into the huge wooden beams overhead, the five Americans applauded and asked for more. Without hesitation the Swiss began again, pleased at the appreciative response to their music.

It was another of those unexpected moments that so often occur when people travel. Portraits of life that become frozen in time, never again to be repeated, yet which live forever in the collective diary of one's own experience. Personal events that never fade from memory. Instances which can only be absorbed by those who share them, for once the synergy disappears within the limitations of that brief span of time, it can never be recaptured or duplicated in quite the same manner. It is the essence of travel, which becomes internalized within those who are fortunate enough to be united by it. It enriches one's life, because such moments are one of a kind, unique in all the world. The knowledgeable traveler quickly learns that a journey is an exercise in creating a series of vignettes that are, in the purest sense, nothing more than memories in the making. The best thing to do is to allow those memories to take their own form, to happen at their own pace, in their own time and within their own realm.

The singing ended. There was another round of applause before Beth spoke up and said, "Your singing is lovely. Thank you very much."

"Where are you from?" asked one of the young men.

"The United States. North Carolina. We love your country. It's very beautiful," Beth replied.

The old man pointed toward Lawrence and smiled. Then he pointed to himself and nodded. Lawrence knew that he was emphasizing that they were the elder statesmen of each group.

"My father does not speak English," said the young man, "He never had to learn it. He is 92 years old."

Though Lawrence was probably the same age as the grandparents in the Swiss clan, he was certainly the oldest member of his own group, and he responded by saying, "I am 70 years old today. Today is my birthday."

There was some muttering around the table as the younger Swiss translated for the older family members. When the head of the clan understood, he grinned and nodded. Soon they were all bowing and smiling and muttering to each other culminating in a spontaneous burst of applause directed at Lawrence. There was more conversation, which continued for several seconds before the old head of the family got a gleam in his eyes and whispered something to one of his granddaughters. The whispers circled the table until all were in agreement. There was a pregnant moment of silence and then the old man looked up at Lawrence, holding out his hand palm up facing Lawrence as if he was directing traffic.

Lawrence looked back at him and said, "OK, but what do you want me to do?"

The elderly Swiss gentleman pushed his hand outward with a sharp thrust, as if to say, "Be quiet, but don't leave."

Lawrence stood perfectly still. He wasn't sure what was going on, but he made no further effort to speak or to move. The old man raised his other hand slowly and slightly higher than the first, bringing it to a full stop in midair. At the precise moment, when the timing was just right, he began conducting his little Swiss family choir.

"Hoppy birssday to you. Hoppy birssday to you. Hoppy birssday, hoppy birssday. Hoppy birssday to you!"

There was a huge cheer of approval from the Americans who clapped loudly and thanked their new Swiss friends.

"Wonderful. Just wonderful," said an appreciative and emotional Lawrence who was overwhelmed by the simple, but lovely gesture of kindness.

Moments later, the commotion, and a chorus of "thank yous" and well wishes reached its climax as the two groups parted ways after what had been a splendid conclusion to a magical evening.

Dawn came late to the village of Andermatt. It began with little more than a pinprick of light at the crest of the mountain before daylight melted the shadows of night from the hillside and spread sunshine down into the valley. Fran was awakened from a deep slumber the next morning by a series of crashing sounds emanating just below her balcony. She threw back her comforter and went out on the ledge to see what was causing the noise. In her haste, she forgot that the events of the previous day had once again left her unprepared for the trip, causing her go to bed clad only in her black panties. As she leaned over the railing of the balcony to discover the source of the commotion, a garbage collector looked up, waving happily with a smile broad enough to crack his face open at the ears. Fran waved back, remembering from the minute she raised her arm that she had nothing on from the waist up. Little wonder the garbage man was so friendly at that hour of the morning.

Fran darted back into her room, shutting the doors behind her as fast as she could, though by then the damage had already been done. As she sat down on her bed, laughing to herself at her foolishness, it occurred to her that just two days before she had been laying in the sun at the pool in Monte Carlo in virtually the same condition, and thinking nothing of it. Now, she was embarrassed at being caught in the buff by an unsuspecting trash collector, and the perplexing thing was that she couldn't figure out why her perception of one situation should be so dramatically different from the other.

Except for a few other minor difficulties the trip had come to an end. On the way out of town, Jake found a self-service filling station, which was easy enough to use once he understood the system. Since the directions were written in German, it took him considerably longer than usual to top off the tank, but eventually he prevailed, and then all that remained was the drive back to Sion.

Sally Mae persisted in her odd assortment of mishaps, the worst of which was catching the metal buckle of her torn purse in Hannibal's back seat and ripping a five-inch gash in the leather. Jake was never so thankful to have insurance for a car as he was when he returned Hannibal to the rental company with its broken window, scratches, dents and torn seat. And Hannibal was never so thankful to be home, free from the five terrorists that had been the source of so much torture throughout Europe for more than a week.

At the gala farewell bash at the mountain resort, the North Carolina gang seemed like visitors from outer space having been away from the group since the first night. Jake made up an elaborate story about the problems they had dealt with trying to dry Lawrence out, and eventually taking him to a detoxification center to see if they might be able to help him. Lawrence never did catch on, but as Beth, Fran and Sally Mae mingled with the other guests, they perpetuated the tale and embellished it whenever possible. By the time the return flight landed in Philadelphia, Lawrence was the object of great pity, Jake was regarded as a folk hero among the other tour members, Sally Mae was looked upon as a bumbling natural disaster to everyone she came in contact with, and Beth and Fran had inaugurated a lifelong friendship.

For Beth, the trip had been arduous in many ways, but it had also presented invaluable learning experiences that she later carried over to her travel writing career. She had learned much about people; people she knew, and people she didn't know. She began to formulate ideas and opinions about other cultures, and the need to be tolerant, respectful and mindful of differing points of view. She learned the value of research before traveling, and she learned about random acts of kindness as a means of survival, as well as support. Beth had grown during her ten-day sojourn to Italy, France and Switzerland. She had learned as much from the failures as she had from the successes. Her fear of the unknown had diminished greatly by the adventures of the "fabulous five", and at the same time, Beth learned that travel is purely an interactive and personal undertaking that has a singular significance, regardless of how many people travel together.

Not long afterward, Beth began reading travel essays and narratives of prominent writers. She began writing down quotes by writers who had preceded her and expressed their thoughts about the process of travel. Over time she amassed a voluminous collection of statements and points of view from writers, essayists and poets ranging from Mark Twain to Rudyard Kipling to John Steinbeck, Thomas Wolfe, Charles Kuralt and others. They, as well as her travels, had altered her life, forever. Not always comfortably or happily, but always as a process of growth and as a permanent place in her soul.

There were three quotes that remained etched in Beth's heart regarding the crossing of the Alps with Hannibal and her four mates. The first was an anonymous saying which stated that "no matter how many times others have been there before, every place is undiscovered until you discover it yourself."

The next came from Somerset Maugham who wrote that "the good traveler has the gift of surprise."

And the third was perhaps the most poignant, because Peter Matthiessen must have had a crystal ball when he wrote it. "Here I am, safely returned over those peaks from a journey far more beautiful and strange than anything I had hoped for or imagined—-How is it that this safe return brings such regret?"

As the years passed, the lessons from the adventures with Hannibal would become increasingly meaningful for Beth, and even more powerful through the memories of the success of Lawrence's 70th birthday. Deep down inside, she hoped that one day, someone not unlike herself would perhaps discover something that she had written about travel, adventure, people or life, and save the quote as a lesson to share with others about their own travels.

MIDSUMMER ON THE GOTA CANAL

The field was such a brilliant shade of yellow that it hurt Beth Jacobsen's eyes to look at it. In fact, the colors and textures of the surrounding farmland and meadows had a richness beyond anything she had ever seen. So rich that the terrain looked like a vast patchwork quilt laid out by some omnipotent hand.

"It is rape," said the driver as he steered his Volvo along the winding roads of the Swedish countryside. "We grow it in the summer as food for the animals. It only lasts a few weeks."

The vistas were stunning, especially when a rectangle or square or some odd configuration of the rape would burst upon the passing scene carving out sharply defined islands of gold into the terrain. To be unaffected by the constantly changing panorama was impossible. Each new landscapte seemed more picturesque than the last, forcing Beth to take notice regardless of how breathtaking the previous scene might have been.

Perhaps it was only an illusion, but colors appeared bolder to Beth. Because she was so far north, the angle of the sun caused the light to become more concentrated and penetrating. The traditional red houses with white trim weren't just red any more, they were crimson. But it wasn't only the reds. Every other color was enhanced, and the vivid yellow of the rape was especially dazzling, though nearly blinding in its intensity.

After spending several days in Stockholm, Beth was making her way northwest toward the tiny village of Grythyttan. The Swedish countryside

88

was lovely in all its mid-June splendor, but Beth had also been smitten by Stockholm and its magnificent archipelago. Over the years she had learned that her personal taste in travel leaned toward discovering small, out of the way places rather than big cities. For Beth there was always a time-consuming orientation process in her introduction to a major city which dictated that she must visit all the well-known sights and monuments. Regardless of how often they had been documented in magazines and guidebooks, Beth had always felt a personal obligation to do the necessary research on her own. Once that mandatory exercise was completed however, it was the hidden, tucked away, unknown places that beckoned to her.

Stockholm was different somehow. As Beth had expected, it was sophisticated and cosmopolitan, but it also had a small town charm and charisma that most metropolitan areas don't have, and she found that ambience particularly captivating. Maybe it was all that water. Stockholm thrives on the water. Built upon fourteen islands, it is a city that has no choice but to have a unique personality.

In three short days, Beth had seen much of Sweden's capital. She had visited the palace and the *Grand Hotel*. There was a tour of *Skansen*, the famous outdoor museum featuring architecture from every corner of the country. She had been overwhelmed by the warship Wasa that was raised nearly intact from Stockholm Harbor in the 60s after resting on the sea floor for more than 350 years. Gamla Stan, otherwise known as the Old Town, with its delightful maze of cobblestone streets, had been a charming place to spend an afternoon. Another highlight was the magnificent town hall where all the Nobel Prizes, except the Peace Prize, are awarded each year. And then there was the Kings Garden, in the heart of the city, attracting a steady array of sun worshipers at almost any hour until the last beams of daylight grudgingly fade from the heavens.

Beth had never really thought of Swedes as being sun worshipers before, but it made perfect sense to her now that she was there. She nicknamed them "turtles" because the moment a ray of sunshine appeared anywhere, heads would simultaneously turn toward the light with necks stretched to the max in order to soak in as much of the warmth as possible. The icy cold of winter with its long hours of darkness made summer a season to savor, and the "turtles" absorbed every available beam of light.

As the car continued making its way through the winding backroads of Sweden, Beth reflected upon her assignment. She was writing a feature newspaper article centered upon the Midsummer festivities, which annually celebrate the longest day of year. In much of Sweden, Midsummer is a day when the sun doesn't set until around 11 p.m., then rises anew by two in the morning. Further north, above the Arctic Circle, is the phenomenon of the "Midnight Sun" where the sun never goes down. Rather it dips to a low point just above the horizon before arching its way back into the sky. It had already been an adjustment for Beth getting accustomed to the seemingly endless hours of daylight. The only way to ensure that she would get any sleep was to close all the curtains in her room, in order to make it as dark as possible. The abundance of daylight was not conducive to a good night's rest. One day during lunch Beth had even overheard a conversation between two golfers planning to schedule a 9 p.m. tee time with the intent of completing nine holes by sunset.

While the central theme of the article was the Midsummer Festival of Light, Beth also planned to write a sidebar feature about some interesting and unique places to stay in Sweden. According to her schedule, she would spend two days in Grythyttan and then move south again to Soderkoping in time for the holiday. Beth knew nothing about either place, relying solely on information provided by the Swedish Tourist Board that these would be worthwhile destinations to write about for her newspaper.

As they drove along Beth became fascinated by the unusual design of the rural roads in Sweden. They were actually three lanes in width with a cruising lane on either side of the highway and a passing lane in the middle. The next, and most obvious, question that came to mind was what happened when two cars decided to pass at the same time. As far as Beth could remember she had never read anything about a serious problem with head-on collisions in Sweden. In fact, she recalled that Volvo's were typically rated among the safest brands of automobile on the road. Beth analyzed the situation for a while, until at last she noticed how the Swedes had reached a solution. Everyone was driving with their two left wheels on the tarmac and the right two wheels on the shoulders! Everyone. On both sides of the road! The result was that there were now two lanes left in the middle for oncoming cars to pass without being forced to crash head-on. Apparently Swedes had accepted the procedure as standard driving technique and merely went about their business without ever giving it another thought. Just another example of necessity being the mother of invention.

After many miles of driving in silence, Beth made an effort to engage her chauffeur in conversation. "Thor, how long does it take to get to Grythyttan?" she asked.

"Not long. A couple of hours I think," he replied.

"Is Grythyttan a nice place?"

"Oh yes. Very nice."

"What is it like?"

"Very small. Just a tiny village."

Beth could see this was going to be more difficult than she thought. The driver's name was Thor Jorgenson. He was a pleasant person in his late 50s, balding with a roundish face that matched his roundish physique. The tourist office had assigned him to show Beth around and to take her wherever she needed to go, but Thor wasn't working in the capacity of a guide so much as he was an escort.

When he spoke at all, Thor spoke English very well. In fact, most of the Swedes that Beth had met spoke excellent English. And, unlike many other Europeans, they seemed to enjoy the opportunity to communicate with Americans in their own tongue. The reason was simple really. Sweden is the fourth largest country in Europe, yet it is sparsely populated, and virtually the only place in the world where Swedish is spoken. In order to conduct business and to communicate with the rest of the world, it is necessary for Swedes to be conversant in another language, so English became the primary second language of the country.

As an American traveling alone in a foreign land, the lack of a language barrier made getting around considerably easier for Beth. At the same time however, she had always been a proponent of the national pride displayed by the citizens of other countries for their native language. It was part of their identity. Part of their character. A major facet of their culture. And for Beth, who was woefully monolingual, learning a few words of another language, and understanding their origins, was as much a part of a travel experience as the journey itself. She enjoyed the challenge of words rather than being intimidated by them, and she was glad to see people show high regard for their linguistic heritage.

Beth had also realized rather quickly that it was very much a Scandinavian trait to be overly reserved. At first she had thought that everyone was just being rude, but she later observed that, in general, Swedes are basically shy people until you get to know them. The shyness is a facade that can sometimes take quite a while to penetrate, so Beth was not surprised by the brevity of Thor's responses to her questions.

The solitude of the journey was refreshing in a way. It was free of the meaningless, idle chatter that so often accompanied the initial period of getting acquainted. Besides, it also offered Beth time to soak in her new surroundings, and to reflect upon some possible storylines for her article.

As she stared out the window watching the countryside roll by, Beth had a flash of inspiration. It was a wonderful idea for obtaining insights about Sweden from the people themselves, and it was so simple. For the next few days, in every interview she conducted, Beth would make certain that she asked each person the same question. It would be an unofficial, non-scientific mini-poll of what Swedes really thought about their own country. Then she would take the various answers she received and find examples that reinforced what each person told her. In essence, she would be writing the story about Sweden from the points of view of the people who lived there.

Beth was excited. She couldn't wait to learn the results of her informal survey. The concept was to get as many varied opinions as possible by polling Swedish citizens from all walks of life. She decided to begin immediately.

"Thor, if you had to choose only one thing that you could tell other people about Sweden, what would you say?" asked Beth in a self-satisfied tone.

Thor didn't hesitate. "That is very simple. Just look around. I would tell them about our nature. Fresh and clean. You are looking at it now."

Beth couldn't deny the response. For the past hour she had been awestruck by the pageantry and tranquility of the Swedish countryside with its kaleidoscope of colors. Especially those brilliant lemon-yellow fields. Thor's answer was all Beth needed. For the remainder of the drive she absorbed herself in the environment, allowing all the natural wonder of Sweden to unfold around her.

From Stockholm the trip was slightly over two hours. To say that Grythyttan was tiny was an understatement. It was little more than a series of shops lining the perimeter of a traffic circle in the center of town. There were a few of the three lane country roads radiating like the spokes of a wheel from the central roundabout, and several back streets which led to a medium sized lake, but other than that, the only buildings of prominence were those belonging to the inn.

Beth had traveled enough by now to know that first impressions weren't always accurate, but she was getting curious as to the reason the tourist board had recommended this place. Obviously, she would soon find out.

The inn was called *Grythyttan's Gastgivaregard*, and the proprietor was a gentleman named Carl Jan Granqvist, whom Beth would meet later that evening. The primary building of the establishment extended about fifty yards along a stretch of the main road leading into town. Situated at what amounted to little more than a wide spot that snuggled beside the shoulder of the road, the inn barely had enough space for cars to park beside the building, giving the overall scale of the place a toy-like atmosphere.

It was mid-afternoon when Beth and Thor arrived at the hotel. Thor had a room in the main building, but Beth would take up residence across the street.

"I will show you to your room," said the hostess. "It is very lovely. There are only three rooms in that entire building. Mr. Granqvist did all the decorating of the rooms in the inn himself."

"How many rooms do you have in all?" asked Beth.

"A total of 45. There are 20 in this building, and 25 more scattered throughout several other buildings. Yours has three, another has five rooms and one has seven. We even have a building with only one room in it."

Beth was beginning to get a better understanding of why the tourist office had chosen Grythyttan, and its inn, as a location for her article. In all there was a total of eight furnished buildings. The main section of the property with its 20 chambers was the largest, but there were seven other buildings on the grounds with the number of rooms ranging from as few as one to as many as seven.

At first Beth wasn't thrilled about the idea of staying across the street instead of in the main building. It made her feel like an outcast. But the more she thought about it, the more intrigued she became. Besides, the hostess had told her that the room was only about 100 feet from the main entrance, and the isolation offered additional privacy that was particularly appealing.

"We go now? It's OK?" asked the receptionist.

"Oh yes," said Beth. "Just show the way. I'll follow you."

When the Swedish woman opened the door to the room, Beth was thrilled beyond imagination at the place she would call home for the next couple of nights. The irregular contours of the room created all sorts of nooks and crannies that Granqvist had exploited to the fullest. No space was wasted. Every angle was utilized in a manner that was a welcoming visual feast for its occupants while expressing the sentiments of comfort, hospitality and warmth.

The canopied four-poster double bed was appointed in floral pastels, while the rest of the space was accented by antique Swedish furniture that flourished in exterior light from a bay window that looked out to the street. Lace curtains framed the window allowing the maximum amount of light to filter into the room.

"This was once part of the stable many years ago," offered the hostess.

"You're not serious. Really? I can't imagine such a thing. How many years ago would that have been?" asked Beth.

"Well this barn dates to the 17th century, and then it was abandoned in the early part of this century. It is an interesting story about this hotel. Mr. Granqvist can tell you about it this evening at dinner. He owns almost all of the buildings in our village, and as you can see, he has made most of them part of his inn."

"Well this is definitely the most elegant stable I've ever slept in. Come to think of it, it's the only stable I've stayed in," Beth answered warmly.

"I will leave you now. If you need anything you can call us on the phone, or just walk across the street. It is a little bit different I think. Yes?"

"It certainly is. It certainly is," said Beth in a voice filled with curious wonder.

The hostess tiptoed out of the room, quietly closing the door behind her. Beth took a few moments to become oriented. The décor was tasteful and subtle, and there were all kinds of hidden amenities waiting for her to discover.

With dinner still several hours away, Beth decided to explore the village and get some exercise in the process. An hour later, after strolling through town and down to the lake, she returned to the sublime confines of her room. Then she soaked in a long, hot bubble bath before cuddling beneath the fluffy softness of the comforter on her bed, and falling asleep the moment her head touched the pillow.

When Beth awoke it was nearly 6:45. Dinner was scheduled for 7:30. She took her hunter green dress out of the closet and pulled it down over her head, zipping it up the back. Her gown accentuated the mounds of her cleavage in precisely the manner she desired, allowing her to feel especially sensual by showcasing her femininity while also making a classic statement of elegant sophistication.

She completed her ensemble with a simple, single strand of pearls and matching earrings. The combination of deep green and white set against the reddish-brown tint of Beth's shoulder-length auburn hair was striking, and she sensed it. She knew all too well that she looked chic, stylish and sexy, and she liked the way she felt as she strode confidently across the street to greet her companions for the evening.

It was shortly after seven when Beth walked into the main section of the inn. She was early, but she wanted to make a brief site inspection of the property before joining Thor and Mr. Granqvist for dinner. Every aspect of the hostelry was as lovingly appointed as Beth's room. Granqvist's attention to detail was exquisite, clearly reflecting his personal sensibilities and tastes. There were large drawing rooms with ample areas in each for several conversations to occur simultaneously without infringing upon the space of others. One room featured a grand piano for cocktail parties and after dinner sing-alongs, while another sported an oversized fireplace that could accommodate massive logs when a crackling fire was in order.

Beth was sitting by the fireplace enjoying a glass of Merlot when Carl Jan Granqvist made his entrance. There was no mistaking who he was. It took only a matter of seconds to realize that this was a man who enjoyed living to the fullest. That fact was evident in the decor of his establishment, but it was even more obvious in his flamboyant personality.

Granqvist was a tall man with a winning smile that erupted in a volcano of personality. There was none of the "reserve" in this man that Beth had witnessed in the other Swedes she had met. He was rather gangly in his movements and mannerisms, yet he was so well attired and manicured that his countenance compensated for any awkwardness. As Granqvist flitted from patron to patron with welcoming handshakes, he assumed a posture whereby he would thrust his upper body to the rear and arch his back with glee when responding to his guests.

It wasn't necessary for Granqvist to be talking to communicate. His body language was as telling as his speech. Now and then he would cross his arms and gaze intently at a guest, as if hanging on every word and phrase, then he would throw his arms high into the air and laugh, or slap his cheeks "Jack Benny-style" when the guest concluded the story.

At other times Granqvist would clasp his hands together about chest high in front of him, before pulling them apart to waggle his right hand limply from the wrist. At the same time he would toss in a comment such as "You don't mean it," or "Do tell," or "I don't believe it," thereby giving total credence to the discussion, creating a party atmosphere while adding a mood of hilarity and chaos in the room.

With abnormally large teeth protruding in front of his mouth, Granqvist had a "Bugs Bunny" kind of a face. He was not by any stretch of the imagination handsome, but his demeanor was so infectious and charming that he compensated in a way that almost made him into a living caricature of himself. He was the type of person who people gravitate to because he made them feel comfortable, and joyful, merely by being in his presence.

Granqvist also had one other endearing quality. He was one of those unusual people who seemed to be capable of suspending time. That exceedingly rare individual who can cram 30 hours into every day because they are so wonderfully adept at getting the most out of each one of them.

When Thor finally arrived, he looked bewildered by all the commotion in the parlor, as if he had not expected so much to be happening. He spotted Beth and walked over to her. Then for the next several minutes he watched Granqvist work the room meeting and greeting everyone as if each of them were his lifelong friends. When all the members of the gathering had been properly welcomed, Granqvist came over to Beth and Thor.

Granqvist looked at Beth and proclaimed, "I am Carl Jan Granqvist. Just call me Carl Jan. That's what most people do. I hope you enjoy your stay at our little inn. It's not the *Waldorf*, but then neither are the *Ritz* or the *Savoy* are they? Still we call it home," he said loudly with the impish, playful grin that had already affected everyone else in the room. "My, my you are ravishing my dear! How perfectly lovely you are. What a gorgeous dress, I must say."

Beth could not contain herself. She knew the compliment was sincere, but she had to smile. In the presence of Carl Jan it just seemed natural to feel lighthearted and happy.

"Thank you for your kind words. I'm Beth Jacobsen, and this is Thor Jorgenson. Your inn is just magnificent. You must be very proud," Beth said.

"Yes, it has been a wonderful project. I have many interests, and the hotel allows me to pursue most of them."

Though it was the first time Thor had met Granqvist personally, he had known of him by reputation for many years, and he made the most of the opportunity of the introduction to join in the conversation. He turned to Beth and said, "Carl Jan is quite well known all over Sweden. He is regarded as the finest connoisseur of wine in our country."

Beth was impressed. "Really. How exciting. I suppose that means we don't have to worry about the wine selection for dinner tonight."

"You are most kind, Mr. Jorgenson, thank you very much," said Granqvist humbly, while graciously acknowledging the compliment. "We do have a very nice wine cellar in the hotel. I will show you after dinner, perhaps. It's downstairs where the dungeon used to be. I made the other part of the prison into a cheese cellar as well. You will see, but first we must dine, yes?"

As Carl Jan turned toward the door extending his right arm to show the way, Thor leaned over to Beth and whispered, "He's also famous for his cuisine. He's a gourmet chef."

"But of course," she uttered under her breath. "Would we have expected anything less?" Beth looked down at the floor, smiled to herself and shook her head in amazement. She was both amused and incredulous at the abundance of talent combined with the wealth of personal charm exhibited by this Swedish Renaissance man.

At Carl Jan's urging, Beth and Thor moved forward, making their way into the dining room. Beth wanted to hear more details regarding the story of the inn during dinner. After all, here she was sitting down to eat with one of Sweden's foremost food and wine experts, a man who had converted a dungeon into a wine and cheese cellar, and an entrepreneur who had quite literally remodeled an entire town into a hotel.

As anticipated, everything about the dinner was superb including the two selections of wine Carl Jan had chosen from his cellar. Caesar salad preceded a main course of smoked salmon and reindeer with cloudberries, followed by champagne poured over lemon sorbet.

"Tell me about your hotel, Carl Jan," said Beth as the culinary event proceeded. "What is the history of this place?"

"It's not very complicated really. I have lived in this area all of my life. For many, many years Grythyttan was an "up and down," and for that reason it was once a thriving community. Not large mind you, but quite prosperous."

Beth didn't understand what Carl Jan was saying. "An up-and-down?" she asked. "What exactly is that?'

"Of course they don't exist today because there is no need for them, but in olden days, when people used to travel by horse and carriage rather than automobiles, villages like Grythyttan were very important. You see it wasn't so possible to travel quickly, or to be able to go the great distances we can today. An up-and-down was always someplace about halfway between two major areas where travelers would stop to eat and to rest for the night. It was also a place where the horses could be stabled and fed before going on, so these villages became quite necessary. They got the name of up-and-down because people would come "up" from Stockholm or go "down" to Stockholm from other towns north of here."

"I see. So Grythyttan survived because of its location along the wagon paths to and from Stockholm."

"Precisely, and for nearly 300 years this little town was quite wealthy. This main building was the original inn, but other portions of the hotel were formerly stables or blacksmith shops or something that was here to make the community function. The prison was next door because in that time there were highwaymen, you see. Thieves. And so the dungeon was built down below. We don't need it today. At least not for robbers, so I decided to convert it to a wine and cheese cellar. It's much more practical that way, don't you agree?"

The proprietor had a deliberate manner of speaking, which only added to his mystique. His voice seemed to come from the depths of his throat, and he had a way of adding syllables to words, which extended them so that they hung in the air. Or he would pause in mid-sentence before continuing with a thought. At times his tone became boisterous, and at others it would soften so much that he was barely audible. In some regards he sounded rather like a college professor, from whom some people might infer an air of pretentiousness, but with Carl Jan his mannerisms were completely natural and indigenous to his outgoing personality.

Remembering the earlier comment by the receptionist about the advent of motorized vehicles causing Grythyttan's demise, Beth asked Carl Jan to continue.

"When automobiles began to replace horses for transportation, there was no need for towns like Grythyttan. At least not as before. And so we died. Quickly. For a number of decades this village was abandoned. Deserted. How do you say it, a "ghost town." The buildings and stables only grew older, dustier and more run-down with each passing year. So I bought the properties that nobody wanted, and I turned the whole town back into an inn. But I knew this had to be a special place, someplace quite different you see, because I knew there had to be a reason for coming here other than for sleeping."

"So you decided to specialize in elegant food, superior wines and a unique atmosphere," said Beth completing the story.

"But of course. I, too, like all of these things. They are my passion. If I am going to enjoy them anyway, why shouldn't I invite people to come share them with me? It is a nice idea, isn't it? We try very hard. People must have a wonderful experience when they come here. That is what we want to do for them."

"Is there anything else? Do you have any more surprises?" Beth inquired. She assumed the story was over, but once again Carl Jan caught her off-guard.

"Only one or two things," Granqvist replied. "You shall see very soon."

Beth couldn't begin to imagine what else her host had in store, but whatever it was she knew it would be grand, and she also knew it would be unusual. Dinner concluded around 9:25, and then, as promised, Carl Jan escorted Beth and Thor down to the dungeon for a tour of the wine and cheese cellar.

In typical Granqvist style, the tunnel to the cellar was illuminated by hundreds of candles. The visit was only a few minutes old when Carl Jan glanced at his watch. "My God," he exclaimed, "it's getting late. We must go."

"Go?" Beth wondered. "Go where? There was no place else to go." Or so she thought.

Carl Jan quickly shooed Beth and Thor out of the dungeon and down the corridor of the tunnel. When they reached the top of the stairs and were again outside, Granqvist said, "Wait here. I will be right back to get you."

Neither Beth nor Thor had an inkling of an idea as to what was happening. Carl Jan was only gone a couple of minutes when his black Volvo screeched to a halt at the entrance of the inn. "Get in. We don't want to be late!" cried Granqvist urgently.

Beth and Thor hastily moved around the car. Beth practically flopped into the front seat while Thor jumped in the back.

"Where are we going?" asked Beth.

Carl Jan didn't answer. The wheels of the car spun wildly, shooting pebbles and small bits of gravel in every direction as the Volvo lurched toward the roundabout a few hundred yards away. They went three-quarters of the way around the circle and headed down a long straight country road. When they were finally on their way and things had calmed down slightly, the hotel owner replied, "We are going to my villa. The concert begins in just a few minutes!"

"Concert? In your villa? What do you mean?"

As the car raced through the soft evening twilight Granqvist supplied more information. "During the summer I have chamber music concerts at my home in the country. We have performances four nights a week, sometimes five. I invite members of the Stockholm Philharmonic to stay at my inn, and in return, they perform for my guests at my villa. But I live about fifteen or twenty minutes away, and since I am the host, I must not make everyone wait."

Upon arriving at the Granqvist mansion Beth was certain they had set an all-time speed record for getting there. The villa was a two-story stone building that faced a sloping lawn, which ended at a small pond about 100 yards away.

From the second story, where the performances were held, Beth could see the peacefulness of day's end overtaking the setting across the water. The air was calm, and the absence of a breeze left the pond mirror-smooth. Stillness enveloped the surrounding woodlands as twilight seeped into the forest with a protective layer of serenity. Except for the crickets, the occasional croak of a bullfrog and the coo of a dove now and then, there was no sound.

Beth walked to a large drawing room in the center of the mansion where the musicians were busily tuning their instruments. As she entered the room an usher handed her a printed program for the concert. By now nothing should have surprised her, but in her wildest imagination Beth had not guessed that Carl Jan would go to the trouble of having programs printed for these nightly chamber music events. She was now even more pleased with her decision to dress up for the evening. Casual clothing would have been perfectly acceptable, but Beth suddenly felt even more elegant than before, as if she had magically burst into a scene from some exotic foreign film with subtitles, and she took comfort in the knowledge that she was appropriately attired. Lawrence Jacobsen, Jr. had educated her well.

The little "concert hall" had seating for about 75 people. Over the years, the locals had come to love these occasions, and they, too, were invited to attend along with the guests of the hotel. The program was divided into two segments. The first lasted approximately 45 minutes and the second about half an hour. There was a 15-minute interval in between during which refreshments were served and people could explore the upstairs grandeur of the Granqvist estate. A few guests made their way downstairs to walk around the grounds, but most remained on the upper level.

As the end of the program approached around 11:15, Beth could see the final traces of daylight yielding to the canopy of night outside the huge upstairs windows. It was difficult to imagine that she was sitting in a villa in the backwoods of Sweden listening to a Mozart concerto as the sun was setting just before midnight. It was a delightfully strange experience, as well as cerebral, and most certainly sensual. More and more Beth had come to appreciate the hidden sensuality of travel. It was one of her favorite travel writing secrets, and among her top ten poll of hedonistic occasions, this event ranked with the best of them.

By 11:30 the concert had concluded and the guests had departed. Beth and Thor returned to Carl Jan's Volvo at a considerably slower pace than before, and rode back to the inn. Though the day had officially ended, it was still bright enough to make out the detail of trees and buildings without benefit of artificial light.

When the trio reached the inn, Carl Jan stopped at the main entrance to drop Beth and Thor at the door. "Please join me for a drink. Go ahead inside, and I will meet you there in a moment," said the hotel owner.

Beth and Thor got out and sauntered into the room where the grand piano was located. Already there were 50 or more people standing around talking quietly, sipping nightcaps and listening to the piano music. Nearly all of them had been at the villa for the concert, and now as midnight was approaching they were rounding off the occasion with a final cocktail for the evening. It was a regular occurrence at the inn, even on nights when there were no performances.

Carl Jan was the last person to enter the room, and his presence altered the entire dynamic of the setting. What had been the hushed tones of polite conversation mixed with the gentle sounds of a cocktail piano quickly became a scene of ragtime music and animated chatter, even though it was short-lived. Over the next 45 minutes the group gradually dwindled until there was only a handful of people remaining.

It had been a remarkable evening. One that Beth would never forget, but she knew it was time to let it go. She thanked Carl Jan for his gracious hospitality and kissed him on the cheek. Thor was at the far end of the room wrestling to keep his eyelids from crashing shut when Beth came over to give him a hug before departing for the night. She then made the short walk across the street to her room with barely enough time to undress before collapsing into bed and a deep dreamless sleep.

During the night a cold front moved in dropping the temperatures to an unseasonably cool level and turning the sky the color of pewter. It was late in the morning when Beth arrived back at the main part of the inn. Rather than wait for the elaborate smorgasbord the restaurant prepared for the noontime meal each day, Beth decided to have brunch. She was also hoping to catch Carl Jan so that she could continue the interview she had begun at dinner on the previous evening.

After finishing her first cup of coffee, Beth was pouring a second when she heard the unmistakable voice and laughter of Carl Jan in the lobby. He was bidding farewell to three guests, personally extending an invitation for them to return. Moments later he fluttered into the breakfast room, spoke briefly to a couple of people who were sitting in the corner, then came over and sat down with Beth. As Granqvist ordered a glass of orange juice, Beth asked, "Do you have some time right now to tell me more about yourself and the hotel?"

She was hoping Carl Jan would say "yes" because that would free up the remainder of the day to walk around town, catch up on her notes, perhaps read a little and even relax with a glass of wine in the garden. Beth was thrilled when Granqvist replied, "But of course, my darling. What else would you like to know? I am most delighted to accommodate you in any way."

For the better part of an hour Beth chatted with Carl Jan about his hotel, his philosophy and outlook on life, his passion for food and wine and a myriad of other subjects. As the interview came to a close Beth looked up at her host and asked, "One final question Carl Jan. Can you tell me what you believe is absolutely the best thing about Sweden?"

"Oh, it's the landscape." Granqvist answered quickly. "We have such wonderful forests and lakes and so many natural places. There's no other answer. It must be the nature."

No other answer or not, it wasn't the response Beth was looking for. She had asked the question twice now and received the same result on both occasions. Though her work was not finished, at least Beth had the interview behind her. The remainder of her visit to Grythyttan could now be spent in observation, and the best part was that she still had time to enjoy the village and the genteel ambience of the inn for herself.

Dinner produced another adventure into the fine art of food preparation, followed by coffee in the fireplace room and later the traditional late night cocktails.

By the next morning the weather had turned even worse. Added to the cold and gray came a steady drizzle that would follow Beth and Thor all the way to their next stop at Soderkoping. Beth felt a tug of remorse at having to leave the tiny oasis known as Grythyttan which had been created from the heart and soul of a man who knew much about the quality of living. Carl Jan Granqvist was one of those deliciously lovable characters who made traveling so personally rewarding for Beth, by adding to her lifelong treasure chest of memories.

Beth and Thor made their farewells and then climbed into the car to begin the next leg of their journey. The staff had prepared a basket of food for the trip, complete with two superb bottles of wine selected by Carl Jan to carry along as a reminder of their visit. As the car eased away from the inn, Beth could see Carl Jan waving in the rear view mirror, and she could hear his distinctive voice in the distance. "Goodbye Beth Jacobsen. Goodbye. You will return one day. Goodbye."

Thor's Volvo eased up over a small hill and around a curve to the right at the edge of town, and in the process, Carl Jan Granqvist vanished from Beth Jacobsen's life.

Soderkoping is another picturesque Swedish village with Lilliputian qualities. It is southeast of Grythyttan and below Stockholm to the west, but Thor was able to drive there directly without returning to the capital. Though Soderkoping is about three times the size of Grythyttan, it retains a miniature scale that made strolling through the 800 year-old town a pleasant and exhilarating exercise.

It was the day before the Midsummer holiday. Beth and Thor had reservations at the *Soderkoping's Brunn*, which is the oldest spa in Sweden dating to the year 1774. The heyday of the property came during the 19th century, and though by modern standards it remains an impressive two-story building, it must have really been a showcase of elegance during its prime.

The owner was a beanpole of a gentleman by the name of Stig Ekblad. At nearly 7 feet tall he had an "Ichabod Crane" look about him that naturally made him tower above everyone else in the community. Like Carl Jan Granqvist, Stig had a winning personality which exuded charm and sincerity, but it was sprinkled with a healthy dose of that Swedish reserve Beth had come to know so well, and he had nowhere near the outgoing presence of Granqvist. Ekblad was ever conscious of his height, but he capitalized upon his stature by taking full advantage of the situation with an infectious sense of humor.

In Swedish the word "brunn" translates to mean "spa" in English, so Beth and Thor were simply residing at Soderkoping's spa. It had a marvelous location on the outskirts of the village, but it was easily within walking distance of the town. The spa featured its own park, which spread for 70 acres around the property culminating along the banks of the Gota

Canal just a few hundred yards beyond. There were numerous bike paths and walking trails, and a small stream divided the park with its slow moving, meandering waters. Already there was evidence of preparation for the festival that would take place the next day. With so much space on its grounds, *Soderkoping's Brunn* was the ideal location for all the activities that would soon be underway.

As usual, Beth quickly settled into her room and prepared to do a sightseeing excursion through town. She was always restless upon arriving at any destination, so whenever possible, a familiarization tour was the first item on her agenda. With the weather still raw and damp Beth donned a thick sweater and her raincoat before venturing among the narrow streets of Soderkoping for the next couple of hours.

It was close to four in the afternoon when Beth returned to the spa. Despite her precautions, the briskness of the Swedish climate had penetrated her soul, and she entered the inn looking for a comforting place to rest. Off to one side of the main dining room was an intimate little parlor that was being warmed by a fire. It seemed odd to be sitting by a crackling fireplace in the middle of June, but it was a welcome discovery for Beth after her stroll. She ordered a cup of hot tea and a bowl of soup to further dissipate the effects of the cold, and decided that once she was sufficiently rid of her chill she would indulge herself with a massage.

The steaming liquids eliminated Beth's goose flesh and, at the same time, took the edge off her hunger. Now thoroughly satisfied, she was prepared to engage herself in an hour of digital manipulation as she walked to the reception desk to make an appointment for a treatment.

Fifteen minutes later Beth was savoring every relaxing probe of her road weary muscles as each touch by the masseuse eased away the tensions in places in her body that she never knew existed. Afterwards, she returned to her room to read for a while and to organize her notes. With the promise of a long celebration ahead for the Midsummer's holiday the following day, Beth ordered dinner from room service and went to bed early.

With so many hours of daylight, it was easy to become disoriented about time, which had happened to Beth more than once during the trip. There had even one morning in Stockholm when she had looked out the window to be greeted by brilliant sunshine, only to be stunned moments later when she discovered it was just 4:30. So despite the fact that the Midsummer's weather was gray with a melancholy overcast, Beth was still uncertain as to how early, or late, it was when she first heard the sounds of a parade marching down the street toward the hotel.

It was more of a small procession than a parade really, with local people strutting through the streets, recruiting marchers as they went by. Horns blared and drums banged as the growing entourage swaggered along, proudly waving a huge blue and gold Swedish flag. As the crowd passed each house, people would come to their windows, or out on their balconies to wave to the marchers who would wave back and encourage them to join in. Beth heard the parade several minutes before she saw it. She glanced at her watch and saw that it was a little before 9 a.m. Climbing out of bed she went outside and looked down the street from her second story landing. When the marchers appeared from behind a building three blocks away, Beth could she that though they were all bundled up in coats and sweaters nothing was going to deter them from enjoying their celebration. The crowd continued to increase with new revelers joining in along each block as it made its way down the street. By the time it reached Beth, there must have been several hundred people in the throng.

After a hasty shower, Beth made her way down to the front lawn of the spa. Already it seemed that the entire population of Soderkoping had grown to three times its size. People were gathered everywhere. Many adults, especially the older ones, were outfitted in traditional costumes, while most of the little girls under the age of ten, and all of the toddlers, wore garlands of flowers in their hair that had been woven together by either their mothers or older sisters.

Beth began filing through the crowd listening to the conversations and observing the various traditional projects that were in progress. One of the main attractions was decorating the Maypole, which had more than its share of volunteers of all ages. The giant log was perhaps 2 feet in diameter and 25 feet long so there was plenty of space for everyone to wrap vines and flowers all around it. At the same time, there were five or six burly men undertaking the task of digging the hole into which the pole would later be lowered for the raising ceremonies. The upper portion of the pole was encircled by a crown of flowers which dangled from the top by six woven strands of vines. Scattered throughout the property were tents filled with people preparing a multitude of snacks and refreshments such as pretzels, Belgian waffles, cotton candy and the like. In another corner of the grounds, there were fifteen or twenty tables snuggled beneath large umbrellas where Stig Ekblad was making crepes as fast as he could. The demand was far greater than Stig's ability to maintain the supply of his creations, keeping the gangling innkeeper in a perpetual state of motion slinging batter everywhere as though that would help speed up the process.

Beth managed to make her way to the spot where Stig was cooking. She couldn't help but laugh at his predicament. Sweat was pouring from his brow as he worked feverishly with the batter and his spatula. At the same time however, he was laughing and talking with townsfolk and guests who were in no great hurry to be served despite the delay in his efforts. The smoke rising from the griddle had a delicious sweet smell as it wafted into the air. With Stig's extreme height, it was necessary for him to bend way down to reach his paper-thin pancakes. Occasionally the steam from the grill would puff into his face at the same moment he leaned over, forcing him back with his eyes full of tears from the smoke and the heat. He was not giving in however. His mission was clear, and he was focused upon it. Everyone who desired a crepe would most certainly have a crepe, regardless of how much Stig had to sacrifice to complete his ordeal.

Beth looked around for Thor. She hadn't seen him all morning. She finally noticed him sitting on the grass near the temporary bandstand, which had been constructed, along with a sizable dance floor, just for the occasion. Shortly after midday the band started to play and the dancing began. It was the custom to limit the first portion of the program to traditional music and folk dances performed by townspeople dressed exclusively in native outfits. Later in the afternoon, the music became more contemporary and everyone was invited to participate in the dancing. Many families also got involved by forming large circles on the main lawn where someone would lead them in whimsical ditties such as *The Chicken Dance* and *The Hokey Pokey*.

Fortunately the rain held off, and the cool temperatures failed to dampen anyone's spirit or prevent any activities from taking place. The scene had a comforting air of nostalgia to it. Like an old-time Fourth of July. It was simple in scope, but it was the uncomplicated gaiety, and the spirit of genuine fellowship that gave the festivities their character and charm. The celebration was totally unpretentious. No gaudy displays of commercialism, no radio and television coverage, no cheerleaders and fanfare. Just hundreds of people enjoying their Swedish heritage and the traditions of their country. It was also completely spontaneous and serendipitous, reminding Beth of her childhood, and causing her to reflect upon those days that were now forever lost in the helter-skelter race to the 21st century.

By early evening it was time for the raising of the Maypole which was greeted with great anticipation and enthusiasm. The burly men who had dug the hole eased the log into its base by pulling it into place with long tethers attached to the top. At the climactic moment just before the Maypole lodged into its resting-place, the band struck up a rousing fanfare as everyone cheered the successful accomplishment of the task. Afterwards long tables were set up for an elaborate smorgasbord and everyone joined in the feeding frenzy. Beth was amazed at the boundless spirit of these people as each successive event brought renewed surges of energy.

At one point someone decided that the weather was cool enough to create a huge batch of "glugg" bringing about enthusiastic cheers of endorsement from the throng of partygoers. Glugg is a favorite hot drink in Scandinavia consisting of mulled wine with some fruit added. It is traditionally reserved for the Christmas season because of the bitter cold during that time of year, but on this day everyone agreed it was all right to enjoy a little bit of Christmas in June. It was certainly not a typical feature of a Midsummer festival, but there was no resistance to the mixing of traditions when the warm, potent liquid made its appearance upon the scene.

The eating and drinking continued far into the evening along with the music and dancing. Stig was no longer involved in the crepe making process, taking full advantage of the opportunity to immerse himself in the frolic. At one point during his merrymaking he invited Beth and Thor to finish off the evening with yet another drink in the more private surroundings of the inn after the day's activities had ended.

By 10:45 or so, the raucous elements of the daylong festivities had quieted, but a fair number of people remained on the premises to help Stig's staff with the cleanup. It had been a joyous occasion filled with song and dance, food and fellowship. Beth went into the spa and walked over to a comfortable sofa by the fire in the parlor. Soon after, Thor joined her. Stig was still busy with housekeeping chores, but when he was sufficiently satisfied that everything was well in hand he, too, came to the parlor.

Beth ordered a glass of Chardonnay and spent the next half-hour in casual conversation with Stig and Thor. It was a low-key sort of interview about a wide range of subjects. As the conversation wore on Beth began looking for the appropriate opportunity to spring her survey question on Stig. Eventually the subject of tourism arose, providing just the opening Beth was seeking. She looked directly at her host and asked, "Stig, the other day I posed this question to Thor, and I am curious to see what you will say. If you were telling someone about Sweden and you could mention only one thing to get them to come here, what would it be?"

Stig was not as quick with his response as Thor and Carl Jan had been, but when he spoke, the answer was the same. "Oh I should think it would be the glory of our vast wilderness. When people come here they have access to lakes, they have access to forests, and they can see birds and animals in the wild. We cherish our nature. We are very proud of it."

"Three for three," said Beth to herself. She looked over at Thor who smiled knowingly. The conversation continued for several more minutes before Stig excused himself to approve the final stages of the cleanup and to release his staff. At the same moment, Beth and Thor decided it was time to retire for the night.

While most of the villagers slept in after their day of celebration, Beth was up early the next morning. She was scheduled to take an excursion on Sweden's famed "Blue Ribbon" known as the Gota Canal. It only took a few minutes for her to walk from the spa to the landing where the steamer, *Wilhelm Tham*, was docked. When Beth arrived, the boat was still covered with the decorations of the previous day, though they looked somewhat tired and wilted from all the activities. She had hoped for a break in the weather, but no such luck, so she bundled up and made the best of the situation.

The Gota Canal is a marvel of engineering. Completed in 1832, it took 22 years and more than 58,000 men to finish the project. The original purpose was to connect the east coast of Sweden with the west, a link between the Baltic Sea and the North Sea, by using existing rivers and lakes combined with an artificial waterway that would unite Stockholm with Gothenburg. In its time, it was the fastest way across the country. Today, at speeds of just under five miles an hour on the canal, it is probably the slowest.

Over the course of the four day journey, ships pass through an intricate system of 65 bridges and 65 locks which elevate them more than 300 feet above sea level at the highest point, before lowering them again at the opposite coast. In the process, the boats traverse two major lakes, Vattern and Vanern, during their snail-like adventure from one side of Sweden to the other. The canal itself is narrow with a maximum width of about 70 feet, and it is shallow as well, reaching a depth of merely ten feet.

Beth was excited about her upcoming voyage. She would only experience one short leg of the itinerary, but it was supposedly a picturesque stretch which highlighted the engineering achievement of the canal, while offering a firsthand view of the manmade wonder at the same time. Beth had seen the pyramids of Egypt and the treasury of Petra and the breathtaking splendor of the *Sistine Chapel* in all their magnificence, but this was something completely different. Of course, the canal couldn't begin to compare with the grandeur of such well-known wonders of the world, but it was certainly unique. It was interactive, participatory and, best of all, it was relatively unknown outside of Sweden.

With three sharp toots on the horn, the *Wilhelm Tham* cast off at 9 o'clock sharp. The steamer glided away from the pier. A light drizzle began to fall, but Beth was able to take shelter under an overhang on the upper deck so that she could observe the passing cyclorama of the landscape.

As the boat navigated its way slowly along the canal, Beth could see huge tracts of the golden fields of rape. From her vantage point on the upper deck, it gave her an even greater appreciation of the countryside than what she had previously witnessed from ground level in Thor's car. Now and again a red and white cottage would dot the landscape, or an occasional castle would emerge from the crown of a nearby hillside or from behind a cluster of white birch trees. On the left side of the canal was a towpath, which many people used as a walking trail. Now and then, walkers would appear almost from nowhere and immediately take up the challenge of marching along the shoreline. It became a sort of casual competition with the ship to see who could go the fastest. In places where the canal narrowed, the boat came so close to shore that the walkers would carry on friendly conversations with passengers as if they were long, lost friends or relatives. It was a magical scene where the most important event of the day was the steady gliding movement of the *Wilhelm Tham* along its appointed course. All that existed in the world was a sublime sense of here and now, captured within a peaceful realm where the pace of the day adapted itself perfectly to the idyllic rhythms of the setting. Time became meaningless. Non-existent. Mother Nature was in charge, and she would not be hurried.

Before long the boat arrived at the first lock. Beth had been wondering why every few feet there were birch logs dangling from the perimeter of the steamer, and now she knew. They were bumpers. The locks along the canal were only 23 feet wide, which was only slightly over a foot more than the width of the boat itself. So it was not uncommon for bumps and bangs to occur as the ship settled into the concrete capsule that would lift it to another level of the canal.

People continued to gather at the lock to offer moral support for the raising of the ship. Some merely stood by and observed. Others slogged along the towpath in their rubber boots trying to get ahead of the boat. When the ship was safely wedged into its box, the rear doors of the lock closed behind the *Wilhelm Tham* with a resounding thud, and water began spilling over the front barrier causing the boat to gradually rise about five feet. Once the water stopped bubbling, gurgling and churning all around the boat, a lock attendant eased the front doors open toward the new stretch of canal that lay ahead.

The rain had ceased. Vapor steamed off the mirror-smooth water, which was enhanced by reflections of houses and trees, creating twin images between land and water, serving to double the peacefulness of the canal. A long line of sheep strolled along the towpath at the shoreline, and in the distance Beth could see several deer grazing at the edge of one of the fields of rape.

Some passengers with binoculars dangling from their necks were ready to track any sign of a finch or a wren or a nightingale or a heron. Others were intent on naming every species of wildflower in sight, proudly identifying daisies, buttercups, peonies and any other growing thing they could spot. In many places, forests came right down to the water's edge, creating a stillness, and an eerie silence that seemed to have a sound all its own. Unseen voices could be heard far in the distance, while muted conversations on deck were filled with "ooohs" and "aaahs" at each new panorama.

As the *Wilhelm Tham* prepared to enter a new series of locks, another passenger turned to Beth and said, "This is one very impressive ditch."

"So it is. So it is," Beth thought to herself nodding in agreement.

Because of the design of the canal at one location, Beth was able to hop off the boat during the pause, allowing her to witness the process from the shore. It was a series of locks, which were constructed in such a way as to literally form a staircase for the little steamer. It would take the captain more than an hour to maneuver the vessel some 52 feet higher than its original level. Beth watched the ship gradually climb the elaborate aqua-escalator, fascinated by the ingenuity of the engineers who had conceived and designed the project.

During the course of her journey, Beth learned that each lock was different according to its individual logistical situation and geographical setting. The same was true of the various bridges along the route. There was even one spot where a bridge and a lock converged, forcing automobile traffic to wait while a drawbridge was raised to allow the ship to enter the lock.

The cumulative effect of all this was that each place along the canal seemed to have its own unique character and personality. The stunning colors, though muted by overcast skies, enhanced the beauty of the countryside, giving it sharply defined contours and a vividness that exploded into a vibrant canvas of intense, brilliant textures. Combined with the serenity of being able to observe wildlife in its natural habitat, the journey had an aura that Beth simply could not translate to words.

When the ship finally completed its multi-leveled ascension, Beth and the other passengers re-boarded and set sail again.

Before departing from Soderkoping, Beth had obtained permission from Captain Ake Sjoren to join him briefly on the bridge for an interview. She always relished the special occasions when she was allowed to go "behind the scenes" for her story. For some reason such instances instilled a sense of power within her at having access to people and places she would otherwise never get a chance to reach. For Beth it was one of the perks she enjoyed most about her career.

Captain Sjoren was a stocky chap who had been navigating the quiet waters of the Gota Canal for nearly 20 years. During those two decades he had never become bored with the repetition of the route. In fact, the opposite was true. Each new crossing was more stimulating than the last, and it all had to do with the wonders of nature that were constantly changing before him. For the captain, these gentle transitions through the rhythms of life were the greatest stress relief he could imagine, and his career on the canal was filled with memories of creation in its purest sense.

Beth knew the answer before she asked the question. Based upon the previous three responses, there was no doubt in her mind what the captain would say. Especially in light of his many years of piloting a boat on the canal. Just to be certain, Beth decided to ask it anyway. "Captain, what would you say is the very best thing about Sweden?"

"How could I say anything else but our wonderful nature. It is a joy to cross this country every week and to see all the things happening along this canal. I see the forces of nature at work. There are storms. There are magnificent sunrises and sunsets. I see the seasons change. I see new colors and wonderful light. For me every day is a living photograph. I live in a world that looks like Eden. Someone told me once that "Nature is solace for all things." Our nature is not just the best thing, it is the most important thing. Swedes have a passion for their environment. How could they not?"

Beth could not disagree. She had seen the passion in everyone to whom she had posed the question, and the Gota Canal only reinforced what they had said. At first Beth was disappointed at having obtained the same answer from everyone, but now she was invigorated by it. The results of her poll were not what she had expected, but that didn't matter any more, they had still provided her with a theme for her article, which in many ways was even stronger than the one she had anticipated.

It was now late in the day. Beth's portion of the journey was coming to an end. She had become so engrossed in talking with the captain that she didn't notice the little potholes of blue that were beginning to punch their way through the thick layer of clouds overhead. Slowly the holes widened and merged. By the time the *Wilhelm Tham* made its scheduled stop at Norsholm, the ugly gray had been washed away by the sun into explosions of billowing white clouds.

The journey had been a delight with its intimate scale and toy-boat sensation. People had come from everywhere to watch; all kinds of people who had stopped to observe the anachronistic little ship ply its way along the only route it had ever known. The locks were always the largest gathering places. They seemed to be a kind of crossroads with picnic tables, a lock keeper's house, flowers in window boxes or perhaps even a vegetable garden.

Waving was the universal sign language of the canal. Everyone had a greeting: lock keepers and bridge attendants; cyclists on the towpaths; fishermen everywhere; yachtsmen flying the flags of many countries; kids of all ages. In the afternoon, as the boat glided through the countryside, one old man even honored its passage with a serenade on his violin.

Thor was waiting for Beth at the landing, resting comfortably, eating an ice cream cone and facing the sun "turtle-style" so as to soak in every ray of its warmth. The temperature seemed to have risen by several degrees, and with it, the palette of color returned even bolder than before, as if someone had raised a prism into the atmosphere and let it drip over the world.

When Beth arrived back at the spa, she was reflecting upon the day, contemplating what she would do for dinner when she saw Stig standing at the reception desk. After a few minutes of conversation, he suggested that she take a picnic basket and ride a bicycle along the shore to Mem where the Baltic met with the entrance to the canal. The weather was now sunny and warm, and Beth greeted the idea with great enthusiasm. She went back to her room to freshen up and change, and by 8 p.m. she was back in the lobby.

The towpath along the canal was the perfect means of solitary exploration. Beth was now totally immersed in all the natural wonder of the Gota Canal that she had seen from the ship. Evening was easing to its close, quietly preparing for a restful slumber that would awaken early with the summer dawn of a new day.

It was an easy half-hour ride to Mem. When Beth arrived she took her picnic basket and walked to a peninsula of rocks where a tiny lighthouse signaled to the sea. She reached for the bottle of wine in her basket, poured herself a cup and then leaned back against the base of the lighthouse.

It had been a trip Beth would never forget: the spectrum of rich Scandinavian light made brilliant by the loving hand of God; an entire town converted into a hotel by an eccentric man with a zest for the best things in life; a lovable crepe-making giant who lived in a spa; a holiday celebration filled with perpetual daylight; and a boat ride through paradise.

Water lapped gently against the rocks and the air was so calm that Beth could hear the dull flapping of wings as birds returned to their nests. Still others glided gracefully along invisible currents of air while a soft breeze whispered through the sea-grass.

"They were right," Beth thought. "All of them. Nature is indeed solace for all things. Sweden is truly a wonderland of nature, and one of the best kept secrets in the world."

Beth was content. She, too, was now one with nature. The sun hung low in the sky shooting a fiery golden stream of light across the water. Beth turned toward the sun, leaning her head back as far as she could to take in all of its delicious warmth.

It was wonderful being a turtle.

MIXED NUTS ALONG
THE AMALFI COAST

"Hey Beth, there's a guy named Earl Richards on the phone," shouted Fred Hatcher across the newsroom. "You wanta talk to him, or should I take a message?"

"Tell him to hold, I'll be right there," Beth Jacobsen yelled back. Whenever Earl Richards called, Beth would drop everything to get to the phone. Richards had been the east coast public relations person for TWA for nearly twenty years, and a call from him usually meant an invitation for a press trip to some exotic destination.

Beth first met Earl as a result of a referral from Vivian Timblin who was a fellow travel writer from a previous trip. On that occasion, Richards had hosted a group to St. Kitts when the airline was inaugurating service into the Caribbean. He had been looking for a good media contact in North Carolina, believing that it was an up and coming travel market, and when he received no enthusiasm in Charlotte, he was delighted to discover Beth Jacobsen in Winston-Salem. The feeling was mutual, and Beth jumped at the opportunity. Charlotte's loss was her gain, and she couldn't believe her good fortune at having ready access to an international airline, especially an American carrier.

"Got your bags packed?" asked a jovial Richards when Beth picked up the phone.

"Always. Are we going someplace really neat?"

"How about some Italian spas down in the Gulf of Naples?"

"You mean massages and facials and all that good stuff?" asked Beth.

"You got it. And lots of good food too," answered Richards.

"Sign me up," said Beth without hesitating.

"Well that was easy. We've got six other writers besides you, and there's one stow-away who's actually a dentist doing a site inspection for a possible convention. We fly into Rome for the first night, then travel down to Naples and over to the Island of Ischia for a few days. Then we come back to Rome for the rest of the trip. I'll send you a press kit with all the information. Have you ever been to Rome?"

"No, this'll be new territory for me. Anybody going that I know?"

"Let's see. I've got Maggie Sisken from Memphis. Then there's Burt Henry. He's a freelancer writing for the *Los Angeles Times*. The dentist's name is Dr. Joseph Boyd. Jack Hendricks is writing for *Travel Holiday*. He's an interesting story. His real job is full-time editor of a porno magazine, but every now and then he accepts a travel assignment to stay legitimate, and, of course, so he can get a trip out of it. Then there's Terri Blake with *Glamour* and Janice Carlton who writes for *Town and Country*. You've probably heard me talk about Vince Jackson with the *New Orleans Times Picayune*, but I don't think you've ever met him. There's you and then Maria Manzetti who represents the hotels where we'll be staying."

"Wow that sounds like a pretty impressive group. How'd I manage to get in with all those folks?"

"C'mon Beth. You know you're on the primo list when "Magic Earl" starts makin' his rounds."

Beth knew he was right. In fact, some of the writers on past trips had given him the nickname "Magic" because everything always seemed to work out just right when Earl was in charge. Though she had only traveled with him on two other occasions, Beth learned right away that Earl was not the typical PR guy. In the first place, he never made demands, or harassed writers about when their stories would appear. He took the philosophy that if the people he invited didn't produce, then they weren't asked again. It was that simple. Secondly, he always made certain that every trip he put together had at least one good "hook" for a story and usually two or three. Having been a writer himself once, Earl never planned an itinerary without having something of interest on which to hang a good travel story. Finally, and most important, he believed that it was much more necessary to have a compatible group of people traveling together than the so-called prestige of their publications. His idea was that people who enjoyed each other's company would automatically produce good stories and, at the same time, return with positive feelings about the trip. It was a winning combination, and an excellent philosophy.

Beth also knew that Richards really did keep a short list of select people from which he chose his participants. He never specifically wrote it down, but he used the list as his core resource for invitations, and then modified from there according to the needs of the client he was working with, and the writers they might want to include. Over the years Earl's stable of writers had done numerous trips together, creating an encyclopedia of memories that not only made for lively dinner conversations but, over time, had also established lifelong friendships.

Beth and Earl continued talking about the itinerary, dates for the trip, the hotels and other details for several more minutes. When she hung up, Beth was officially headed for sunny Italy, and another chapter in her travel writing career was about to begin.

The TWA first class lounge was teeming with people preparing to embark to the four corners of the globe. It was always a fascinating place for Beth, especially when she considered the idea that this was a nightly occurrence. Travelers filling plane after plane, taking off for exotic places. Rio. Hong Kong. London. Athens. Moscow. And Rome. Rome. On this night, she herself could be counted among the number in that group.

The first class lounge was a nice perk for travel writers. Not only was it a good meeting place, because it was relatively small and quiet, but it was also an easy location to round everyone up when the time came for departure. And, of course, it was comfortable, too. Beth looked up from her book just as Earl Richards made his way into the room. She was reading *The Italians* by Luigi Barzini, a fascinating series of essays written in the 60s about the Italian way of life, good and bad. From a documentary perspective it was one of the best books she had ever read about Italy. That, and another book by Barbara Grizzuti Harrison entitled *Italian Days*.

Earl was a tall, lanky chap of about six feet four or five. He had one of those curly hairdos that made him look like he had just stuck his finger into a light socket. His other trademark was his Coca-Cola thick eyeglasses, which he used for distant vision. In order to read, Earl had to remove his glasses and practically swallow a newspaper, magazine or periodical, perusing it from about three inches away. He also wore an ill-fitting raincoat, which appeared to be about two sizes too short for his height. And he carried a briefcase containing his bible of information about contacts, schedules, writers and other details he needed to ensure that everything ran smoothly.

Beth now knew the routine by heart. The first thing Earl would do was go to the reception desk and determine the load factors for the first class cabin. Whenever possible, Earl would try to upgrade everyone to first class. His term for the front cabin was "riding the big chair," and everyone who had ever traveled with him before always kept their fingers crossed that he would have them flying in front of the curtain instead of behind it. Richards had a policy about upgrading, however. If it wasn't possible to get the big chair for everyone, then no one got one. That didn't usually happen though, because with his oversized body, nobody enjoyed the first class cabin any more than Earl himself.

It was still too early to make a final determination about the load factors, but at least Richards now had an idea about his potential for success. The next task was to make a quick scan of the lounge to see if any of his gathering had arrived. Earl looked around and immediately spotted Beth, and two others who were sitting in different parts of the room. When Earl caught

Beth's eye, he walked over and gave her a hug before excusing himself to meet with his other two companions. After a few moments Earl brought them over to where Beth was sitting and made the necessary introductions.

"Beth meet Maggie Sisken of Memphis and Burt Henry from Denver. Burt is writing for the *L.A. Times*, and Maggie's family owns the newspaper in Memphis. This is Beth Jacobsen with the *Winston-Salem Journal* in North Carolina."

There was a lot of handshaking and general getting acquainted conversation, except for Earl who already knew everyone. Instead, he took time to "catch up" by making an informal survey of what each of them had been doing since the last trip. He had a fondness for journalists, and probably knew more about newspapers, magazines and various travel publications, and their writers, than just about anyone else in the industry.

It didn't take Beth long to make an evaluation about the two new characters in her life. Burt was definitely a curmudgeon, and Maggie was the classic Southern belle. Beth could tell from Burt's conversation that he was not a happy man. He was as surly on the inside as his gruff exterior. At well over 70, Beth sometimes wondered why people like Burt even bothered to stay in the travel writing business. He had been everywhere and seen everything at least twice. Maybe three or four times. It was one thing for Burt to remain in a bad career choice in his own hometown, but why spread the grief to other people around the globe? Maybe it was for financial reasons, or the benefits, or because of family pressures. The trouble was that travel writing didn't pay very well, except for an elite few, and even if it did, after he had already seen the world once, why bother to challenge it again if he didn't like it? Especially when there were more lucrative opportunities elsewhere. Beth could tell right away that there would be nothing on this trip that excited Burt. Furthermore, it seemed odd that he was even part of this group, because he certainly didn't fit the profile of most of Earl's selected travelers.

Burt was one of those people who was always disheveled. His mustache was unevenly trimmed. His salt-and-pepper hair was slightly uncombed.

His tie was pushed to one side, his jacket was wrinkled and his pants looked as if they hadn't been pressed for a couple of weeks. He was also a cigar stub smoker. Over the course of the trip, no one would ever catch sight of Burt lighting up a fresh cigar. It was as if he was breaking them off halfway down the shaft before he even began puffing away. Already Beth was mentally planning her seating arrangements for upcoming meals during the next eight days, and Burt was not included as a partner, if she could help it.

Maggie, on the other hand, was extremely pleasant, even though she was obviously a social climber. As the oldest daughter of a family owned and operated newspaper, prestige was important to Maggie above all else. Prestige of the places she had been, as well as the number of destinations. Quantity was definitely important. There was also prestige in the people she met. If Maggie could hobnob with a countess, have tea with an oil baron, spend an afternoon on an international jet-setter's yacht or dine with a celebrity in some far away port of call, that represented the ultimate moment of prestige.

Youth had long since passed Maggie by, but it hadn't been kind to her when it was in flower, either. She was clever however, and coy. Maggie knew exactly how and when to charm anyone into getting whatever she desired. Part of it was her drawl, which has been one of the most powerful secret weapons that southern women have possessed since long before *Gone With the Wind*. She milked her accent to perfection, getting more syllables into words than seemed humanly possible. She did possess a fun-loving personality, and a delightful sense of humor, but at the same time, Maggie Sisken was always playing "the game" as hard as she could, and she never missed an opportunity to take full advantage whenever possible.

"Weeelll yooouuu knnnooowww just last week I waaass haavvviiinnng dinnnneeer wiiittth a Suuullltaaannn from the Middle Eaaassst. Heee waaas suuuccch a diiivvvinnne felllooow, aaand weee got alonnng faaamousssly. I wiiish yooouuu could haaave met hiiim. Eaaarl waaas niiice enough to arraaange a tiiicket fooor me so thaaat I could visit thiiis gentleman in

Neeew Yorrrk. I stayyyed at the Piiierre you knnnooowww. I wouldn't waaant the Suuullltaaannn to feeel uncommmfortabbble," would be a typical comment from Maggie. She was the kind of person who made everyone nervous just listening to her because you wanted to hit a switch somewhere that would speed her up.

As part of his ritual, Earl returned to the reception desk to make another inquiry. There would be several more such visits right up to the final few minutes prior to departure. Earl Richards was a highly social animal, but he never socialized during this portion of the trip. He was too busy. This was his territory, and he made certain his people were properly looked after. Once the plane began to taxi for takeoff, well, that was another matter, but until the mammoth 747 backed away from the gate, Earl was all business.

He was at the reception desk when Maria Manzetti arrived. She tapped him on the shoulder and said, "Hello Earl. Am I the last one to get here?"

"No there are a few more to come yet. How're you doin'? Hotel business good these days?" asked Earl.

"Same old thing. You know, lose a few properties, pick up a few new ones. It's a funny business, but I guess every business is funny if you stay with it long enough."

"Speaking of funny business, I've got some for you right now, so I'm glad you're here," said Richards.

"Is something wrong?" asked Maria.

"Not really, but I need your input. The flights to Rome are pretty full tonight. We've got two planes going out. The first one stops in Milan, then goes on to Rome. The second is non-stop to Rome. The first one leaves about an hour earlier than the other one, but they both arrive in Rome within a half-hour of each other. The problem is, I don't think I can get everybody up front on one flight, but if we split the group, then we can all ride in comfort. That's the dilemma. What do you think?"

Maria was easygoing and always flexible. She would do anything she could to accommodate anyone, and the fact that both planes were scheduled to land within a half hour of each other was no big problem. "Sounds fine to me," she replied, "By the time everyone clears customs and gets their luggage the time difference shouldn't matter much anyway. I say let's split up."

"Great, that's what we'll do then. Now let me get this right, we've got nine people flying tonight, correct?"

"That's right. Doctor Boyd is already in Italy, and he'll join us in Rome. Everyone else is leaving with us," said Maria.

"OK, then why don't you and four others go on the non-stop flight because that's the one that gets in first. I'll take the other three with me. All of our luggage has already been checked or will be checked on my flight because we were originally scheduled to take that one. Rather than complicate things we'll just leave it that way and pick up everything once we get there. How does that sound?"

"Good plan," replied Maria. "That was easy enough. Now, if there aren't any other problems to solve, I think I'll go over and say "hi" to the others."

It was shortly after 6 p.m. Earl would leave with his party at 7:25, while Maria's flight was scheduled to depart at 8:30. Ordinarily the extra hour of waiting would have been an inconvenience, but in this case, it was really a matter of sitting in the lounge or sitting on the plane so there wasn't a great deal of difference.

Three other writers had joined the group by the time Maria introduced herself. Jack Hendricks, Terri Blake and Janice Carlton were now deeply engaged in meaningless get acquainted conversation with Beth, Maggie and Burt. Only Vince Jackson was missing, and he was due to arrive at any moment. Maria made herself known to everyone and filled them in on the plan that she and Earl had arranged for the flights. The decision was met with a cheer of rousing enthusiasm. The "Big Chair" had a special ring to it that had a tendency to make people very adaptable. Earl had worked his "magic" again, and no one was complaining.

Within fifteen minutes, Vince Jackson appeared on the scene to complete the entourage. It was an eclectic group to say the least. Most writer's tours were, but this one may have set new standards for eccentricity, and the word "eclectic" was about to be redefined.

Airport arrival areas are by their very nature frantic. Rome was different. It was chaos. Perhaps because it was Italy things were supposed to be that way. Whatever the reason, the congestion, suitcases, luggage carts, support personnel, police officers and other assorted paraphernalia that accompanies the transition from the planes to the outside world had converged into one huge mob scene in the middle of the baggage claim area. As anticipated, Maria and her traveling mates arrived first, but there was no hurry to get to the carousel since everything was coming in on the second flight anyway.

The writers stood away from the crowd, biding their time until the others in their group arrived. Earl and his crew were not far behind. Maria spotted them immediately because Earl stood out by a full head above everyone else as he led the way through the sea of people.

The task of retrieving luggage was the usual hassle. Somewhere in the recesses of her travels, Beth had created an image in her mind of a trip being likened to an inverted hourglass. A typical hourglass is bulbous on both ends with all the congestion in the middle. But traveling by air was just the opposite. All the congestion was at the extremities with a huge bubble of freedom in the center. Arrivals were never quite as bad as departures because of the anticipation of the journey ahead, but the final battles to reach the plane at the end of a trip were nothing short of sheer torture.

Soon the large metallic carousel began its slow clockwise rotation. Gradually passengers spotted their belongings and forced their way through the bodies in front of them to recapture the traveling components of their lives. One by one the writers retrieved their possessions, stacking them awkwardly onto luggage carts for the short transfer to the waiting motorcoach outside. From the time the bags began to move, it was only a matter of ten minutes or so until everyone had reclaimed their suitcases and was ready to go. Everyone that is, except Burt.

The number of bags was thinning out. And so was the crowd. It was increasingly easy to work to the front of the conveyer. In fact, Burt was now standing alone at the edge of the machine, but only the same few lonesome bags kept coming around again and again and again, and his were not among them.

Earl walked up beside him. He was helpless to do anything, but at the same time, he was trying his best to be of assistance. "Goddamned TWA lost my luggage," growled Burt. "I knew we shoulda all traveled together. We were askin' for it when we split up the group. Well, what am I gonna do now? Any suggestions?" he asked Earl with disgust.

"Let's go to the TWA office over there. We'll file a claim, and when they locate the luggage I'll have them send it out to us at the hotel. I'm sorry about this. Do you have anything at all with you or did you check everything?" replied Richards.

"I always bring my shaving things and an extra set of clothes in my carry-on. I've been traveling long enough to anticipate this kind of crap from the airlines," snarled Henry.

"I know it's a problem for you and I do apologize, but we'll get your baggage back as quickly as we can. Meanwhile, when we get to Rome, if you want to pick up a few other things to wear, just get what you need and save your receipts and we'll reimburse you," said Earl.

Secretly Earl knew that if the luggage didn't turn up right away, there was a bigger problem looming than he was revealing to his disgruntled passenger. Since the group would only be staying one night in Rome before traveling to Ischia the next day, there would be no way for the luggage to catch up with them. If it wasn't located pretty soon, then surly, gruff, grouchy old Burt was going to go for quite a while without his belongings.

Everyone else was on the bus when Earl and Burt finally got there. Burt was still muttering unpleasantries to Earl, and carrying a small satchel containing his toiletries, a spare shirt, a pair of pants and a change of underwear and socks, when they boarded the coach. The rest of the group had become strangely quiet as the two men got on. Burt sidled his way to the back of the coach and plopped down with an audible sigh. Earl took the front seat, trying to remain as far from Burt as possible after the ordeal of the previous half-hour.

Beth made herself comfortable by a window. She always tried to make the initial drive from the airport to the hotel a personal orientation program by gathering overall impressions of the landscape and the architecture. As the countryside discarded itself past the windows yielding to the remnants of a once glorious civilization and the striations of history from other centuries, Beth reflected upon Barzini's writings in *The Italians*. She recalled the thoughts of others from Barzini's research. People who had written poetically and eloquently about Italy. Henry James, for example, first visited Rome in 1869, and on his first day he wrote in his diary, "At last, for the first time, I live."

Even the Russian's had been affected by Italy's magic. The revolutionary, Alexander Herzen, pointed out, "There is only one country in Europe which can give you a feeling of peace, which can make you shed tears not of disgust and disillusionment but of delight, and that country is Italy." Beth began to visualize the words, trying to recapture the emotions that had caused her predecessors to react as they did. The bus continued to roll through the increasing confusion and congestion that was Rome. It was a serendipitous pageant unfolding before Beth's eyes. People unaware of her curious gaze and thoughts went anonymously about their daily rituals without realizing that they were in some small way performing a dance of life that would profoundly affect her forever.

In the final years of Percy Shelley's all too brief life he spent most of his time in Italy, making occasional visits to Rome. In *Prometheus Unbound* he wrote, "The bright blue sky of Rome and the effect of the vigorous awakening Spring in that divinest climate and the new life with which it drenches the spirit even to intoxication were the inspiration of this drama."

Many who have written passionately about Italy came from northern Europe. Compared to the unpredictable weather conditions north of the Alps, the glorious days of perpetual sunshine were so beguiling that they were impossible to ignore. Heinrich Heine once put it this way, "Our German summers are but winters painted green. The very sun wears a flannel coat. In this yellow flannel sunshine fruits do not ripen. Confidentially speaking, the only ripe fruits we have at home are cooked apples." Equally affected by the spirit of Italy was the Russian poet, Gogol, who wrote, "Who has been in Italy can forget all other regions. Who has been in Heaven does not desire Earth. Europe compared to Italy is like a gloomy day compared to a day of sunshine."

But there was more. Something that went far beyond the climate to make such a dramatic difference in a person's attitude and perception of life. There was something more powerful. Something intangible. Many places bask in the rays of the Mediterranean sun, but Italy was infectious. Italy was a tonic for the soul.

It came as no surprise to Beth, now that she was there, that Barbara Grizzuti Harrison had an on-going "love affair" with Rome, or that Barzini had become so infatuated by his homeland. Beth had barely set foot on Italian soil, she had not even stepped off the bus, yet she could sense a powerful magnetism drawing her into the cast of a vast, eternal and infinite drama that had been enriched by so many players before her. No place she had ever been had quite affected her like this. She could feel the words flowing from her brain like a fountain. She didn't even have to think about them. They just came. Italy was a destination that would write itself.

Even so, Beth knew that her initial sensations were no different than those of all the others who had come before her. Words had burst forth for them as well. There wasn't anything new that she was going to experience that someone hadn't felt before. Nothing she would write would have gone unexpressed by others. The only difference was that now she was part of the experience, and the things that she would write would be a personal reinforcement of her feelings combined with those who had preceded her. Beth took solace in that. In a sense, she felt as if she now belonged to an elite group, a club of sorts, and she was comforted by the idea that those who followed would go through precisely the same orientation program in order to become a member.

Hotel Mediterraneo is located near the railway station at the crest of the highest of the seven hills in Rome. It is also the tallest building on the hill, owing to the fact that it was built under Mussolini's regime and therefore the building codes of the time were ignored during its construction. It is a spacious property and very comfortable inside, but it does have the same bulky, cold appearance of contemporary fascist architecture. In short, it looks like something Mussolini would have built. One benefit is that because the building is so tall, it features a lovely rooftop terrace that provides a delightful view overlooking the city, and a great place for a nightcap, especially in the summertime.

For over 125 years the Bettoja family has been operating hotels in Rome. Though the *Mediterraneo* is relatively new by comparison to the other properties, it is regarded as the flagship facility in the chain. The present owner, Angelo Bettoja, is married to an American woman from the state of Georgia. In her youth Jo Bettoja had been a model on assignment for *Vogue* when she met Angelo, fell in love and cashed in her return ticket to the U.S. Since modeling was now no longer a part of her life, Jo and another Italian modeling colleague took it upon themselves to travel throughout Italy collecting family recipes in small villages around the country. When they had gathered enough, they created an Italian cooking school in Rome overlooking Trevi Fountain, using Angelo's hotels as the residence for their students. It was an ideal story for Maggie to sink her social-climbing teeth into. Since the final day of the itinerary featured an outing at the Bettoja's 300-year old villa, it would offer the perfect opportunity to latch on to Jo after the graduation ceremonies for her current class. Ample time to obtain all the details for her article.

After checking in to the hotel, Earl mentioned he was going to get some exercise by walking down to the Colosseum if anyone wanted to join him. Vince Jackson said he'd tag along, and Beth was also eager for a bit of exploration.

"I've seen it," said Burt, "It's just a broken down old pile of rocks. The whole city's crumbling as far as I can tell. I'm gonna go find a coupla things to wear, then I'll probably sit at the bar for a while."

"You guys go on and I'll see it when we do the city tour." added Jack Hendricks. "I'm gonna wash up a little, and then I'm gonna check out a few of the smut shops in town to see what kind of erotica they're pushin' these days. It's tough doing two jobs when you're on a trip."

Janice and Terri wanted to settle in a little to shake off the effects of the overnight flight. Maria had a couple of meetings to attend to, and Maggie wanted to do some research on Jo Bettoja. "Yooouuu knnnooowww, III thiiink I'll juuussst staaay in my rooom fooor awhiiile and reeead up on Mrs. Bettoyyya. I waaant tooo dooo an extensiiive inteeervieeew wiiittth heeer wheeen weee cooome baaack to Rooome. Is thaaat OKaaay wiiith yooouuu, Earl?"

"Fine by me," answered Richards, "But listen everybody, cocktails are at 6:30 up on the terrace on the top floor of the hotel, and dinner is at 7:30. So we'll see you on the roof at 6:30."

Like Burt Henry, Vince Jackson had been almost everywhere. Unlike Henry, Jackson still had a rich enthusiasm for travel. He had keen interests in a variety of subjects, and the most rewarding aspect of his years of touring the world was that he could now concentrate on specific little articles that were particularly noteworthy to him. No longer was he resigned to the broad overviews that most travel writers had to produce. Now he could focus upon the intricacies that brought a destination to life.

Vince had managed to keep his weight in check over the years. He was in excellent physical condition for a man approaching 60. His hair was still dark and combed straight back. He was one of those men with a heavy beard that got darker as the day progressed. Even after a fresh shave, Vince always seemed to have a trace of five o'clock shadow. His voice was soft and pleasant, unhurried, giving the impression that at any given moment he was content in his surroundings. One of his biggest assets was his curiosity about other people, which added poise to his already genteel personality.

The guys appointed Beth as the designated tour leader, but her map was only partially helpful. Except for a few major landmarks, which were easily recognizable, the hodgepodge of streets was difficult to identify. Street names supposedly could be found on the side corners of buildings, but that only proved successful about a third of the time. The other 66 percent of the effort was pure guesswork.

The trio ambled along Via Cavour, the main thoroughfare in ancient Rome, searching for the best route to the Colosseum. Along the way, if possible, Beth wanted to stop at the *Church of St. Peter in Chains* to view Michelangelo's sculpture of Moses.

The Moses is one of only two sculptures by Michelangelo in Rome. The other being his Pieta in *St. Peter's Basilica*. Beth knew from her reading that the little side trip to see the Moses was actually a short cut to the Colosseum anyway. Besides, it didn't matter to her two male companions. They were in no hurry to get anywhere else, and they were equally interested in seeing Michelangelo's work for themselves. After several blocks of searching for the proper route to the church, they arrived at their destination.

It was a pleasant, easy stroll getting to the church through the serpentine back streets of Rome. Earl and Vince talked shop mostly, catching up on old acquaintances and reporting the latest news to each other. Vince and Beth were still going through the process of getting to know each other, but occasionally Earl would fill in the gaps with information he could share about either of them.

The Moses was breathtaking. After her first misadventures in Italy with her father, brother, Fran and Sally Mae a few years back, Beth had become fascinated by the genius of Michelangelo, and later she had done quite a bit of research about him. Now for the first time she had an opportunity to compare and contrast some of his work, and she could tell that her studies were paying off.

Beth had read that Michelangelo never produced a sculpture that was proportionally correct. He was always keenly aware of the perspective from which it would be viewed. In the case of Moses for example, it was originally intended to be seen from below. Therefore his right leg and head give a distorted impression of the work when seen from eye level as we do today. But from below the long face would have been shortened, the torso telescoped and the feet and left hand partially hidden. Experts say that the sculpture is now most effectively seen from the front where the focus is drawn to the right because of the direction of the head, the extension of the powerful left arm and the tucking back of his left leg.

There was an English speaking tour in progress when Beth and her companions arrived, and though it wasn't technically kosher to do so, they tagged along to hear the final details of the explanation. "In it's original concept, the Moses was to be the right hand corner figure of a massive tomb for Pope Julius II which was never completed," said the guide. "It was intended that the Moses would sit above another sculpture known as The Rebellious Slave which was to be one of six figures of slaves in the finished work. Today, four of the unfinished slaves can be seen at the *Accademia* in Florence, while the other two are displayed at the *Louvre* in Paris."

The guide continued, "While Michelangelo's David is a celebration of the human figure, Moses is also a masterpiece of human form even though it is clothed. Much of the artist's genius lies in the fact that he was able to express the power of this particular figure through the draping of his garments. It has long been an accepted belief that Moses is a combination of the personalities of both Michelangelo and Pope Julius. The term for this blending of characteristics was known by Michelangelo's contemporaries as "terribilitia." The translation means "a frightening power or sublimity." If you look very closely perhaps you can see the portraits of the artist as well as Julius, which are said to be hidden within Moses' beard."

"As with many of his works, Moses appears to contain a psychic force, which Michelangelo was able to either incorporate into the stone or to extract from it. It matters little, for the final result is enhanced purely by the magnitude of the artist's undeniable ability to express the perfection of his craft, regardless of the philosophy one chooses ultimately to believe."

"Most of the questions which first arise about the sculpture of Moses from visitors relate to the horns protruding from his head. The most popular theory regarding the horns is that they resulted from a mistranslation of the Hebrew word for "rays of light" because ancient manuscripts describe Moses as being surrounded with a halo. Interestingly enough, in the ancient world, a head with horns was often seen as a symbol of divinity, honor and power, so there is some conjecture about whether Michelangelo was aware of this and incorporated that idea into the sculpture."

After a quarter of an hour visit with Moses, the lecture concluded. The trio left the church and made their way down to the Colosseum. The approach to the Colosseum from *St. Peter in Chains* opens out just above Via dei Fori Imperiali. It is an excellent vantage point to get an overview of the majestic size of the structure, as well as its relationship to the Roman Forum and the Palatine Hill, which was once home to many Roman emperors.

"Well, Burt Henry was right about one thing," said Beth as they neared the structure which had long ago become the symbol of the city. "It is beginning to show some signs of age."

"Don't give Burt too much credit," said Earl.

"Imagine the spectacles that took place in there for four hundred years."

Earl was looking at his pocket guidebook that he always carried with him. "According to this, it's over 150 feet high, and officially opened in the year 80 AD with gladiatorial events that lasted for 100 days. The capacity was 50,000, and there were 80 entrances. And here's an interesting bit of trivia, supposedly it was designed so the crowd could empty the whole place within five minutes."

"Any more tidbits of knowledge you can pass along?" asked Beth.

"Actually yes," answered Earl. "The original name was the Flavian Amphitheater because it was constructed during the age of the Flavian emperors. Technically that's still the correct name, but the people preferred to call it "The Colosseum" because there was once a colossal statue of Nero standing nearby. The statue no longer exists, as you can tell, but it is believed to have been the largest bronze statue in antiquity. When it was finally removed, it took 24 elephants to perform the task!"

"Vespasian. He started the whole thing didn't he?" asked Beth.

"Excellent. You know your history very well," replied Earl. "As a matter of fact, according to this, he wanted to make a majestic statement to the world that Rome had returned to its unquestioned role of power after a bitter civil war. Remember the line, 'When the Colosseum falls, so falls Rome and all the world?' Well Vespasian said that and it's a common saying even today. So there you have it, a nutshell history of one of the finest architectural achievements in the history of the Roman Empire."

Beth and Earl were leaning against the railing pondering the scale of the Colosseum while Vince was in the process of clicking off a few pictures. Nobody saw the small band of dirty faced children approaching, including Vince who was so preoccupied with his picture taking that he didn't look up until they were about 15 feet away. By then it was too late. Beth and Earl were oblivious to the incident until it was already in progress. The whole thing happened in a matter of seconds. Vince had taken his eye away from his camera just long enough to see the four children walking toward him. Three little boys and a girl ranging in ages from about 11 to 13 moved closer and closer to Vince, appearing as though they were just being playful and innocent. In a flash they surrounded him, distracting the writer who was now busily shooing them away. In that momentary lapse Vince realized what had happened. His wallet was gone. The children remained where they were, but in that instantaneous blur a fifth child appeared out of nowhere, and raced away with the wallet, passing it off to a waiting adult accomplice far down the street.

Vince yelled out as soon as he knew that his pocket had been picked. "My wallet, it's gone! They've got my wallet! Where is it you little bastards?" Vince was now in the process of searching the four gypsy children who were in the original group that had approached him. Beth and Earl rushed over to help, asking questions and searching the children as well. But it was a scam the children knew all too well. Part of their routine was to stand around acting bewildered by these crazy tourists who were suddenly accusing them of theft, all the while knowing that their little diversion had allowed the stolen wallet to be thoroughly stripped of its contents and disposed of by then.

"Son of bitch! I should have known better, dammit! First time I've ever been caught like this. I've read about it, heard about it, knew about it and damned if I didn't get zapped the first time I let my guard down."

Vince was more frustrated than angry. He kept blaming himself for not being smart enough to see what was happening. He knew that he hadn't been in any danger. The kids were thieves, but they weren't out to hurt anyone. The search continued, but it was evident that the tiny perpetuators of the crime were no longer involved, and their role now was to simply stand around pleading their innocence.

"What did they get Vince? Do you know what you had in there?" asked Earl with concern.

"Well it could have been worse. They got some money, but not much else. I had about $400 with me, but the rest was really just a Mastercard and my driver's license. Don't need the license here anyway. I can replace that at home, and I can cancel the Mastercard when I get back to the hotel. So other than the $400 bucks I'm pretty lucky, I guess."

Beth was thinking that a $400 loss would have been devastating for her, not to mention the sensation of being violated in broad daylight by a mob of street urchins. It was a difficult lesson to learn, even if it had happened to someone else, but it was not an uncommon occurrence in Rome. Gypsies worked the streets in crowded tourist areas like the Colosseum, the railway stations and the Spanish Steps. There were even thieves on motorbikes who would streak past pedestrians walking along sidewalks, slashing the straps of a woman's purse with a razor and speeding down the street before she even knew what happened. If a person took proper precautions, and didn't let their guard down, the chances of being a victim were greatly reduced because the gypsies usually wouldn't attempt to rob someone who was aware of their methods. For the moment however, the sunshine of Rome, and the magical words of all those writers which had seemed so poignant just an hour before, were now sadly taking a backseat to reality.

The wine cellar at the *Hotel Massimo d'Azeglio* was the first acquisition of the Bettoja family when they began their venture into the hotel business more than a century ago. It is an ideal place for a grand welcoming dinner, and would have been equally perfect for a farewell gathering. The elusive Dr. Boyd was now in attendance completing the traveling ensemble. He was a mousy sort of chap with beady little rodent eyes, closely cropped hair and a pompous attitude that seemed to say he was only gracing everyone with his presence out of necessity. In Beth's eyes he had the appearance of what she had always imagined Pontius Pilate to look like.

He was certainly the best-dressed member of the party, male or female, with every aspect of his wardrobe custom tailored and precisely coordinated. There wasn't a hair out of place nor a wrinkle to be found anywhere in his garments, and there was an air of arrogance in his personality that was distinctly distasteful. He was certainly an outsider. It was obvious that it had never occurred to him that he should be a part of the group anyway, and that he intended to remain as aloof as possible with no desire whatsoever to join the inner circle of the riffraff with whom he was traveling.

On this night there was a dramatic shift in the conversation at dinner from the idle chatter that had dominated earlier portions of the trip. Now there was common ground to discuss, mishaps though they were, and there was lengthy debate about airline baggage handling, Roman gypsies and various offshoots such as how best to cease payment on credit cards, trying to purchase new clothes in European sizes and so on.

There were also bathroom evaluations for the rooms and the amenities provided therein. This was a common topic among the women of a group because females often rated their surroundings according to the quality of their hotel bathroom facilities. Ever since her first press trip with Ian Lampley, and even before that, bathroom surveillance had been a significant aspect of Beth's modus operandi, so she was pleased to learn that she was not alone in the ritual. Besides the reconnaissance missions, there were several people who had been unable to get their televisions to operate because they couldn't figure out how to use the remote, and they knew they wouldn't survive for a week without access to CNN.

The multi-course meal was superb featuring antipasto, soup, pasta, chicken, veal and dessert all enhanced by an exquisite selection of Italian wines and topped off with coffees and after dinner drinks. It was further enlivened by a number of artifacts generously supplied by Jack Hendricks who had made some eye-opening purchases during his brief excursion into the world of Italian erotica. Though short, it had been a most productive tour resulting in a set of phallic key chains, ceramics depicting graphic, and seemingly impossible, sexual positions, a few items of underwear and a postcard of the David in the state of arousal. If nothing else, Jack's treasure hunt became the ultimate icebreaker. By 11 p.m., the group had deteriorated to its lowest common denominator. Its personality was now thoroughly defined by its cast of characters, plus the added events of lost luggage, a robbery, pornographic memorabilia and an elegant dining experience. Only one person remained to join the entourage; Enzo, the bus driver, and the group would meet him in the morning.

It was a sleepy band of reporters that passed by the burly coach driver on the way to their seats the following morning. Enzo spoke no English, and had no desire to learn any. He was Italian through and through and that was good enough for him. At 6 feet 3, 250 pounds, give or take, the heavy-set, barrel-chested driver was extremely large for an Italian. He was actually top-heavy. From the waist down Enzo was slender for his bulky size, but above the level of his belt he could have been a professional wrestler. He was not a big talker, nor was he particularly fond of the gestures so typical of Italian conversation. Instead, he seemed to prefer expressing himself

with a series of low growls and grunts, which he did with masterful execution, leaving little doubt about his intent or the meaning of it. He also liked
music. American rock and roll was his choice, though he despised the idea
that he was escorting Americans through Italy and would therefore have to
make concessions to them about his musical tastes.

At this stage in his life Enzo enjoyed quiet, peaceful surroundings. He
was unprepared for the rowdiness of his passengers and their raucous
American playfulness. Still, he had a job to do, and he would fulfill his
appointed tasks to the best of his abilities. Enzo was really a lovable creature
who rather enjoyed cultivating his image as being a grouch. It was a little
game that he played with himself and his guests so as not to reveal the true
kindness in his heart. In truth, he was a pushover. On the surface he and
Burt may have appeared to be two of a kind, but there was no question
that, by comparison, Burt was the real thing when it came to surliness.

The missing luggage was still missing, failing to turn up during the
night. Earl kept smiling and putting a cheerful face on things, but he
knew that Burt would probably not see his bags again until they got back
to Rome. The trick was not so much keeping Burt happy, which was
impossible anyway, but making certain that he had a proper opportunity
to replenish his God-awful wardrobe without creating so much negativity
among the others that it would have a corrosive effect on their attitudes.
That would be the most damaging thing that could happen. On the other
hand, in Vince's case, Earl had known him for years, and he was sure that
the gypsy incident would in no way diminish the enjoyment of the tour
for the rest of the writers.

It was a pleasant day for the drive to Naples. The sky was streaked with
long lines of crisscrossing clouds that gave the appearance of vapor trails.
The air was warm with a slight trace of humidity, the kind of day that
made a person feel optimistic. Three and a half hours later, in the early
afternoon, Enzo pulled the motorcoach up to the docks at the port of
Naples where a ferry would transfer the group to Ischia.

Enzo unloaded the bags from the bus before driving to a garage where the coach would be housed until the group returned three days later. He would rejoin his passengers later for the ferry to Ischia where another coach would be waiting to be used for transportation on the island. While Enzo was taking care of logistical matters, the others had a fair amount of free time for shopping, browsing and picture taking. Jack took off on another search for strange implements of sexual behavior; the doctor sought out the seclusion of a fine restaurant; Beth immersed herself, and her camera, into the pageantry of life around the square and the docks; Vince and Earl went hunting for the best gelato in Naples; the other women went shopping and Burt did the same.

It wasn't difficult for Beth to become absorbed in her surroundings. Snap! It was a photographer's paradise. Click! A collage of humanity. Flash! The piazza was buzzing with the rhythms of the day and a passion for living. Fishermen sorting their catches and hosing down the decks of their tiny boats. Vendors lining the pier with buckets of fresh squid. Laundry lines filled with sheets and pillowcases and personal items strung between ancient mustard colored buildings. Gray haired old women dressed entirely in black peering from third story windows, observing the same daily rituals they had watched continuously from the same locations for decades. Small groups of men, two, three, sometimes four, flailing arms and hands with gestures to emphasize their points of view; the topic being secondary to what really mattered, which was the flair and the amount of expression with which the opinion was expressed. Sidewalk cafes with waiters clanking dishes and glasses as they flitted through their mazes of tables. Tethered children crying and reaching for elusive, brightly colored balloons. Lovers walking hand in hand so infatuated with each other that nothing else existed.

There were smells too. And sounds. A feast for the senses. People shouting from hidden doorways and alleys. Distant voices from upstairs apartments singing opera that permeated into the clamor of the streets, creating a theatrical backdrop for the elaborate outdoor stage. Motor scooters zipping helter-skelter between people as if they had been choreographed not to run into anyone or anything. Fruit and vegetable stalls, and freshly cut flowers. This was a place where participation was mandatory, yet it was also a place where one could remain anonymous. Indeed it was a pageant, a carousel, a parade and a circus all wrapped into a single piazza, performed under a canopy of sunny, blue Mediterranean sky, and orchestrated by life itself.

Beth had read accounts of the people of Naples living their lives in the shadow of Mt. Vesuvius. There has been a sense of foreboding and pending disaster there for nearly two thousand years since the eruption of 79 AD buried Herculaneum and Pompeii in a graveyard of lava and ashes. In those days Pompeii was a coastal city. Today it lies inland, roughly a mile from the sea. Now Vesuvius hovers over Naples as a perpetual reminder of the awesome power of nature and the fragility of life, and that fact alone has a significant impact on Neapolitan lifestyles. Unlike the San Andreas fault in California, where Americans know that eventually the mother of all earthquakes will wreak havoc upon the west coast, Americans are essentially optimists. They get on with their lives with a sense of invincibility, believing that if and when it happens, it won't be nearly as devastating as the predictions have forecast it to be. Italians, on the other hand, know that they are mortal, and anything that can snuff out that life force is given complete and total respect.

Barbara Grizutti Harrison made a similar observation in *Italian Days* when she stated that, "Italians know they are going to die. (Americans have not quite got used to the idea.) You cannot live your life in Italy without getting used to the idea—without breathing in the idea—that to dust you will return. This knowledge oxygenates the blood of Italians, and it is this knowledge that animates the living dust we call flesh. The beautiful young men and women live so beautifully in the moment because they know they are **OF** the moment."

Whatever the reasons, they mattered little to Beth. She was overcome by the pageant. Barzini described it as "animation, a show," and Beth was enraptured by it. There was a touch of decadence all around her. A freeing of the spirit. A release of energy that evoked an intoxicating confidence. It was a sensual banquet, all so splendidly pagan, yet so indefinable. There was no way for Beth to express what or how she felt. She only knew that she was caught up in it, that she had internalized it through her pores, and that it was real, and it was wonderful.

By now Enzo had returned, having concluded his business faster than anticipated so the group was able to make their departure to Ischia earlier than scheduled. There was a hydrofoil leaving in fifteen minutes, and the added speed of the craft would save even more time than taking the slower ferry. Maria purchased the tickets, then everyone lugged their suitcases aboard for the 45-minute ride to the island.

Hotel Regina Isabella is located in Lacco Ameno several miles from the main town of Ischia Porto. The hotel had achieved a certain notoriety in the 60s when Elizabeth Taylor stayed there during the turmoil of her torrid love affair with Richard Burton while filming the movie *Cleopatra*. Approximately twice the size of her sister island of Capri, Ischia is also half as crowded.

During World War II, Ischia was a popular R&R location for German soldiers, while Capri became a haven for the Americans. Partly for that reason, Capri is better known today to American travelers than Ischia.

Ischia is often called "The Isle of Eternal Youth" because of its abundant thermal springs and lush vegetation set against the backdrop of the sea. For the Germans it is the ideal location for a spa with services ranging from *fango* mud baths, natural mineral springs, body wraps, massage therapy and hydrotherapy to countless other treatments, all packaged neatly under the umbrella of glorious Mediterranean sunshine.

The aquamarine and turquoise waters of the Gulf of Naples contrasted dramatically with the soft pastels of the buildings, giving the setting an appearance of being a living watercolor. Combined with the vibrant tile floors from the mainland village of Vietri, and its archways filled with sheer flowing curtains, the hotel had a light, breezy atmosphere which evoked an imaginary merger between indoors and out. For Beth, the accommodations alone were therapeutic enough without ever taking advantage of the first treatment, but she wasn't going to let that prevent her from indulging herself in all the pampering she could endure. And she was quite certain that she could endure plenty. There was a manicure, a pedicure, a massage and a *fango* treatment in her future, and before long she would be a willing participant in a grand sensual physical makeover experience fit for the gods.

After an afternoon at leisure, dinner was scheduled back in Ischia Porto at a little hideaway recommended by Maria. As in Rome, the evening meal proved to be another exercise in overindulgence, but for the ladies, it also provided an opportunity to display their latest acquisitions from the world of fashion. The highlight of the evening however, was not the women's clothing, it was Burt's.

The forces of nature had long ago taken their toll on Burt, and Italian clothing was not at all agreeable with his physique. Decades of smoking uncounted half-cigars and drinking vats of liquor combined with massive periods of inactivity had created a sort of reverse metamorphosis whereby the butterfly was turning into a caterpillar. On his best day Burt could be described as looking like a sack of shrink-wrapped potatoes. There were bulges in the most unwanted locations, while his slumped posture and shuffling manner of walking only magnified his lumpy features. Though his new wardrobe was not yet complete, Burt's purchases had at least been stylish. Stylish, that is, had he been a twenty year old Adonis with five percent body fat instead of a replica of the Pillsbury Doughboy trying to squeeze into one of Michael Jackson's skin-tight costumes.

Burt was now outfitted in a spiffy white shirt with a tapering waistline that narrowed severely at the bottom. It was obviously a quality piece of merchandise because the two lower buttons were performing the Herculean feat of straining to remain fastened from the pressure of the flesh that was bursting behind the seams. Diamond shaped gaps formed between the buttons with little blobs of hairy skin poking through the holes. Similar difficulties occurred at the neck where the top button squeezed off the circulation to Burt's head, spreading a rosy color across his face, and which occasionally left him wheezing for air. He also sported a pencil-thin red necktie, which in no way filled in the gap between his collars, nor did it in any manner shield his exposed bits of torso. In short, Burt was now the human manifestation of an Italian sausage, and Beth was forced to empathize with him, even if he was a grumpy old lout.

Maggie had fallen in love with the restaurant, showering it with multi-syllable southern accolades throughout the evening. "Myyy, myyy, myyy oh myyy, isn't thiiisss rooomaaantiiic? III deeeclaaare I've jussst diiied aaand gooone to heaveeen. I've juuussst nevvver seeen anyyythiiing liiike iiit."

Though rambling, she was correct in her assessment. *The Orange Garden* was indeed a unique dining experience. The outdoor patio was tucked into a square formed by the walls of the four surrounding buildings. The contours that comprised each wall were varied to such a degree as to establish a distinctive flavor around the perimeter of the tiny piazza. In one corner, an ancient stone staircase led to the back door of an apartment building. On another wall a second story balcony covered with bougainvillea protruded over the courtyard. There was a myriad of little platforms and stairways and alleys going everywhere, heading off into the night toward unseen locations. Above the glowing red, green and white lights that crisscrossed the patio, freshly washed clothing hung unabashedly from clotheslines that stretched between the two buildings. Rather than detracting from the ambience however, the laundry was an integral part of the natural habitat, entirely appropriate to the occasion, which would have altered the character of the setting completely had it not been there. It was all part of the charm, accentuating the magic, as if to punctuate the notion that life surely did go on just as it had for centuries.

The last rays of daylight vanished into an ebony sky, while the tables filled with cheerful diners bathed in the amber glow of flickering candle-light that splashed against the honey-colored buildings. A gentle breeze

caressed the night. Conversations wafted into the air, periodically interrupted by outbursts of laughter from different corners of the patio as the
cumulative effect of bottomless glasses of wine increasingly added to the
gaiety of the occasion. All that remained to complete the scene was music.
Then, as if on cue, at the precise moment that Beth had realized its
absence, there came the strumming of a mandolin from the lower right
hand corner of the piazza. Softly at first, then bolder and faster.

Diagonally across from the mandolin, on a slightly higher platform, a
concertina joined the performance. Next a guitar could be heard from the
flower-filled balcony above, and finally an accordion played from behind,
creating a 360-degree serenade filled with romance, enhanced by the
moonlight and the intoxication of the wine. Italy had cast its enchanting
spell once again.

Enzo was waiting patiently in the bus when the boisterous band of revelers made their way out of the restaurant. It was only a momentary lapse,
a temporary letdown to be sure, but even Burt and Dr. Boyd had mellowed enough to the point of being tolerable. Beth wouldn't have gone so
far as to say they were charming, but for a brief period of time at least,
they had actually become somewhere close to approaching pleasant.
Almost human. It came as a great surprise to everyone when Burt and the
doctor spotted a lively tavern at the far end of the street, and suggested
that since the night was still young, it required a nightcap. Normally in
such situations, once the planned activities were dispensed with, a group
would split into several factions based upon variables such as age, sex,
experience, personal interests, the itinerary and a host of other things.
Rarely did a group remain intact for after dinner festivities, but on this
night, whether it was the wine, the relatively early hour, the location so far
from the hotel, the charms of Italy or a combination of all of those things,
the entire entourage was ready for more. The person most shocked by the
decision was also the person most inconvenienced, because now Enzo was
forced to continue waiting patiently until someone finally petered out.

Inside the nightclub a live band had the place jumping with a well-chosen selection of international dance music. For Janice Carlton, who was an accomplished competitive ballroom dancer, it would have been a perfect location were it not for the fact that there were only five men in the group, four of whom were non-dancers. Only the doctor had any sense of rhythm, or knowledge of how to move around a dance floor, and even then, he was barely passable when compared to Janice's level of skill. Janice was certainly the only female who was going to be a participant. For the others this was purely a spectator sport. The question was how and when the men were going to get involved, and that's when Beth concocted a plan with Maria.

"Maria, I've got an idea for Janice's dancing partners," said Beth.

"What have you got in mind?" asked Maria who could see the conniving glint in Beth's eyes as she formulated her scheme.

"Let's have a contest," answered Beth.

"Ooohhh, thaaat's a wonnnderfuuul ideeea. Whaaat kiiind of coooonteeest dooo yooouuu haaave in miiind?" asked Maggie gleefully.

"Well the band is playing different kinds of dances, and Janice knows them all. Now we can't do the kind of dancing she does, but if the guys are any sort of gentlemen at all, they should offer to dance with her."

"Go on," said Maria smiling with anticipation.

"We'll write the names of five dances on separate pieces of paper, and then we'll have a drawing. Each guy will make a selection and whenever the band plays a certain style, whoever has that particular type of dance will ask Janice to join him."

Jack was within earshot of the conspiracy and knew right away that he wanted no part of it. "Count me out," he said. "I'll be the judge, but you can forget about me doing any dancing."

"Thiiis souuunds liiike fuuun," said Maggie clapping her hands with joy.

"OK, we'll let Jack off the hook, but which dances do we want to write down?" asked Maria.

"Let's see. I think we should have a Tango," Beth replied.

"Oooh I knooow. We neeed a Saaamba," giggled Maggie.

"Good choice," said Maria, "And how about a Cha-Cha, too?"

"Terrific. Now we only need one more," said Beth.

"Rumba!" they all shouted simultaneously.

The concept was not met with the same enthusiasm from the men, but they knew they were trapped because a refusal was tantamount to insulting Janice. Had they been remotely sober, every one of them would have probably opted to be like Jack, but as it was, in their inebriated state, the gloves were off, the inhibitions weakened and the challenge taken.

First up was Dr. Boyd, who had drawn the Cha-Cha. Everyone knew that this was going to be as good as it got, and that everything that followed would only be downhill from there.

"It's just three steps and a shuffle, that's all you need to do," said Janice. "If you can follow, I'll lead you."

"I took lessons once, but I only got as far as the "cha," so I'll probably only be able to do a step and a half and a "shuff" if you know what I mean," answered Boyd.

In a matter of seconds the couple was on the floor tripping the lights less than fantastically, flailing away at the Latin rhythms in an attempt to appear coordinated. Twice Boyd moved past Janice on the turn, losing her in the process, but other than that he moved well enough to keep most of the laughter contained to the writer's corner of the room.

The band provided a momentary reprieve by playing two unlisted dances, but it wasn't long before it was Earl's turn in the spotlight to display his skills at doing the Samba. "You know I went to a Samba school in Rio once," said Earl, "I was going to learn the Latin Hustle, but the Samba seemed more dignified. So don't be surprised if I'm actually quite artful at this."

"I guess we'll find out soon enough, won't we," said Janice. "When were you in Brazil?"

"Maybe fifteen years ago, but it'll come back to me, you'll see," answered Earl.

"Right," said Janice sarcastically.

As they made their way to the dance floor, the height difference in the couple became glaringly obvious. Janice, who was nearly a foot shorter than Earl, was staring directly at his Adam's apple. The music commenced and the two dancers began to move with all the precision and grace of a gazelle performing a mating ritual with a giraffe.

"Step, close, step, close, dip, spring. Bend a little at the knees. That's all there is to it," laughed Janice hysterically as Earl tried to follow her sensual, hippy movements.

"I've got the step-close all right, but those dip-springs are killers," shouted Earl above the music.

"On the beat," said Janice. "Earl! Earl! The music has a beat, sweetheart. Hear it? Listen."

"Oh yeah, I've got it now. Dip, spring, close, close, dip, whoops, step, close, spring, dip. Gees that's tough."

"It's rhythm Earl. They call it rhythm. Once you get the timing it's easy. Step, close, step, close, dip, spring. Got it?"

When Earl dipped, Janice sprung. When Janice sprung, Earl stepped. Then suddenly during a rare surge of coordination, Earl swung to his left crashing his backside into the oncoming buttocks of an obese woman who was concentrating so fiercely on what she was doing that she didn't see him coming. Their momentum, plus the force of gravity, flung them to the floor where they found themselves piled into a heap with Earl squashed beneath his oversized assailant. To his credit, Earl continued to move his upper body to the beat of the music until four men were able to lift the woman from her spread-eagled position on top of him. By the time the fat lady had been safely returned to her feet, the music had mercifully ceased, and Earl went back to the table, drawing a standing ovation from his fellow travelers.

There was a momentary lull and then the band went into a Rumba. Now it was Vince's turn. "I can't do this," said Vince. "I don't know the Rumba from rheumatism," he said with no confidence.

"Look Vince, remember how you moved the other day when the gypsies got your wallet?" asked Janice.

"Yeah," said Vince suspiciously.

"Just do that and you'll be close enough," smiled Janice.

Vince was a surprisingly quick study, and much more adept than anyone expected him to be, picking up the basic flavor of the steps without embarrassing himself in the least.

"The biggest thing is the transfer of your weight, and the pronounced hip movements," said Janice. "Once you have that feeling then you've just about got it. It's a very sexy dance."

"Listen darling, you're young and you're pretty. And you've got the hips and all the other equipment necessary to make this thing work, but you could put me in a body suit, stick a rose in my mouth, and I'd still look like I was chasing gypsies down the street."

Vince did look rather Latino standing next to Janice with his dark slicked back hair and his better-than-average-for-his-age physical characteristics. She complimented him well, bringing out the best aspects of his motions, and in the process, making Vince look more accomplished than he really was. Vince was pleased with his accounting of himself, but when his dance was over, he knew that the denouement was about to begin.

Pudgy little Burt had drawn the Tango. With his height, and any sort of dancing coordination or poise at all, Earl would certainly have been the most likely candidate in the group to attempt the Tango. Burt, on the other hand, was definitely the least likely. Moving to center stage a sense of calm and a look of enjoyment came across Burt's face. Part of it was the wine, but more to the truth, he knew this was as close as he would ever get to being near a female as divine as Janice. If he had to force himself to maneuver his way around the dance floor for the next three minutes, he was going to make the absolute most of the opportunity. Burt was now in sensual overdrive.

Burt's new shirt was being put to the ultimate test. The tension against the threads of his buttons was enormous, creating a mounting fear that they would eventually yield to the pressure, expelling small plastic projectiles across the room at any moment. Burt put his arm around Janice's waist. Janice reached as far as she could around Burt's rotund little body, grabbing a chunk of one of his love handles to steady herself for the first long glide across the floor. Burt went into his crouch, practically buckling at the knees, figuring that even if it resulted in surgery the next day, a chance like this would never come his way again.

From a distance Burt resembled an explosion in a mattress factory. Though he and Janice were the same height, Janice appeared taller. She was lithe, graceful and beautifully proportioned. By comparison, Burt was stocky, clumsy and asymmetrical. Zero hour was upon them. The band began to play. There were four long gliding strides forward followed by a quick turn and a pause. At the outset Burt had little trouble with the steps, though his stocky legs caused him to extend himself to the limits to keep up with Janice. Pulling a hamstring was distinctly within the realm of possibility, and the chance of throwing his back out during a turn was also very much a reality.

After surviving the first forward thrust, Burt became cocky. He stiffened his back to an upright position as best he could, snapped his head back with a burst of bravado and stuck out his jaw. His eyes glazed over, staring straight ahead while listening intently to the music. Thus far the movements themselves had not been a problem, but the pauses were another matter entirely, because they severely affected his momentum.

Next came four more long glides across the floor followed by a second snap turn, and this time a deep arching dip to the rear with a high leg kick. Burt wasn't prepared for the kick. He had considerable doubt as to whether one leg could maintain his weight, regardless of how briefly it was called upon to support him. Burt raised his right leg about a foot off the floor. Looking to his left, he saw that Janice had her leg fully extended above her waist and over her head, but there was absolutely no way he was going to undertake that challenge. Janice quickly brought her leg down to the floor with a flourish that ended in a crisp, precise stomp. Burt tried to do the same, managing only to kick his left shin with his right heel, nearly undercutting himself to the floor. He let out a blood-curdling scream of pain that was masked only by the next burst of music, and then with no time to recover, he found himself stretching across the floor once again.

Disaster awaited at the other end. Burt was fine up to the moment when he and Janice stopped. It was when he extended his left arm and reached out to catch his turning partner in an attempt to whip her back to him that he got in trouble. The "whip" was clearly a failed strategy. Janice collided with Burt, immediately knocking him to the floor and flat on his back. Without hesitation Burt displayed amazing athleticism, which could have only been driven by a sudden, unexpected burst of adrenaline. Somehow he immediately popped back to his feet like one of those punching dummies with weights in the bottom.

The worst was not over, however. Now it was Janice's turn to extend her arm and spin Burt. Had the first catastrophe not taken place, the second might also have been avoided, but the domino effect was now overtaking the choreography. Burt was dazed and disoriented, and the dizzying effects of a spin would do nothing to alleviate the problem. Furthermore, Janice was stronger than Burt. She was young and fit and didn't realize the strength of her pull when she jerked Burt toward her. Burt only grazed past her outstretched arm for a split-second as Janice was unable to restrain her twirling partner. He turned like the uncontrolled swirl of a tornado with no sense of where he was going or how he would stop.

The old curmudgeon spun out of control, like a top, across the room. Dancers saw him coming and separated in the middle of the floor as if Moses was parting the Red Sea. Burt could see his life flashing before him. As he was spinning, his mind raced in search of a solution. The only thing he could come up with in the blur of his dilemma was to stick his right foot out sharply in front of him in order to create a brace that would hopefully and mercifully stop his movement. It was a brilliant strategy. Partially. Burt slammed his foot to the floor, which did indeed minimize his speed. Unfortunately, his right foot continued to slide forward, forcing him into a fully extended split, with one leg in front, one behind, 180-degrees apart, and his crotch smashed squarely upon the floor. It was a maneuver that would have done any Olympic gymnast proud. An unqualified 10 performance with an unparalleled degree of difficulty. Burt's legs extended straight out from his body in opposite directions, establishing a position that any betting person would have laid odds was impossible for him to achieve.

Once it was determined that Burt was not hurt, several men assisted him to his feet. He brushed himself off and wobbled back to the table. Despite his misfortune, he couldn't resist the urge to strut with pride, as if the entire incident had been done solely for the amusement of his companions. Everyone knew better of course, but the truly amazing thing about the episode was that Burt's new shirt had survived the ordeal, miraculously remaining intact.

Enzo could hear the voices before he could see the group. Accustomed as he was to waiting, his Roman blood was boiling at the imposition of an additional delay at his expense. He hated this rowdy bunch of Americans. They were loud and brash and always causing him trouble. It was payback time. The little herd of people crossed the street laughing hilariously as they recounted the events of the past hour. When they were safely across the road and eager to board the bus, Enzo revved his engine, shifted gears, stepped on the gas and pulled the coach two long blocks further down the street.

The writers stood on the sidewalk in stunned amazement. Enzo was punishing them for their lack of consideration. Earl was the first to arrive at the new location, banging on the door with the flat of his hand, demanding to enter to the bus. "Hey Enzo, let us in. We want to go home," shouted Earl.

Enzo looked out of the window with a sinister grin as he lurched forward again to drive several more blocks down the road.

"If we keep this up he may have us walking all the way back to the hotel," said Earl as everyone started walking again.

This time when the group arrived Enzo begrudgingly granted entrance to his vehicle, and the weary band of dancers climbed aboard without saying a word. Enzo growled incoherently at each one as they passed by, just to make certain they understood his message. The drive back to the hotel was quiet with one obvious exception, an occasional low moan of agony from Burt.

Beth was up early the next morning taking pictures. She walked out by the pool, which nudged against the sea and gazed across the Bay of Naples. The prism of morning gave softness to the layers of color rising into the sky. Vesuvius was silhouetted above the horizon as the sky began to burn into a brilliant orange ahead of the sunrise. Beth loved this time of day when the stillness of the night prepared a new palette for the morning and calmed the water with a mirror-smooth surface. The little bay was filled with a kaleidoscope of fishing boats cloning themselves with perfect reflections in the glassy water.

Sounds were different at that time of day. Beth could even hear the wings of birds flapping as they made their way across the sky. The sea lapped gently upon the beach in soothing wavelets that curled along the shore with their unique form of serenity. There were voices in the distance; far away conversations indicating that the world was gradually waking up with a pace that would soon accelerate into its daily rush of activity. Coming from and going to. All waiting for sunset, and with it the return of more peaceful, fleeting moments of reflective solitude.

Beth turned to go back to the hotel. As she walked beside the pool, she heard the sound of a curtain being drawn from one of the rooms on the third floor. She glanced up to see the silhouette of a male figure pushing open the sliding glass windows, moving into the daylight and out onto his balcony. It was Earl. Beth continued to walk as she watched Earl stretch his arms high into the air toward the sun. She was ready to wave to him when she realized that Earl was facing the morning in all his naked glory. He brought his arms down, planting his hands squarely upon his hips with his feet spread wide as if he was some sort of gladiator greeting the day.

Beth was far enough away so that she was unable to make out any significant amount of detail, but she was still close enough to plainly see Earl's privates dangling freely between his legs. That was plenty close enough for her. When she realized the situation, she immediately turned away and grabbed a deck chair. Beth quickly sat down, momentarily taken aback by her unintended voyeurism. She began to fumble with her camera, hoping that Earl hadn't spotted her. She continued to fiddle with her lenses and her camera bag until she guessed that sufficient time had elapsed for Earl to go back into his room. Slowly she turned to look in Earl's direction. When she saw that he was no longer there, Beth hastily gathered her things, ran to the hotel and up to her room.

Earl never mentioned the occasion to Beth, so she was never quite sure whether he had seen her or not. She certainly had no plans to make any references about it to him, however. Upon reflection, Beth recalled the day that she, Fran and Sally Mae had taken the bold step of going topless at the pool in Monte Carlo. She remembered how liberating it had been, and how invigorated she felt. Perhaps she shouldn't have been so embarrassed after all, and perhaps Earl wouldn't have been either. Still, she had no intentions of asking him. It was a conversation she was not ready to pursue. On the other hand, Beth was slowly adapting to a new way of thinking. Maybe the Europeans had it right after all. Maybe given the right place, at the right time, she, too, might one day find herself basking totally in the altogether just as Earl had done.

After two days of touring the island, savoring the sun and submitting to the luxuries of decadent, unlimited, sublime pleasure, the group returned to the mainland for a two-night stay along the Amalfi Coast. There was a midmorning sightseeing excursion of the hillside village of Positano, followed by lunch at *Hotel San Pietro*. Positano was once a sleepy fishing community tucked within a huge indentation along the coastal road between Sorrento and Salerno. It became a haven for artists, writers and poets, but it wasn't long after, that tourists discovered it, and some of its quaintness and charm faded. Even so, it is still one of those marvelous little places that captures the imagination of all who visit.

Enzo drove the motorcoach along the serpentine ribbon of road that led from Positano to *San Pietro*. It was defined as a road, but it was really more of a narrow ledge providing access from one end of the coast to the other. At one particularly sharp bend, the road widened into a space large enough for Enzo to park the bus in front of a small chapel overlooking the Gulf of Salerno. If there was any evidence of a hotel it could not be found from the highway.

Everyone got off the bus and waited for Maria to lead the way. Several people walked to the waist-high wall to take in the majestic view of Positano, which from afar was now hugging the sides of the cliffs that plunged into the sea.

"We go this way," said Maria walking to the left side of the chapel and then to a stairway leading down behind it. "This is the *Chapel of San Pietro*."

The group followed Maria down a narrow, flower-strewn staircase until they arrived at an elevator. Maria pushed the button and seconds later the doors parted to allow everyone to get in. When the doors reopened it was like an invitation into an emperor's palace. The marble floors had a coolness and a luster that had a way of luring people into the magnificently appointed lobby, and just beyond a tile patio beckoned with its stunning location perched at the edge of a precipice that dove into the sea far below. The tiny huddle of people moved through the lobby like a giant amoeba, walking ever so slowly with heads turning from side to side in an attempt to absorb everything. Cantilevered terraces and sloping gardens basked in the sunshine that splashed across the hotel's southern exposure during the day, and bathed it in the cool, romantic glow of moonlight at night.

"Magniiificeeent. Juuust maaagniiificeeent," said Maggie who was eagerly plotting in her mind a way to make sure the owner knew exactly who she was. "Mariiia, caaan weee taaake a tooour laaater?"

"We'll do that after lunch," answered their host.

Normally room inspections were not popular items on a travel writer's agenda because there was little for them to write about so they became a nuisance and a waste of time. Hoteliers could never quite understand that, in general, the destination came first and accommodations became the frosting for a delicious dessert. In the case of the *San Pietro* however, the hotel was so unique, that this was one time where there would be an exception without any grumbling from the writers. Everyone was eager to see more of it.

The idea for the hotel was conceived by its original owner, Carlo Cinque. Cinque was not an architect, but he was a designer. He was also a master of elite tourism. The property was extremely small at first, offering little more than a getaway for members of Cinque's family. As time went on, he gradually began adding rooms to accommodate friends and guests. The result was the *San Pietro*, which annually receives acclaim as one of the top two or three resort hotels in Europe.

For some reason that even she did not understand, Beth had never been one to get overly enamored of elegant hotel accommodations. That wasn't to say she didn't thoroughly revel in the pampering of a five-star property whenever the opportunity afforded itself to her. It was simply that her philosophy was that a destination always took precedence over the number of amenities at her hotel, and if, by chance, she was also able to participate in a "lifestyle of the rich and famous," so much the better. *Hotel San Pietro* was different. For Beth it was the ultimate place to stay. It was a destination unto itself.

Beth had stayed at fancier, more elegant places. A few hotels she had been to had even overwhelmed her. Places so service-oriented that she could hardly brush her teeth without someone standing there ready to assist her. She had dined in restaurants that served microscopic portions of food at exorbitant prices, which were supposedly justified by the so-called "presentation" of having the chef sprinkle some colorful herbs and sauces around the perimeter of the plate. No, what *San Pietro* had was completely different and innate. It didn't have to work at being what it was, it just was. That's what made it so special.

Though everyone was ready for lunch, the interest in the hotel seemed to be taking precedence over their stomachs, so Maria adjusted the program and held the tour first. While Cinque may not have been in the category of Frank Lloyd Wright or Eliel Saarinen, his creation still had to be regarded as an architectural wonder. If there was no other feature than the mere fact that the hotel was almost invisible from land or from sea, it would have been enough to inspire awe. Except for the main patio, and the swimming pool, the entire property had been literally excavated into the rock, thereby preserving the scenic beauty of the coastline. When combined with the hanging gardens that cascaded everywhere from the cliffs, the hotel was virtually shrouded by the mountainside making it difficult to see its physical structure, even from the water.

Each room was different, and each was exquisitely decorated. In addition, every room had a sea view, and none had any curtains in either the bedrooms or the baths. There was no need. Several rooms had sunken marble bathtubs, which snuggled against huge picture windows, all designed to allow guests to see out, but no one else to see in, creating a sense of being totally united with nature. In one room there was a sunken tub large enough for four adults, which immediately prompted Earl, Vince and Jack to remove their shirts and hop in to have their pictures taken as "three men in a tub."

Another room had a bed so large that it had actually been constructed inside the room because it would not fit through any of the doors. Several other rooms featured full-sized marble statues and fountains, including one with a sculpture of a nude masculine figure standing with a continuous stream of water flowing from its prodigious, horizontal phallus.

The group was still buzzing about the hotel when they sat down for lunch in the open-air dining room off the main lobby. As with other meals, the wine poured in abundance, causing Jack to become particularly lightheaded by the time the dessert cart made its way around the table.

"None for me," he said as the cart came by. "I'm takin' Beth with me to the pool to get some pictures for my magazine."

Beth didn't quite know how to respond, but she wanted to see the pool anyway, and she didn't need to experience the parasitic joy of having another dessert latch onto her hips, so she obliged. Earl decided to tag along just for fun, so while the others engorged themselves further, the three mavericks made their way across the lobby and headed for the beach.

The elevator to the pool area was a single shaft that bored down through the rock some 83 meters before opening out to a grotto that lead to the seclusion of a sun deck and the eternal expanse of the sea. From the lobby on the main floor to the beach took a full 45 seconds on the elevator with no stops in between.

Jack was in rare form as he staggered from the elevator out to the stony beach and up to the sun deck. "Now look Beth this is what I need. I'm looking for some kind of really sexy shot that I can put on the last page of my magazine. Something really spiffy. You know like a beautiful woman with huge breasts, just laying there all naked and oily in the sun."

"In case you haven't noticed, breasts don't interest me much," said Beth. "Besides you don't really think I'm stupid enough to believe that you would run a picture in your publication without permission or some kind of model release. And furthermore, plain old boobs are too tame for your magazine. I know you need something more provocative than that. If you see someone you like, just point her out to me and I'll try to get a picture. It'll give me a chance to practice shooting with my long lens anyway. You tell me what to shoot and I'll do my best, OK."

"OK, OK. You made your point. Earl can help though. He's got an eye for this sort of thing."

"Right." Beth's response was filled with sarcasm and amusement.

"Good, then we can hide up in the rocks where nobody can see us. It'll be more candid that way," said Jack enthusiastically.

For the next half hour or so, Jack and Earl climbed all around the rocky cliffs overlooking the sun deck, ever on the lookout for new arrivals to remove their tops and lay out in the sun, trying to pick just the right subjects for Beth's lens. Neither of them had any photographic sensibilities whatsoever, but they went through the motions of determining the best possible angles and evaluating the array of "talent" that was unsuspectingly modeling down below for their ultimate photo. In the process they were constantly tripping over the steps or sliding off the rocks as they peered around corners or from behind flowers, all the while laughing and shushing each other like a couple of schoolboys trying to be unobtrusive as they lived out their voyeuristic fantasies.

The sun deck and pool were beautifully positioned with the rock face to one side and a view of Positano to the other. Beyond the edge of the deck was a ladder leading down to the sea, which was only a few feet below the level of the patio. There was a small snack bar back in the shade of one corner of the pool. From the water, the pool area was one of the few ways of locating and identifying the hotel. The other was the tiny *Chapel of San Pietro* perched high above on the edge of the main road. By now, the two middle-aged adolescents had played enough and decided to return to the main floor of the hotel. Beth had snapped a few pictures, but nothing that would in any way impress Jack, even if there had been a legitimate opportunity for publishing something in his magazine.

The drive from *San Pietro* along the high coastal road to Amalfi was only ten kilometers, but it took three quarters of an hour to get there, partly because of the meandering route and partly because of a stop for the traditional group picture. Enzo was in deep concentration trying to maneuver the motorcoach along its treacherous path when Maggie spotted the ideal location for the photo up ahead. She raced to the front of the bus waving her arms and shouting, "Eeenzzzo swwweeetheeearrrt, caaan weee stooop the buuus sooo weee caaan taaake a piiiccctuuure? Pleeease Eeeenzzzo, daaarlllliiing. Ooohhh yooourr sooo sweeet."

Enzo slowed down at the small overlook and pulled over as close as he could to the side of the road. He grumbled something under his breath in Italian and brought the bus to a halt high above the sea. The view was indeed breathtaking, there was no disputing that, but Enzo had had his fill of these American writers, and he knew exactly what was coming next. He was going to be appointed group photographer.

Everyone searched for their cameras, then got off the bus. There was a wide assortment of photographic equipment, but in general, most of the cameras were relatively simple and uncomplicated to use. Only Beth and the doctor had what might be regarded as anything approaching profes-sional camera gear. There was the usual commotion and arranging of bod-ies as everyone suggested the best way to compose the shot. Enzo took each camera and lined them up one by one at his feet to be sure that he had them all in order. Dr. Boyd was the last to hand his camera over to the bus driver, and because it was an expensive, state-of-the-art piece of equip-ment, he went through an involved explanation of just how everything worked and exactly what to do. Not one word of which Enzo understood. After his short sermon, Boyd went to the end of the row of cameras and placed his opulent rig gently on the ground beside Beth's. Even the strap on the doctor's camera was of the highest quality. It was a wide leather band with padding at the rear to keep it from chaffing his neck. The strap alone probably cost more than most of the other cameras.

There was still some shuffling going on as everyone huddled closer and closer together to make certain they would all be properly framed in the picture. The little crowd of ten people was standing in front of a stone wall that looked out toward the irregular fingers of coastline protruding into the sea. Below the wall was a sheer drop of several hundred feet to a rocky bay where waves crashed and sprayed upon the boulders with a coat of white foam before returning to the transparent blue-green brine of the bay. It was late enough in the day for the light to cast a warm glow on the group, highlighting the greens of the hillsides and accentuating the sugar cube stacks of houses in the background.

At last everyone was standing still. Enzo looked through the viewfinder of the first camera, then backed up slightly to accommodate each member of the group into the shot. There were seven people in the front and three more in the back kneeling on the wall, peering between the others. "Reddie," said Enzo in broken English, "Is OK. Now say 'fettuccciiineee."

Everyone laughed and simultaneously said, "Fettuccciiineee." Snap! Enzo had his first picture. Just nine more to go. Or so he thought. The burly bus driver had determined that the only way to make certain not to duplicate his work was to place each camera on the wall after he took a picture with it. He turned to his right, taking a step forward with his left foot heading toward the wall, but as he made his pivot he accidentally caught his size 13 shoe in the strap of Dr. Boyd's camera. It was a recipe for disaster. Instinctively Enzo tried to shake his foot free, but his reaction had the opposite result of what he was trying to accomplish. Instead, it caused the strap to rise even further on his leg. In the process, the doctor's camera swung into the air in a wide arc before smashing violently onto the ground. Enzo was now staggering forward still shaking his left leg trying to free himself from the camera. This time the lens swung around hitting the tarmac at a 45-degree angle. The bus driver was now hopping on his right foot while frantically shaking his left leg at the same time, crashing Boyd's camera to the ground over and over again with each successive motion as he stumbled out of control toward the precipice. Only the wall prevented Enzo from plummeting to the craggy rocks below.

Enzo reached out for the edge of the wall in desperation to stop his momentum and catch himself. In one brief moment of fear he gazed panic stricken over the stone barricade, then pushed away quickly in horror at the thought of his possible fate. He sat down gasping for breath, gulping in large quantities of air with his massive chest heaving in and out in terror. The doctor rushed toward him in similar horror at finding bits and pieces of his camera strewn along the road in the path that roughly followed Enzo's tracks during his struggle for survival.

Both Boyd and Enzo were now panicked, but for entirely different reasons. The doctor flailed his arms furiously at the bus driver, then began to inspect what had moments before been his camera, and which was now reduced to little more than an expensive piece of junk. When Enzo saw the doctor coming toward him he became immediately defensive, but he was in no mood to put up with any of Boyd's badgering. As far as Enzo was concerned, he had narrowly escaped a face to face meeting with St. Peter, and he was not about to take any abuse from an uptight, spoiled American dentist who could afford hundreds of cameras if he wanted them.

It was a scene played out daily on thousands of street corners in Italy. The only difference this time was that one person was speaking English while the other was equally vehement in Italian. Two men gesturing frantically, screaming at the top of their lungs as they chastised each other for their inadequacies. It was a classic confrontation; a study in the art of expression. Words had no significance. Only the gestures mattered because the wild, erratic arm and head movements made it unnecessary to hear a single verbal exchange from either party in order to have total understanding of the situation.

The rest of the group was laughing hysterically at the entire scene. For the moment there was no guilt that Enzo might have been seriously injured or that Dr. Boyd had seen his camera reduced to rubble before his very eyes. Perhaps it was the personalities of the two combatants that made the scene so humorous, or perhaps it was simply relief that the events had not happened to any of them. Whatever it was, the occasion resulted in sidesplitting laughter that produced several additional moments of hilarity when it was referenced at various times during the trip.

Hotel Santa Caterina is a gem located at the outskirts of the once prominent seacoast village of Amalfi. It is owned and operated by two sisters, Guissie and Nene, who are constantly decorating and renovating it with their own personal touch. Situated along a bend in the road, the facade of the hotel in no way indicates the surprisingly large size of the property with its lemon groves and terraces of fig trees, bougainvillea and peonies sprawling along the coastal side of its buildings. Like *San Pietro*, it too features a spectacular elevator to its pool area. The project took a year to complete because the elevator shaft is literally built inside the rocks.

A porter guided Beth to her room through a succession of passages, corridors, niches and vaults that opened at each turn to another glorious unexpected perspective. Beth's room was simple but elegant with charming tile floors from the neighboring village Vietri. It featured a small private balcony looking toward the village of Amalfi and out to the Gulf of Salerno.

Though not as decadent or elaborate as *San Pietro*, *Hotel Santa Caterina* has its own special charm. It retains all the contagious spirit found only in Italy, where life is a constant procession of indescribable qualities that make it unique in the world. Beth moved out to her balcony and stood trance-like for several minutes gazing out toward the vast expanse of water below. It was open and free, and the soft sirocco breezes whispered against her skin. There was a poetic atmosphere that lingered among the gentle currents of air. This was a place where one could follow celestial rhythms as they made their way across the water, shimmering golden pathways by day that merged into sparkles of moonlight that danced like liquid stars upon the surface of the sea at night. Beth knew this was a place where dawn didn't break, choosing instead to ease across the hillsides, caressing each little nook and kissing every little contour along the way.

Beth reflected upon the observations of Norman Douglas in *Siren Land* when he noted that Italians become so preoccupied with other things, they fail to recognize the beauty of their own country. "There are wondrous tints of earth, sky and sea, in these regions, flaring sunsets and moons of melodramatic amplitude that roll upon the hilltops or swim exultingly through the aether; amber hued gorges where the shadows sleep through the glittering days of June and the mad summer riot of vines careening in green frenzy over olive and elms and figs; there are tremulous violet flames hovering about the sun scorched limestone, sea mists that climb in wreathed stateliness among wet clefts, there are thousands of joys like these." Standing there, seeing it for herself, Beth knew exactly what Douglas meant, and she knew that he was right.

Dinner was a blur for Beth. She had little desire on this night to be polite with idle chatter. She only wanted to finish the formalities of the meal and go back to her cocoon where she could once again savor the solitude of absorbing herself in the magical charms of the Amalfi Coast.

It was still early when Beth left the others in the dining room. She had left the doors to her balcony open as wide as they would allow, letting the breeze fill the space, blowing the curtains inward and beckoning her to step forward to observe the twinkling lights of Amalfi. The tiny amber orbs of light in the village had the look of fireflies flickering upon the indigo mountainside. Far beneath her balcony Beth could hear the surf crashing its eternal rhythms upon the rocks. Nighttime sounds. Comforting noises that signified continuity, embracing the ever present passage of time while also creating a sensation of timelessness.

Beth went back into the room and picked up her copy of *The Italians* by Barzini. She opened it to a familiar passage and reread the words. "Italy is one of the last countries in the Western world where the great god Pan is not dead, where life is still gloriously pagan, where Christianity has not disturbed the happy traditions and customs of ancient Greece and Rome, and where the Renaissance has not spent itself."

Beth continued reading. "Italy is the world's earthy paradise, where sin is unknown, man is still a divine animal and all loves are pure; the right milieu for legal, illegal, natural, semi-natural, unnatural or merely bizarre honeymoons, affairs, liaison, and escapades."

Beth put the book down on the dresser and stood mesmerized by the night-cloaked horizon beyond her balcony. She was intoxicated, engrossed by an all-consuming natural high. Slowly she unbuttoned her ivory colored, satin blouse, allowing the cooling winds to embrace her skin. She removed the garment and tossed it on the bed. Something hypnotic was happening, and Beth was willing to yield to the euphoria as she unzipped her slacks, letting them fall limply to the floor. She gently unhooked the front of her bra, freeing her breasts to the bewitching evening air, releasing them to the succulent ambience of Italy. Lowering her black lace panties down over her knees, the lingerie momentarily clung to her calves before collapsing lifelessly on top of her slacks. Beth stepped away from the tiny mound of clothing, still enraptured by the allure of Amafi's seductive embrace. She was naked, and it felt marvelous.

Beth turned out the light, standing motionless in the darkness, allowing the sensuality of the moment to envelop her. Then she moved quietly to her balcony and reclined on a lounge chair, reveling in the simplicity of it all, and the serenity of being one with nature. It was a peacefulness Beth had never known. Now she understood what Earl must have felt that morning she caught a glimpse of him standing naked in Ischia. She felt no shame. No inhibitions. Instead she felt pure. Complete. Fulfilled and in control of herself. Moments later, Beth was asleep.

When the group arrived back in Rome, the city had lost some of its previous luster for Beth. To be sure it was still as alive as ever with all of its crumbling layers of history and its frantic pace, but the difference was that the Amalfi Coast had been such an overwhelming and unexpected treasure that Beth was now being forced to readjust to an urban lifestyle.

Burt had grown even more grouchy when he learned that his luggage was still somewhere in the nether regions of Europe. By now he had more or less unofficially established himself as the group information center because he was always stationed at the bar puffing away at his cigar stubs and drinking whiskey sours as fast as the bartender could make them. If anyone needed to know where the others were, all they had to do was stop by the lounge and Burt could fill in the details.

During his ordeal Burt finally gave in to the fact that he needed another pair of pants to compliment the other features of his new wardrobe. Sadly, he had not learned from his earlier shopping experiences and somehow managed to acquire a pair of slacks that gradually tapered at the ankles. In addition, the trousers were well fitted in the waist, but the crotch was cut in such a way as to hoist his genitals into a grotesque little wad at one side of his fly or the other. The end result being that when Burt walked into the room all eyes immediately focused on his groin where the bulge in his pants gave the appearance of concealing a small bag of jelly beans. Combined with the other aspects of his unfortunate ensemble, Burt's body had all the semblance of an oversized sack of peanuts that were still in the shell.

The final outing of the itinerary was a trip to the graduation ceremonies honoring the cooking school participants at the Bettoja's villa outside of Rome. It was the perfect opportunity for Maggie to work her social butterfly routine by rubbing elbows with her new found acquaintances. In mere minutes she had arranged a return trip to Italy for herself and her daughter, and had also agreed to introduce Mrs. Bettoja to every prominent citizen of Memphis.

"Neeexxxt tiiime yooour in the staaates, yooou juuust cooome byy aaand seee us. Weee'll haaave diiinnner aaat the counnntryyy cluuub aaand I'll introooduuuccce yooou tooo theee maaayyyor. Heee'll juuust thiiink yooou're wooonnnderrrfuuul."

The 300-year old villa was not a fancy place by any means, but the surrounding countryside was magnificent, and the luncheon was as superb as it was anticipated to be. Cocktails were held outside on the back lawn with the students and writers mingling with each other and offering commentaries on their various activities throughout the week. Also in attendance were the Bettoja's canine pets, of which there were several, each of them large, and all named after Roman emperors.

Enzo spent most of his time inside, near the food, talking with Luccino Visconti who was a long-time friend of Mr. Bettoja. Luccino was the nephew of the great Italian film director of the same name, and he was 120 percent Italian. Before the party was an hour old, he had already made a pass of some type at every female writer in the group. Each member of the cooking school had previously been lecherously approached by Luccino earlier in the week, so he was now officially a major topic of conversation among all the women.

Enzo and Luccino were deep in conversation when Earl walked in and sat down beside them. Earl was his usual jovial self as he began his general chatter. "This is quite a place the Bettoja's have here, Lucky."

It was clear that Luccino did not appreciate being called "Lucky," but he tolerated it and replied, "Yes, they have been very happy here for many years. I have seen their children grow up here. It is a wonderful place to get away to."

Enzo tapped Luccino on the shoulder and said something to him in Italian. Luccino answered back and then Enzo said something else. Suddenly Luccino was laughing out loud saying, "Si, si, si."

Earl was confused. "What did he say?" he asked. "What's so funny."

Luccino looked at Earl with tears of laughter in his eyes and said, "Enzo, he say, do not trust this man. He's been busting my balls all week!"

The completely unexpected response caused Earl to burst into laughter as well. "He's right. Enzo, you're a good man to put up with all of us for so long, but don't ever give up driving your bus to become a photographer." By now Earl was laughing even harder.

Luccino translated for Enzo who nodded in agreement and made an obscene gesture with his right hand before laughing some more. For the next quarter of an hour or more the three men poked fun at each other, laughing uproariously at each successive insult.

The day concluded with a happy ending for everyone. The graduation luncheon wrapped up by mid-afternoon followed by the hour and a half bus ride back to the city. When the group arrived in Rome, Burt was delighted to discover that at long last his luggage had arrived.

No longer would he have to dress like an American trying to look Italian and failing dismally at it. No longer would he have be a poster boy for a Picasso painting.

Dinner was at 7:30, and it was another gala multi-course meal, which in this case, would bid farewell to Italy. When dessert was over, so was the trip. Now all that remained was the torture of fighting through the crowds at the airport the next morning for the return flight back to reality.

Coming home was always the worst part of a trip for Beth. There was no anticipation. All her dirty clothes were stuffed into the suitcase. There were bills and phone messages waiting to be answered, and the memories were still too fresh to be meaningful. They needed time to mature, to properly age, in order to become permanent full-fledged members of her ever-expanding repertoire of people, places and events that made travel a never-ending source of revelation and discovery for her. Furthermore, the hassle of modern air travel with its security checks, customs declarations, baggage claim frenzy and plain old stress only served to make the process all the more tedious.

TWA flight #3 was late arriving in New York so Earl went ahead to help Maggie and Vince because they had tight connecting flights. That left Maria and Beth riding the escalator in front of Burt as they made their way out to the baggage claim area. Jack followed behind Burt. The two men were in the midst of a heated discussion as they stepped onto the moving stairway heading up toward the next level of the airport. In the process, Burt was so intently involved in what he was saying that he failed to notice the right handrail of the escalator was not moving. Halfway to the top Burt instinctively grabbed the railing with his right hand, and as he continued to talk, the forward motion of the escalator drew his arm behind him causing him to lose his balance, falling backwards on the steps. Jack tried to catch him but to no avail. Everything happened so quickly that it created a domino effect on the escalator, forcing other passengers in the rear to fall down as well, crashing back into one another with no other place to go.

Maria and Beth were at the top of the stairs when they heard the commotion behind them. Burt was now flat on his back with both feet high in the air coming directly toward the two women, while Jack was trying to lift his companion's head and shoulders which were pointing back toward the arrival gate area. At the same time, passengers in the back were frantically looking for ways to maintain their balance in an effort to avoid further collisions and prevent the possibility of serious injury. Until Burt's obstruction was removed however, there was little that anyone could do because of the steady movement of the escalator.

Maria and Beth had to react quickly, but they had no plan of action other than to grab Burt by the ankles and guide him up the steps until his body came to rest at the top of the landing where they could move him out of the way. Had Burt been the only person on the escalator that solution would have been perfect, but with the other passengers arriving at the top in a continuous stream of humanity, the only thing for them to do was try to jump clear of the old man's body. Some were successful, others were not. Bodies went flying in every direction across the room as they kicked Burt in the head and chest and fell over each other, stumbling for any clear space possible to halt their momentum. The two women were finally able to maneuver Burt to a corner where he could sit with his back against the wall and catch his breath. He had several small cuts on his head and his glasses were broken, but other than that he was more frightened than hurt. Fortunately, no one else was injured either, and what could have been a potential calamity, had rectified itself in a matter of minutes.

Later when they had all reunited with Earl in the baggage claim area, they filled him in on the latest series of events. By then everyone had had an opportunity to calm down, and the story was now beginning to emerge as a classic for the annals of travel writing history.

The following day Beth called Earl, as she always did on the day after a trip, to thank him for her latest adventure and to be sure to keep her in mind for upcoming journeys.

"Earl, I just wanted to tell you how much I appreciate the chance to go to Italy," she said. "I hope there's another trip sometime soon."

"Don't worry about that, you're on my A-list," answered Earl, "By the way did you hear what happened to Burt?"

All Beth could think of was that the trauma of the accident, combined with the other difficulties Burt had endured, had caused him to go into cardiac arrest, but surely that wasn't what Earl was referring too. "No! You mean something else happened to him after the escalator incident?"

"Yup, sure did. Poor guy. We managed to get him on his plane back home, but his luggage didn't make it. We lost his bags again! Can you believe that?" laughed Earl.

Beth knew Earl well enough to realize that professionally he didn't think the situation was funny at all. On the other hand, the fact that Burt lost his luggage in both directions was one for the books, and to happen to him, of all people, was very humorous in its own dark sort of way.

Several years later Burt passed on to his final reward, and Beth often thought about his fateful journey to Italy with all his trials and tribulations during that trip. But somehow she also knew that up there in curmudgeon heaven Burt was finally able to smile, for at last he had found the ultimate travel destination, and the best part was that he didn't have to take any luggage.

LE MONTANGARD

The tiny railway station in the village of Zweisimmen resembled an elaborate model train layout. There were flower boxes everywhere filled with rainbows of flowers and plants. Irises, roses, chrysanthemums, crocuses and edelweiss. Reds, yellows, purples, pinks. All brilliant and bold.

The miniature station could have been lifted directly out of some Hollywood movie set from the 30s and lowered into the rolling countryside of Switzerland. Several long wooden benches rested neatly against the outside walls of the ticket building offering respite for passengers waiting to catch the next train, but there was rarely much activity except after arrivals and just prior to departures.

There were no platforms. No underground passageways to get from one track to the other, because such facilities were unnecessary for a narrow gauge line such as this. Travelers simply walked across the tracks when it came time to board their trains. The tracks themselves were countersunk into the tarmac to prevent anyone from stumbling or falling.

There was a soothing, tranquil quality to the picturesque ambience of the surroundings. Not so much that time was standing still, just that it wasn't going to be rushed. Yet there was also a rhythm to it all. Switzerland has a way of doing that because everything runs on schedule. Perhaps the Swiss aren't responsible for the concept of "time" as we know it, but over the centuries they have certainly perfected it.

Some people find that kind of precision boring, always knowing exactly when each train, or boat, or bus will arrive and depart, but for Beth Jacobsen it was uplifting. It made her feel positive. It was something to rely upon, that her train would actually get to its destination at the time it was supposed to, and the same was true of departures. For someone traveling on a tight schedule with a focused itinerary that was particularly appealing, and comforting. She knew that she could tell people what time she would be at a particular place, and that she would be met there at that exact moment.

That's why the station at Zweisimmen seemed so calm most of the time. Travelers would go to the little cafe across the street to wait, or they'd walk around the village, or do some window-shopping. Locals could show up just a few minutes before departure and always be certain the train would be there. It was a marvelous system, and after nearly a week of riding the rails through the alpine wonders of Switzerland, Beth was sorry the journey was coming to an end.

Beth was working with a television crew from the local NBC affiliate in her hometown of Winston-Salem, North Carolina. It was a cooperative effort between her newspaper, the *Winston-Salem Journal*, and the television station to produce a series of articles and features about the Swiss Travel System. The paper would run stories each day and promote TV features at night. It was all part of a gimmick to get higher ratings for the television station during "sweeps" month. Though Beth had never done any type of broadcast work before, she was acting as the field producer for the project since she was the only member of the group that had any sort of travel background. Her two traveling companions, a cameraman and a grip, were providing all the necessary technical aspects of the shoot.

For several reasons it had taken Beth a few days to adjust to this particular traveling experience. For one thing, David and Blaine were considerably younger than she was, and that made for a definite generation gap in their priorities and points of view. The second thing was that it was the first time that either of them had ever been out of the country, which meant that everything they did was a totally new experience. Therefore, every move they made became a challenge. Changing money. Clearing customs. Adapting to another culture. Interpreting other languages. Making certain they had all their documents. Trying to guess what to eat from a menu.

Beth had never felt quite so old. Maybe "worldly" was a better way of putting it. It wasn't exactly like baby-sitting so much as she kept praying that in their youthful exuberance her mates wouldn't do something really dumb and innocently create an international faux pas that she'd have to make excuses for later on. On the other hand, Beth appreciated the wide-eyed wonder they expressed as each new day presented exciting opportunities for discovery.

The third part of the equation was adjusting to the rigors of working with television people. For years Beth had thought that journalism was basically journalism, that radio was nothing more than a newspaper with sound, and that television was merely radio with pictures. She was quickly finding out how wrong she had been, having to practically learn another language. Furthermore, the constant shifting between the two mediums was mentally exhausting. Especially when she had "Mutt and Jeff" to contend with all the time.

To a lesser degree, because of her age and experience, Beth was also responsible for the public relations aspects of the project. That meant that when there were any questions or decisions to be made, Beth was always the person to whom the inquiries were directed. As the days went on, the hours of free time had become increasingly shorter, along with her patience.

One thing Beth didn't have to be concerned with was all that electronic gear the crew was using. Normally she traveled with one small bag and a carry-on. Now she was dealing with several cases of equipment for the camera, tripod, tapes, batteries, assorted adapters and cables, lights and on and on. Fortunately, that was a problem for the TV guys to deal with. But they were young and full of energy. They could handle it.

The eight-day trip had started in Lucerne and would end in Montreux. The idea was to follow the route of one of the classic rail journeys of Switzerland known as "The Golden Pass." Actually the Golden Pass is two different rail excursions because it includes the Brunig Panoramic Express, which makes its way through the Brunig Pass between Lucerne and Interlaken, and the Panoramic Express, which goes from Zweisimmen to Montreux. In between there is a brief connecting ride between Interlaken and Zweisimmen.

Lucerne, which was the first stop, is a favorite resort for tourists from all parts of the world, especially Americans, so it was a great place to begin. On day one, the first priority was to shake off the effects of jet lag by taking a nap upon arriving at the hotel and settling in. Generally that was not something Beth would do as a part of her travel routine, but she knew that there was no possibility of getting any work done until her "Munchkins" had rested themselves, so she yielded to the will of the majority.

After a brief snooze, the threesome headed for the Old Town to begin some late afternoon shooting. As always, the village was busy with a mixture of tourists and locals weaving their way through the maze of colorful, charming streets. September was a great time of year to be in Switzerland. Most of the frenzy of summer visitors had passed, and the weather was turning cooler with just the right edge to it. A few wisps of clouds floated gracefully above the peaks of the mountainous horizon, while lake steamers made their appointed rounds back and forth across the lake, and scattered sailboats amplified the peacefulness of the setting. The air was crisp, just right for a sweater, but the briskness felt good, and it was comfortable for moving about while shooting the video.

Now that they had been revived after their short nap, David and Blaine were as uncontrollable as children in their new environment. Everywhere they looked there was another shot. For them Switzerland was one gigantic photo-op, and they were determined to document every scene.

Lucerne's landmark is the Chapel Bridge, which has spanned the River Reuss for centuries at the place where the Lake of Lucerne spills into the river. Built at the beginning of the 14th century, the bridge is the symbol of the city, stretching more than 200-yards across the Reuss. Its most prominent feature is a large octagonal tower that flanks the magnificent covered wooden structure at one end, providing a one-of-a-kind backdrop for the rows of cafes that line the shore of the river in front of the Old Town.

Flower boxes extend like a botanical pathway along the length of both sides of the bridge. On market days, the stalls of fruits, vegetables and flowers add even more color and fragrance to the surroundings. Near the tower end of the bridge, swans glide effortlessly across the top of the rapidly flowing river. When skies are clear, the majestic, snowcapped mountains create a framework for the scene, peering down from the jagged horizon to envelop the perimeter of the lake with a protective barrier of rock. Massive peaks that rise into the sky as if they are piercing the heavens.

That was the picture that greeted Beth and her travel weary television companions as they made their way through town. There was simply no way to describe the awesome magnitude of the Alps that towered over the village of Lucerne. Every place they turned was a potential picture, like walking through a living postcard that had somehow magically transformed itself to life. A breathtaking introduction to the country to say the least, but it was only the beginning.

Blaine was busy lining up a shot across the river toward the Chapel Bridge when Beth tapped him on the shoulder. "When you're finished let's go back into the main section of the Old Town. There are a couple of very nice squares with buildings that have frescoes painted on the facades. It should make some good footage."

"OK. This will only take a couple more minutes," said Blaine.

David was gathering in the totality of the grand panorama, unable to turn his eyes from a dominating structure perched in the distance on the hillside off to his right. "Is that a castle over there in the middle of that hill?" he asked.

"That's the *Chateau Gutsch*. It's a turn-of-the-century hotel that just looks like a castle. I think they have about 40 rooms, and the views from up there are incredible. Everybody wonders what it is when they come here. I guess it's hard not to."

"Well you could have fooled me. I sure thought it was a castle.

You know it's kind of funny about Switzerland," added Beth. "It's been a democracy for so long that they don't really have lots of castles like other countries do. There's a few scattered here and there, like Chillon, and one in Thun and over near Bern, but there aren't very many."

By now Blaine had finished his shot and lifted the camera off the tripod. David reached down and picked up the bag filled with tapes and extra batteries, balanced the tripod on his right shoulder and off they went to the center of the Old Town.

For the next-half hour the television crew shot scenes of the colorful facades on the ancient buildings in the two main squares of the Old town. Though the primary tourist season was over, there was still an abundance of shoppers and sightseers busily meandering to and fro in every direction, adding a festive dimension to the shots. During the shooting, Beth remembered she had once visited an intimate little music box store on her first trip to Lucerne several years before. She recalled how fascinated she had been by the many different styles of music boxes. Beth wasn't certain whether she could find it again, or if they were even in the right square, but she began looking around the plaza to see if she could locate the shop. Sure enough she finally spotted it jammed among the other ancient buildings with a tiny sign on the window that simply read *Olga Portmann's*.

"That's it," Beth shouted with excitement. "Over there. That's the little shop with all the beautiful music boxes. We have to go over there and get some video. You'll love this place."

The next hour was spent browsing and shooting and conversing and shooting some more. Beth was right. It was indeed a marvelous place to look around. The range of boxes went from very simple single melodies to elaborate inlaid designs featuring multi-layered wheels of music that almost sounded like a symphony orchestra. There was even one creation that had two sets of dancers in formal dress spinning in front of a series of mirrors, creating the illusion of a ballroom filled with people. It was a perfect end to a short, but productive, first day in Switzerland.

The schedule called for another full day in Lucerne and environs. Since neither of her companions had been there before, Beth decided to give them a list of things to shoot while she did some research on her own. Considering that Lucerne was nestled in a historic region of the country, she wanted to spend some time around the lake learning more about its legends and its history.

In the meantime, David and Blaine set about the task of shooting an abundance of B-roll footage for their features. Beth had outlined an extensive list of things to cover; the Jesuit Church, the old city walls, the other historic and picturesque bridges along the Reuss, the Lion Monument, the glacier garden, the *Richard Wagner Museum*, the *Transportation Museum* and then, if they had time, some beauty shots around the lake. It was an ambitious program for one day to say the least, but it proved to be an excellent suggestion, because it satisfied both the visual and the historic requirements of the assignment.

Beth had heard the story of William Tell many times, but she never quite understood its significance. Now it was coming into focus as she learned the details of Tell's defiance against the orders of the notorious Austrian Bailiff Gessler. As a symbol of Hapsburg power, Gessler placed a cap on a pole in the center of the town of Altdorf. By edict, the citizens of the village were required to bow in tribute as they passed. Tell had not been informed of the decree, but it wouldn't have mattered if he had, because he still would have refused to obey. When Gessler heard of Tell's insolence, he demanded that the skilled crossbow archer attempt to shoot an apple from the top of his son's head. At first Tell resisted, but in the end, he was forced to comply. Tell was successful with his shot, but he then further insulted the bailiff by stating that there was another arrow in his quiver, waiting just for him if he had missed. Gessler was outraged and immediately took the archer prisoner. Later, during a storm on the lake, Tell managed to escape, and eventually killed Gessler in an ambush as he was traveling along the road to Kussnacht. Over the centuries Tell's legend grew to such a degree that he was immortalized as the national hero of Switzerland, representing the freedom and democracy the Swiss have cherished for more than seven hundred years.

In a declaration of their independence from Hapsburg rule, the Swiss Confederation was born in the region around the Lake of Lucerne in 1291 when three cantons proclaimed their unity by signing a pact of allegiance at Rutli Meadow. That history, combined with the glorious natural beauty of the area, made it easy for Beth to understand why Lucerne is such a popular destination not only for tourists, but also for the Swiss themselves. Thanks to its central geographical location near the St. Gotthard Pass, Lucerne has prospered over the centuries, and even today the pass remains a primary connecting point linking northern Europe with Italy.

Beth spent most of the day on boats, sailing from one historic village to another. Weggis. Vitznau. Gersau. All her methods of transportation were easily covered by the use of a Swiss Rail Pass which was valid not only for the trains, but also for lake steamers, cable cars, funiculars, city buses, trams and rack railroads. Whenever she needed to get anywhere, Beth simply hopped aboard a boat, or whatever other conveyance was necessary at the appointed time, flashed her pass and got off whenever and wherever she needed to stop.

Clouds had rolled in during the night leaving the day gray and moody. Overcast days are not uncommon in Lucerne, but the air was still warm, there was no rain in the forecast and the lake remained calm throughout her journey. All in all it turned out to be a rewarding excursion filled with glorious vistas, a sprinkling of Swiss history and plenty of time to soak in the atmosphere of several small villages.

When Beth returned to the hotel David and Blaine were sitting out front at the sidewalk café drinking a beer. They had managed to get everything on their "shot list," but it was obvious that, despite their youth, the extensive tour of the city in such a short period of time had taken its toll on their energy. With an early call for the next day's program, dinner was brief, washed down by a couple more beers, followed by an early exit to bed.

The Brunig Panoramic train was scheduled to leave shortly after nine. By the time everyone had reshuffled their personal belongings, taken care of all the equipment, made their way to breakfast and finally hustled everything over to the railway station, there wasn't much time to spare. The trio barely had everything aboard the train when it pulled out precisely on schedule. They all slumped into their seats and took a deep breath. It was just after 9 a.m. and already they felt as if they had done a full day's work. Beth smiled at David and Blaine, amused that their anticipated "vacation" had become an unexpected ordeal.

The train ride itself was no escape either. In fact, it required even more hustle than when the team was able to set up a stationary base. David and Blaine only had a limited amount of time to get their footage aboard the train before arriving at the next stop. Furthermore, once a scene had passed by the window, it was gone forever, there was no going back. Even trickier was trying to figure out which side of the train to be on to catch the best shots. There was constant jockeying back and forth in an effort to predetermine which position would provide the best location for the upcoming shot. Blaine would shoot out of one side of the train while David would scout the other to make certain that nothing better was happening over there. Then just when the moment seemed right, they'd swap positions.

In between their attempts at recording all the exterior beauty of the country, the two-man video team also had the task of capturing interior scenes of passengers enjoying the changing panoramas that continuously glided past the huge picture windows. Because of reflections and glare, windows presented a further set of difficulties, and therefore, the oversized windows only magnified their problems. By the time the train pulled into Brienz, David and Blaine were physically, as well as mentally, exhausted, and they still had more than half day of shooting ahead of them. The more she observed the helter-skelter pace of her companions, the more print journalism appealed to Beth.

Fortunately for the crew, the remainder of the day was somewhat less strenuous. After storing the luggage, and any equipment that was not immediately needed, at the rail station, the threesome took off on the Brienzer Rothorn train for a ride high into the mountains overlooking the Lake of Brienz. The little steam-powered cogwheel train chugged for nearly an hour and a half past hillside villages and breathtaking vertical outcrop-pings of mountain vistas. Each time it seemed that the train could go no further, there would be a bend in the track and another alpine peak would emerge. Far below, the lake gradually dwindled into an ever-diminishing pool of turquoise. Due to glacial runoff, the mineral content in the water added a surreal quality to the color of the lake as it shrank into the distance.

All along the tracks the train puffed and chuffed its way in and out of tunnels that were barely wide enough to pass through. Cows and sheep grazed nonchalantly at the base of the heavens, unconcerned with the lit-tle steam engine and its string of carriages. Eventually the first signs of snow began to appear as tiny frozen islands dotting the hillside. Beth was the first to notice the small patches of white and pointed to them. For some reason David couldn't quite grasp what she was showing him. After he finally caught on, a puzzled expression came over his face. "What is that stuff?" he asked curiously. "It must be foam, but what would foam be doing way up here in these mountains?"

Beth stared incredulously at David, not believing what she had just heard. Foam? In the Alps? Did he think that some Swiss farmer had just finished his laundry and thrown out the water here thousands of feet above the Lake of Brienz? "Look again, dummy. It's snow," answered Beth still trying to figure out what David was thinking about.

"Oh yeah, now I see. It is snow. Well, I'll be. But it does look like foam, doesn't it? I mean, it could have been foam."

Beth and Blaine glanced at each other and burst into laughter at David's ridiculous statement. The train inched gradually higher toward the summit of the mountain as clouds rolled across the landscape like balls of misty-white tumbleweed. The snow became increasingly prevalent. By the time they reached the top, people were scrambling to get off the train to seek refuge in the mountaintop restaurant where they could indulge themselves with the coziness of a fire and the warmth of a mug of hot chocolate or bowl soup.

Other than eating, drinking and trying to stay warm, there wasn't much to do at the summit, except to wait for the return train, or the arrival of some blessed rays of heat from the late afternoon sun. Blaine was thankful that most of his taping had been completed on the way up so he could relax during the descent to Brienz.

On day three, Beth and the guys spent the morning in Brienz shooting around the village. As before, they left their luggage and gear at the railway station since they would be coming back shortly after noon to catch the lake steamer to Interlaken. It would be an easy transition to the boat because the dock was less than 100 feet from the station.

With only one main street through town, the mountains rising on one side and the expanse of the lake on the other, Brienz could be toured fairly quickly. The main points of interest were the woodcarving schools and their byproducts, which were the primary source of revenue for the local economy. The artisans were extremely friendly and delighted to participate in the various setups that would highlight their craft on video. With such willing assistance from their Swiss "models," the morning shoot progressed much faster than everyone had anticipated, leaving two or three postcard shots as the only remaining bit of business before stopping for lunch.

While Blaine and Beth were busy shooting, David found a small cafe with a patio overlooking the lake. He ordered sandwiches and soft drinks for the others and then sat back to soak in the sunshine and the soft lapping sounds of the water against the shore. The food arrived just as Beth and

Blaine came up and sat down. Since they were running slightly ahead of schedule, Beth decided there was enough time to order rosti for everyone. The Swiss version of hash browned potatoes was one of her favorites dishes, and she knew her mates would enjoy the traditional Swiss cuisine.

The rosti was indeed the highlight of the meal, but the aftereffect of the extra helpings of food, combined with the warmth of the midday sun, made everyone sluggish, so it was a plodding walk back through town to pick up the remainder of the luggage at the railway station. Fortunately, there was some relief from the overindulgence because the boat dock was so close to the station.

It was a pleasant cruise, lasting slightly more than an hour to travel to the far end of the lake. Occasionally, Blaine grabbed a shot of a waterfall or a scenic village along the shore, but for the most part, everyone just sat back and savored the boat excursion to Interlaken with periodic cat-naps to ward off the gluttonous activities of lunch.

By the time the three explorers were settled into their hotel in Interlaken, it was too late in the day to accomplish anything worthwhile from a video perspective. Besides Beth knew that her partners needed some down time to recharge their personal batteries, so she offered to escort them on an orientation tour of the village. Since Interlaken was a manageable city for novices to navigate, it wasn't long before the guys were ready to break away from their motherly guide in search of more youthful endeavors. Beth, who desired some personal relief of her own, greeted the plan with wholehearted enthusiasm. She had grown weary of trying to keep pace with her two human hormones. As a group, they would not reunite until the following morning, each choosing to pursue individual interests for the remainder of the day.

Interlaken derives its name from being nestled between two lakes; Lake Brienz and Lake Thun. Beth had always believed that from the air the village must resemble a gigantic butterfly with the lakes acting as its wings and the town as the body. She hoped that one day she would be able to fly over the region to see if her theory was correct. Interlaken is also the gateway to the world famous Jungfraujoch which rises nearly two miles above the above the Lauterbrunnen Valley, making Interlaken the origination point for one of the most popular rail excursions in the country. Besides its magnificent scenery, the journey terminates at the highest railway station in Europe, not only making it a touristic highlight, but another example of superb Swiss engineering.

Visiting the Jungfrau was an experience that was not to be missed. At least not for first-timers like David and Blaine. Actually, Beth preferred another excursion which explores the other side of the Lauterbrunnen Valley, and which provides a stunning view of the Jungfrau, the Eiger and the Monch from the village of Murren. Like Zermatt, Murren has no motorized traffic in the village, making it a pedestrian's nirvana. It is a popular skiing community that is literally perched on a shelf of pasture that forms a natural balcony overlooking a precipitous cliff that plunges into the valley. For Beth, the most appealing aspect of that outing over the one to the Jungfrau was that it utilized so many different modes of transportation. In order to complete a round trip properly, Murren requires two trains, a funicular, a postal bus and a cable car, not to mention walking. On the other hand, the Jungfrau is merely a train trip. Magnificent to be sure, but nevertheless a train ride. From Murren, for those who want to go all the way to the summit, there is another cable car to Birg and then on to the Schilthorn. In recent years the Schilthorn has become well known because it was used as the setting for one of the James Bond adventures, *On Her Majesty's Secret Service*. Today the building that was constructed by the film company now serves as the welcome center, complete with a revolving restaurant. Still the Jungfrau was the better known of the two excursions, and therefore the one Beth selected to document in the video.

Beth and her TV crew spent most of the next day taping at the crest of the world before returning to Interlaken by early evening. Despite the wonder of all they had seen, Beth was relieved to be back at the hotel. The cool nighttime air had a softness about it that was soothing, and the chance to be alone for a while was appealing and refreshing.

Beth drew herself a luxurious bubble bath, with water as hot as she could stand, and soaked for nearly an hour. Afterwards she donned the fluffy hotel bathrobe and raided the mini-bar for a small bottle of white wine. The balcony of her room on the third floor beckoned with seductive solitude. Beth found a glass, poured the wine and moved to her perch, where she sat contemplating the twilight sounds of Switzerland.

Soon the soft amber glow of street lamps overcame the remains of the day. There was the distant sound of hoof beats on the pavement as horse drawn carriages made their way through the streets. From the street below came a muffled sound from one corner of the hotel. The sound was pure and sweet, yet lonely and mournful at the same time. Beth stood to see where the music was coming from. She peered over the railing and saw a man dressed in a traditional alpine costume playing an alphorn. At first, she was curious as to why the man would choose that particular spot in which to play his instrument. Then she quickly decided that it didn't matter, choosing to sit back down and close her eyes to immerse herself in the serenity of the lovely tones emanating from the street.

Sometime after midnight Beth awoke in her chair. She had drifted to sleep listening to the alphorn. The night was now chilly, but the air was still refreshing. Beth left the doors to the balcony open wide and moved to her bed. She slid under her down comforter and exhaled a long sigh of repose. In her torpid state of slumber a smile slowly crept over her face. "Foam," she whispered out loud. Beth chuckled to herself, and then the tunnel of sleep overtook her again.

The short train ride from Interlaken to Zweisimmen the next day was merely an appetizer for the final leg of the journey, which was to be the Crystal Panoramic Express to Montreux. The excursion would take about an hour and a half through breathtaking rural Switzerland before descending along a serpentine path through vineyards that eased their way to Montreux and the shores of Lake Geneva. It would be another photographic test for David and Blaine, but unlike the Brunig trip this one featured more open landscape, therefore providing greater opportunities for shots on either side of the train. At least it was that way until the train passed the village of Les Avants. Then it once again became a challenge to be positioned on the side of the coach facing the lake as the tracks zigzagged their way back and forth into Montreux.

Along the route the scenery was typically Swiss-gorgeous though it was not similar to any of the terrain the group had seen before. The vistas were more open with huge tracts of rolling farmland on both sides of the train, but in the distance there were enough alpine silhouettes to remind everyone that they were still in Switzerland. For the most part this was not a mountain experience, though that fact in no way diminished the beauty. Beth was beginning to realize that each of Switzerland's classic rail journeys had its own particular personality and dynamic, thereby making each one a unique experience in its own right.

After a little more than an hour the train passed through Les Avants. Except for brief stops at Gstaad and Chateau d'Oex, there were no other interruptions in the journey. Les Avants featured another of those "toy train stations" set amid a Lilliputian village that had more cows than residents. About 100 yards down the tracks was a small restaurant on the right with several tables shaded beneath large, colorful umbrellas. When trains passed by the patio they came so close that passengers could almost reach out and touch hands with the people who were eating. It was a friendly, light-hearted scene, the kind where everybody waves and smiles to people they've never seen before and, most likely, will never see again. And it was almost as if those greetings were a signal too, that now the journey would take on a completely different perspective with its dramatic descent to Montreux.

Other than the lake and the vineyards, the landmark to watch out for in Montreux is the famed Castle of Chillon. The fortress was originally built in the 9th century to guard the main highway from Switzerland to Italy, but it didn't take on the appearance we know today until the 13th century. Positioned as it is on a promontory of rock that juts into the Lake of Geneva, it has a powerful presence during the approach from the hillside above Montreux. On a clear day the scene is further enhanced by the deep blue expanse of the lake rippling at the base of the majestic curtain of mountains that forms a backdrop for the castle.

Over the centuries, Chillon's dungeons have been used as a state prison at various times, and in the 16th century Francois Bonivard became its most famous prisoner, though he was not immortalized until the early part of the 19th century. During a visit to Chillon in 1816, the poet Lord Byron heard of the story detailing the events of Bonivard's captivity, and later commemorated the tale in his lyrical poem *The Prisoner of Chillon*. As a result of Byron's work, the castle arguably became Switzerland's most popular monument.

David and Blaine worked feverishly to get as much video as possible in their short, downward glide into Montreux. Once again the angle of the light and the oversized windows created difficulties, but as the train pulled into the station they were pleased with the amount of footage they were able to obtain. So delighted, in fact, that they "high-fived" each other like a couple of athletes who had just scored the game winning points to win a championship.

Erika Biehler from the local tourist office was waiting on the platform when the crew got off the train. Because Montreux extends across a long span of the Lake Geneva shoreline, it is a tough location to get around without private transportation, so Erika was prepared by having a van waiting to move all the luggage and gear to the hotel. Once everyone was checked in, David and Blaine went to their rooms to rearrange the equipment in preparation for the afternoon shooting session while Beth remained in the lobby with Erika to discuss the program for the next day and a half.

"We should go first to the castle, I think," said Erika. "It is our best known landmark, and then perhaps we should take a boat down to Vevey. It's market day there, and the setting is lovely. We can also shoot some of the big hotels along the shore from the boat. After that perhaps you can get some nice shots in the old part of the village. I was planning to take you to a folkloric show this evening, but it has been canceled, so instead I think we will go to a very nice restaurant up in the hills. Is that OK with you?"

"Sounds wonderful," said Beth. At first she was disappointed that the evening show had been canceled because she thought it might add a bit of Swiss flavor and local color to the video. But upon further reflection, Beth decided that maybe it would look too "touristy" and just be the same old stuff everyone else always brought back. After all, there was still a full afternoon of taping ahead of them and another day tomorrow, so it might be nice to be able to enjoy the evening without the pressure of having anything more to shoot.

For the rest of the day, Beth, Erika and the two guys gathered more footage in the Montreux and Vevey region of Lake Geneva, returning to the hotel shortly after five o'clock. That gave everyone a few hours to prepare for dinner, since Erika had said she would pick them up promptly at eight.

Beth immersed herself in her customary hot bath and then sat out on her balcony overlooking the lake. She could see France across the water, with its mountains towering above miniature villages. By the time Beth had to leave for dinner the sun was setting behind the Alps and the snow on the crest of the mountains was slowly easing away from white into various shades of pink and gold.

The road had so many twists and turns as it climbed into the hills above Montreux that it took nearly twenty minutes to get to the restaurant. It was a chalet-style building with a pleasant glow coming from the windows and the sounds of music playing inside. Over the door there was a sign that read *Le Montangard*.

"What does it mean, *Le Montangard*?" Beth asked Erika.

"In English it means "The Mountain Man," she answered. "I will tell you more when we get inside."

The interior of the restaurant had a homey, handcrafted look to it. There were two medium sized rooms with tables for dining in both. In the right hand room there was also a small space for dancing. Each room featured a band. One playing traditional Swiss music, the other more international fare. It was a friendly place. The kind of place that had a feeling of hospitality and comfort about it the moment you entered. Beth felt it right away. She didn't quite know why yet, but she sensed there was something unique about the building.

The group sat down at a corner table and watched the patrons dining and dancing and enjoying the music. As soon as everyone had ordered, the waiter brought wine, and then Beth asked Erika again, "Tell me more about this place."

"The owner is quite special," said Erika. "His name is Hans Odermatt, and he is very old. I'm afraid he is not in very good health these days. The poor man, he just works too hard. Hans is the chef, and he does all the cooking himself. His sons help to run the restaurant, but Hans does not allow them go anywhere near his kitchen. He's much too proud to permit that."

"How long has he been doing this?" asked Beth.

"Oh for many years. Decades. Since the end of the war. Hans built this restaurant with his own hands. You see, before he became a chef he was a carpenter right here in the hills of Montreux. When the war broke out he could not stand what was happening in Europe, so he went to Australia. Mr. Odermatt is a very unpretentious and simple man. He loves these mountains, and until he left for Australia they were all he ever knew of the world. But the war was devastating for him, and even though Switzerland was a neutral country, he could not stay here."

Now David was becoming interested in the story. "So what happened?"

"Well, during his time in Australia, Mr. Odermatt learned a little English, and he also learned how to cook. He liked it very much, so after the war was over he came back to Switzerland and went to live in Zurich. In Zurich he enrolled in the chef's school and learned how to prepare everything properly. After that he came back to Montreux and took his life savings out of the bank to purchase an old stable. It cost him about 20,000 Swiss francs, and it was all the money he had left in the world. But as I told you before, Hans was really a carpenter by trade. The cooking was just something he learned because he enjoyed it. And so he took the old horse barn that he had bought, and he began building upon it. Every day he worked on that project until he had it just the way he wanted it."

Erika paused for a moment, reflecting about her story, and then continued. "That old stable Hans Odermatt bought is this very restaurant you are sitting in tonight. He created it with his own hands. It is a labor of love. You see, this little place is his whole life."

"What a wonderful story," said Beth who was happy that her instincts about the place had proven correct. Now the atmosphere seemed to be even more special than before.

"Oh, but wait, I am not finished. There's more," said Erika who was pleased that her companions were intrigued by her story. "After Hans completed the building, he decided that the people of these hills needed a good place to eat. And so with his new skills as a chef he began to cook for them. Perhaps you are not aware of it, but one of the very finest restaurants in the world is just down the coast in Crissier near Lausanne. It's called *Giradet*, and Hans wanted to create something for the people here that would make them just as proud as they are in Crissier of *Giradet*. That is why no one is allowed into his kitchen but himself, and he has been cooking there for forty years."

"I thought this place had a unique atmosphere when we walked in," said Beth.

"Oh it is very special." Erika pointed to an empty table in the far corner of the room. "Do you see that table over there," she said. "No one ever sits there except Mr. Odermatt. When he closes his kitchen every night between 9:15 and 9:30, he comes out with a glass of red wine, and sits in that corner and watches all the guests in his restaurant. It is his little domain, and he loves nothing more than to see people enjoying themselves."

Dinner was now being served. Everyone had ordered something different so they could all sample each other's entrees. Beth was having veal. David chose rabbit. Blaine selected the Cornish game hen. And Erika decided upon salmon. Silence quickly pervaded the table as everyone began the process of entering culinary heaven. Each dish had been lovingly prepared as if it was a work of art in its own right, and the appreciation for its creation was reinforced amid an abundance of "oohing" and "aahing," as well as the plain old smacking of lips.

"You know many famous people have dined in this restaurant," said Erika as the others continued to devour their meals. "We have quite a number of celebrities who live, or have lived in this region, and they all know of this little place."

"Anyone we might know?" asked Beth.

"Of course, yes. People like James Mason and Richard Burton. Peter Ustinov lives over in Lausanne. Hans has cooked for Richard Nixon and David Niven as well. Even for Charles Chaplin, who once lived along the lake. And Charles Lindbergh has eaten here too."

"Charlie Chaplin? Charles Lindbergh? They've been here?" responded Beth in amazement. She was impressed not only by the fact that such well-known people had been there before, but at the historical connections as well. To think that she was eating food prepared by a quiet, unassuming little man who had met all of these people in his lifetime, and who had created wonderful culinary experiences for each of them.

As they continued to savor the magnificent cuisine, Beth saw the figure of the old man emerge from the other room. He was holding a glass of red wine in his hand, just as Erika had said he would. He walked over to his customary place at the table in the far corner of the room. Beth looked at her watch. It was almost 9:20. It was time for Hans Odermatt to observe his domain.

The evening had been one surprise after another, but despite Erika's detailed stories and explanations, she had in no way prepared Beth for what she was now witnessing. Hans Odermatt had a vintage aura about him, and there was no lack of charisma in his personality. He was a character lifted from the pages of some classic novel, though Beth couldn't quite figure out which one.

Hans was a small man, standing only about 5 feet 8 inches tall. He was dressed in a plaid shirt and corduroy pants with hand knitted woolen stockings that met his pants at the knee. His shoes were made of wood, held on by a pair of wide leather straps that bridged the top of each foot. He sported a white apron, plus one of those high cylindrical chef's hats which was slightly tilted back on his head.

There was a rosy complexion to his features that were further reddened by a long snowy white beard hanging almost to the middle of his chest. In short, Hans Odermatt was a dead ringer for a Swiss version of Santa Claus. As Beth stared at him in wonderment, Hans caught her eye. He smiled at her and raised his glass as if to say, "Cheers," and then he continued to survey the rest of the room.

"Erika, we have to interview Hans. This is just too good a story to pass up. Do you think we could come back tomorrow and talk with him?" asked Beth enthusiastically.

"I will have to ask tomorrow to see if it is possible. We would have to do it in the daytime I think. Hans sleeps in the afternoon so that he will be able to cook at night. But we will try."

Beth was excited by the prospect of interviewing Hans and being able to tell his story. The evening had been totally captivating. She was also thankful for the good fortune that the folklore show was called off. Otherwise this experience would have never happened.

The next day Beth went to breakfast early, and then returned to her room to wait for a call from Erika. Shortly after ten, Erika rang to say that Hans had agreed to the interview. They could return to *Le Montangard* at three o'clock.

It was a busy, almost frantic time when the television crew got to the restaurant. David and Blaine had to hustle to set up the lights for the interview because of their limited time, and they were further rushed because they didn't want to keep Hans waiting any longer than necessary. Meanwhile Beth talked with Hans to learn more about him and to see how he would respond to her questions. Whenever possible, she had learned that she liked to do that so the person she was interviewing wouldn't get any surprises from her, and so that she would have a better sense of their personality.

Hans was delightful. There was twinkle in his eye that showed great satisfaction with the world he had made for himself. Yet there was also a humility about him, which came through in his curiosity as to why everyone was making such a fuss to interview him.

As Hans related his story off-camera to Beth, she felt a gentleness within the little chef that seemed to encapsulate his entire person. His message was uncluttered and simple. He wanted only to cook for the people of the region he loved so dearly, and to provide them with a few hours of pleasure whenever they entered his establishment.

At last the setup was complete and Beth was able to begin the on-camera interview. Beth had told Blaine to be certain there was plenty of tape and battery power because she wanted to make sure she got this story. Once everything was ready, the lights came on, the camera rolled and Beth began asking her questions. Hans spoke of his past, relating the same information in his own words that Erika had told on the previous night.

Beth continued to inquire of Hans about the building of the restaurant with his own hands and how he had put his heart and soul into making it unique. After several minutes, Beth noticed a small trickle of water running along the side of Hans' face. At first she thought the heat of the lights might be taking its toll and that Hans was perspiring under the glare. Suddenly Beth realized that she was wrong. He wasn't sweating after all. They were tears. Hans was crying.

The little chef had indeed told his story, but in doing so he felt unworthy of the attention he was receiving. Though his voice remained unbroken and strong throughout the interview, clearly Hans was emotionally touched from relating the details of his own history and the personal joy he derived from his cooking.

Hoping to settle Hans down, Beth decided to take another approach. She had been impressed by the presence of so many famous people that Hans had prepared meals for, so she asked, "What was it like for you to cook for people like Charlie Chaplin and Charles Lindbergh? How did that make you feel to know that they were eating in your restaurant?"

Another tear rolled softly down Hans' cheek, leaving a vertical trail as he looked Beth in the eyes and replied, "You know the rich and the famous are not so important. They don't spend any more money than the peasants do, and the peasants, they come every night."

A simple reply from an uncomplicated man. Beth realized that the little "Santa Claus" chef with the hand knitted woolen socks and the wooden shoes had his priorities in exactly the right place. In her own enthusiasm she had given significance to Mr. Odermatt's story that, in the grand scheme of things, was insignificant to him. And in so doing, Hans Odermatt had made Beth come to understand a valuable lesson about a person's perspective on life.

When the interview was finished and all the gear had been packed away, Hans invited everyone to sit at a window table overlooking the hillside. Hans had one of his sons bring a couple of bottles of wine and some cheese, and for the next hour the group talked about a variety of topics until finally it was time to go.

Beth looked at her host and said, "Thank you, Hans. You have a wonderful restaurant and a wonderful story. I hope that you are here for many more years to come and I wish you continued success."

"I have seen many years come and go. They have been good to me, and my life has been good. You see this little hill outside my window. In the springtime I don't even need a calendar. I can tell what day of the month it is by where the wildflowers are growing on the meadow. For me that is enough."

The journey was over. The next day Beth and the crew took the train to Geneva and flew home. Beth, David and Blaine had seen a great deal during their travels along the Golden Pass of Switzerland. It had been an unforgettable adventure. Especially for Beth who would always remember Hans Odermatt.

Two years later Beth was deeply saddened when she received a letter from Erika informing her that Hans Odermatt had died. That evening Beth went to her favorite restaurant in Winston-Salem and asked for a corner table. She ordered a glass of Merlot and looked around the room, observing all the people who were engrossed in their own private worlds. Then, when the moment seemed most appropriate, Beth raised her glass, and toasted the little chef with the snowy white beard and the hand knitted woolen stockings and wooden shoes. The man everyone called the "Mountain Man."

BLESSING IN BUCHAREST

At first the rustling sound seemed far away, as if it was at the distant edge of a dream. Then it disappeared for several long seconds before returning even louder and more persistently. Now there was something brushing lightly against Beth Jacobsen's cheek and nose. She tried to ignore the intrusion as she huddled beneath her coat, which she had draped across herself to stay warm. Finally Beth yielded to the annoyance, moving her hand from under the coat to sweep the tickling sensation away from her face. It had been a restless sleep at best. A semi-conscious sort of drifting from awareness to slumber that hovered at the fringes between reality and tranquility.

Beth rolled her head to one side and attempted to resume her nap, but the tickling continued to such a degree that she was forced to sit up in an effort to find its source. Though initially confused by her unfamiliar surroundings, she was now awake enough to know that something odd was happening as she peered into the darkness trying to locate the cause of the disturbance.

Beth chased away the remaining clouds of sleep and reoriented herself to her strange environment. She was on a train traveling from Budapest, Hungary to Bucharest, Romania. It was New Year's Day, and the previous two days had been total chaos. The trouble began when, through no fault of their own, the group of college students she was touring with had arrived at the Budapest airport three hours late for their flight to Romania. A ticketing snafu by the travel agency back in the States had inadvertently put the wrong departure time on the itinerary, and as a result, the only flight between the two countries for the next three days had already left at four in the afternoon.

The situation had further been complicated by the New Year's holiday, which made alternative plans not only difficult, but virtually impossible. It didn't help matters that the group was traveling between countries in Eastern Europe, which under the best of conditions, could frequently be an exercise in futility. Furthermore, the missed flight had created a domino effect upon the remainder of the schedule because the primary emphasis of the program was the Romanian portion of the trip, and now that was in disarray. Not only was lost time a factor in attempting to salvage the tour, there was also the additional obstacle of money. Eastern European currencies could not be transferred across borders and exchanged as they are in Western Europe. With the approaching holiday, that presented a monumental financial adjustment when multiplied by twenty students, two faculty escorts and a journalist. Still, that was regarded as a secondary barrier to overcome when compared to the immediate puzzle of trying to determine the most expeditious way to get to Bucharest. In the end, it had taken a full day of frustration, planning, map reading, schedule checking and ticket purchasing to book passage on an overnight train as the only feasible solution to the problem. The final result was that only one day would be lost, though it now seemed like it had been a week.

The monetary situation was resolved when everyone anted up whatever they could afford in American dollars to donate to the cause. Fortunately, the hard U.S. currency spoke a language of its own. There was also a little Hungarian money thrown into the pot, mostly from students who had set small amounts aside as souvenirs, but the bulk of it had been dispensed with in anticipation of the upcoming excursion into Romania. In order to make certain that each person would be fully reimbursed, both faculty escorts took extensive notes of each contribution. Most of the reimbursement money would come from the refund that was due from the aborted plane trip.

This latest adventure had happened rather quickly and unexpectedly for Beth. She was traveling on official newspaper business as a last minute assignment to document an international studies program for Wingate College in Wingate, North Carolina. The school had queried her paper, the *Winston-Salem Journal*, about any interest they might have in sending someone to cover their story. The school would pick up the tab for the expenses, so the paper accepted, and suddenly Beth found herself hastily applying for visas to Hungary and Romania.

The program was called *Winternational*, which was the inspiration of the president of the college, Dr. Paul Wolfe. After several years it had become a major success within the campus community, but Dr. Wolfe saw it as a significant marketing and recruiting opportunity for the college as well. Hence the invitation to the newspaper, and ultimately, the assignment for Beth.

Winternational was a simple concept, but it was also visionary, and, at the same time, extremely ambitious in scope. Each *Winternational* program always took place during Christmas break. Students would spend Christmas with their families and then the following day, they would journey in several small groups to various European destinations. Needless to say, it didn't take long for the idea to become a wildly popular tradition at Wingate. Wolfe's philosophy was that since most of his students came from rural North Carolina backgrounds, it was important for them to be afforded the chance for an international experience, and to witness another culture firsthand before they graduated. Professors were encouraged to submit proposals for courses of study lasting approximately ten days. Students in their junior year were then allowed to sign up on a first-come-first-served basis for the course, and the trip, they wished to pursue. Groups were limited to twenty participants. The most intriguing aspect of the undertaking was that the *Winternational* tours were included as part of the tuition, and therefore each student was guaranteed at least one trip abroad during his or her collegiate experience. In any given year there might be ten to fifteen different international studies programs occurring simultaneously throughout Europe from one small college in North Carolina.

On the day following Christmas each year the Charlotte airport became a madhouse of anticipation and apprehension for frenzied students and parents. Many of the young people had never been out of the state of North Carolina, much less the country. In fact, there was a surprising number who would be flying for the first time in their lives. Yet in just a few hours they would wake up in another country, another culture, perhaps dealing with another language, adjusting to a different monetary system, new customs and experiencing a totally different way of life from their own. It was a grand awakening. Total immersion. Culture shock. To be sure, it was life altering.

The Hungary-Romania trip was unique however, even for the *Winternational* program. It was a bold experiment for the school to attempt a journey into Eastern Europe, especially at a time when the process of traveling there was difficult. Furthermore, the infrastructure for dealing with group excursions to that part of the world left something to be desired. That further added to the challenge of moving inexperienced, youthful travelers through the unknown world of Communism. Despite Dr. Wolfe's personal philosophy regarding global awareness, it was also unusual for him to accompany a group, much less to escort it. In this particular case there were some political considerations involved, however. Wolfe had close personal ties with Howard Pendergraph, the current ambassador to Romania. It was Pendergraph who had been able to cut through the bureaucracy to make the program viable. Those efforts alone were sufficient enough for Dr. Wolfe to seek every possible solution to overcome the problems created by the airline ticketing error.

The final element of the Eastern European package was the students themselves. This was not the typical *Winternational* group. Wolfe had been personally involved in the selection process, and his advisors had made careful decisions in choosing the manifest for the itinerary. They had also skillfully promoted the idea to the parents by making it known that participation was by select invitation only. It was a brilliant strategy that paid off in a number of ways, not the least of which was the PR it generated with some of the school's most prominent benefactors. It was also an ideal opportunity to showcase the concept of *Winternational* and its benefits.

The theme for the tour was to create awareness of the struggle of organized religions to exist under the influence of Communism, and how they had somehow managed to survive. To achieve the full impact of the study in a limited amount of time, as well as to shield the students from total culture shock, the idea was to ease them into the oppression of Romania, if that was possible, by first going to Hungary. Hungary had been "westernizing" for a number of years, so it was decided that Budapest would be a good place to begin. That would allow the adjustment to such radically different political systems to be a gradual process, and hopefully, less severe than going directly to Bucharest.

Beth had been assigned a slightly different schedule for her program because her task was to focus on the entire *Winternational* concept with special emphasis on the Eastern European project. Therefore, she began in Vienna with a group that was delving into the musical heritage of that city. She had joined Dr. Wolfe's program in Hungary a few days later and would continue with them to Romania before going to on Switzerland to meet another group that was exploring international business and diplomacy in Geneva. After the delay in Budapest however, Wolfe decided that Beth should remain with his tour rather than going on to Switzerland.

Beth continued to stare into the darkness trying to learn the reason she had been disturbed from the little sleep she was able to get. The train had stopped, but Beth had no frame of reference as to how long they had been sitting there. In the distance she could hear voices and commotion in the coach up ahead. It was then that her head cleared enough for her to realize that they were at the border. Customs officials were checking passports and searching luggage in every carriage on the train before it would be allowed to proceed.

With the train completely shut down, it was becoming bitterly cold in Beth's compartment. Had it not been for the silver-white orb of a full moon reflecting light off the drifts of snow outside the window, the frigid Balkan night would have enveloped everything in a shroud of impenetrable darkness. As it was, in the absence of color, everything was harshly defined by sinister shades of black and white and gray.

Beth regained her composure and continued to stare in the direction of the passageway outside the capsule of her compartment. Suddenly a woman emerged menacingly from the shadows. Her countenance was both frightening and pathetic as she moved forward toward Beth with her hand out begging for money. She was bundled under layers of shawls and wraps, and she carried a small baby in her arms, which she huddled close to her breast. On her head the gypsy woman wore a triangular babushka so typical of that part of the world. The scarf added the only splash of color to the bleak surroundings.

As the woman came toward Beth, the moon cast harsh patterns of light on her weathered face that was wrinkled beyond its years. The woman had olive skin with deep set eyes that looked even darker in the forbidding atmosphere of the compartment. Her gnarled, witch-like hands appeared threatening with their exceedingly long fingernails, and she carried a small stick with tattered strips of paper at one end resembling a pompom. When Beth saw the stick, she knew that was what the gypsy woman had used to tickle her face. The newborn clutched in the gypsy's arms was little more than a prop for evoking pity from her victim as pleaded for money.

It was an effective scam. The emotion for the plight of this woman and her baby, if it even was her child, was undeniable. Before they left the States everyone in the traveling party had been briefed about such occurrences. Despite those warnings and the precautions, it was impossible to prepare for such an event when it actually happened, or to be unaffected by it. Beth knew that other gypsies would follow, especially if she yielded to her desire to help. She also knew that whatever she did would only provide temporary relief for this woman at best, yet there remained an uncontrollable feeling in her heart that she had to do something. Doing nothing would refute all she had ever believed about having compassion for others.

The gypsy woman's face was pathetically haggard. The starkness of the icy cold of winter, combined with the metallic sheen of the moonlight, and the stillness of the train only magnified the eerie psychological ambience of the setting. And the idea of being stalled in the dead of night somewhere along the desolate border of two Eastern European countries, only seemed to enhance the woeful countenance of the woman's face. She was speaking unintelligible words, probably Romanian, but it wouldn't have mattered. When she spoke, Beth could see the shiny glint of a gold tooth in the front of her mouth. There was sorrow and desperation in her voice as she exposed the sleeping baby's face to the American woman before nestling it back to her bosom, hugging it close to her body.

Beth was torn with inner conflict. She had no Romanian money, but she also knew that dollars were more than acceptable anyway, probably preferable. Furthermore, she considered that in light of the mishap in Budapest there might be a further need to assist her own group with funds, and her allegiance certainly had to be to her traveling companions. Beth fumbled through her purse stalling for time as she tried to figure a solution to her dilemma. It was then that her hand felt something that provided an instantaneous answer to the problem. Cigarettes! Two packages of them. And not just any brand. These were Kent cigarettes. Suddenly Beth remembered why they were there in the first place. During the orientation sessions at the college it was explained that everyone should bring several cartons of cigarettes to pass out to people during the journey. According to their tutor, cigarettes were as good as money in Romania, and Kents, in particular, were regarded with the same reverence as gold. The other item that had been suggested was pocket-sized Bibles to distribute to the members of congregations as a symbol of hope and friendship. So tucked into every spare nook and cranny of each person's luggage was a stash of Kent cigarettes and miniature Bibles.

As a precaution Beth had placed a couple of packs of the Kents in her handbag for the flight to Bucharest, but in the confusion of the previous two days she had forgotten about them. Now she had the perfect opportunity to test her pre-trip instructions for accuracy. Beth pulled the tobacco from her purse, handing both packs to the gypsy woman. It was clear the Romanian had anticipated money, but the cigarettes were the best alternative, and they quickly brought a huge smile to her face. The gold in her front tooth sparkled in the moonlight. Her newfound treasure would be easy to barter for food or money. In some ways the cigarettes were probably more valuable than currency. The gypsy woman continued to smile as she bowed in a gesture of thanks and began to back away from the compartment to move ahead through the train. For the moment Beth felt a sensation of warmth in her otherwise frozen surroundings. Satisfied that she had made a proper gesture, she was comforted by the outcome.

Beth pulled her heavy winter coat up under her chin, propped her feet on one of the seats across from her and leaned her head against the bulkhead of the compartment in an effort to go back to sleep. She could still hear muffled voices in another coach, but she managed to tune them out with little difficulty.

With the advancement of the inspection team, the sounds gradually became louder and more distinct. It wasn't long before the customs officials made their way forward to the compartment next to Beth's where Dr. Wolfe and the other faculty escort, Dr. Durwood Hobson, were sitting. In truth, Hobson was not a member of the Wingate faculty. He was actually the reverend at a small Baptist church in the foothills of western North Carolina. He and Wolfe had been colleagues for more than two decades with Hobson playing a significant role in fund-raising projects for the college on numerous occasions. As a token of gratitude Wolfe had invited him to participate in the trip by serving as a chaperone.

As expected, the two customs officials were humorless individuals who went about their task with efficiency and as much intimidation as possible. The process didn't take long, but it was obvious to Beth from the conversations with Wolfe and Hobson that they were searching each piece of their luggage thoroughly.

By the time the officials arrived at Beth's compartment she was fully prepared for them. Or so she thought. They entered the tiny space abruptly, shining the bright white-yellow beam of a flashlight into her eyes, momentarily blinding her.

"Passport. Quickly," demanded the first official in a tense surly tone.

Beth removed the document from her purse and handed it to him. The official rapidly thumbed through the pages, then turned to his companion and said something in Romanian causing them both to laugh boisterously. Then, almost as quickly as they had begun, they stopped laughing and continued their routine. As the first official returned the passport to Beth, he drew close enough for her to smell the stale stench of alcohol on his breath. The foul odor lingered in the air, heavy from a prolonged day of revelry in celebration of the first day of the year. Beth surmised that their attitudes were likely the result of having to work on a holiday, though it didn't appear that their jobs had in any way impeded their plans for a party. Had the train been moving she might have thought that the slight back and forth staggering of the officials was the result of its motion, but since they were stationary, she knew they were reeling from the effects of several intimate encounters with a bottle of vodka.

Beth was uneasy with their laughter. It had a sinister quality to it. Almost as if there was some kind of dirty joke being told at her expense. It made her uncomfortable. She felt cornered within the confines of her tiny cubicle with the two hulking, inebriated customs officials standing over her. They obviously desired to be someplace other than pulling duty on a train in the middle of the night. Especially on a holiday. Combined with the booze, their demeanor was both unpleasant, and intimidating.

"Bags," said the second official tersely.

Beth pulled her only piece of luggage down from the overhead shelf. The official opened it and began searching through her personal belongings with complete disregard for neatness. Beth could tell that he enjoyed rummaging through her underwear while she watched helplessly, unable to do anything.

After an interminable couple of minutes, the official closed the suitcase without securing the latches having found nothing of consequence.

"Purse! Now," he said reaching out with his right hand.

Beth yielded her pocketbook to thirty seconds of roughshod scrutiny before the official shoved it back at her with a sharp thrust.

"Is all? You have more?" asked the first customs officer.

"Only my carrying case," replied Beth. "That's the only other thing."

Beth had hoped they wouldn't ask about the carrying case because she had her camera and all of her film stored in there. She knew that if they searched that bag they would realize that she was not just another member of the traveling party. It had been agreed by everyone before they left that for precautionary purposes there would be no mention that Beth was a professional journalist. She would simply be regarded as another member of the group. Beth was all too aware that the quality of her camera, and the amount of film she had, would be a dead give-away that she was something other than a casual traveler. Still, she was equally afraid that if she didn't acknowledge the piece of luggage, and then the border police found it, it might be an even worse scenario. Beth took a deep breath and reached up to take the small case down from the rack.

The second official opened the bag and removed the equipment. "Is nice camera," he said to his companion.

"Yes, is wery niiizze. And much film, too."

"You student?" asked the second man, totally aware that Beth was older than the others.

"No. I'm a teacher," answered Beth, lying with hesitation in her voice. "I teach photography."

"You take many pictures."

"I am documenting the trip for our group," said Beth nervously.

"But so many. Vhy so many?" asked the official.

Beth shrugged her shoulders as if to say, "I don't know." Then she smiled sheepishly.

"Perhaps we take film. You need not so many pictures I think." The official looked at his partner. There was a long pause, then both burst into laughter again.

Beth did not respond. She tried to smile, but the intimidation wouldn't allow it. The first official reached over to her and brushed the back of his hand against her cheek. "You pretty. Maybe you give me your picture, yes?"

"If you want," said Beth quietly.

"She is pretty, no?" he asked his companion.

"Yeees. Werrry pretty. Boootiful, my friend." The second man nudged his partner with his elbow and laughed under his breath.

After a few seconds that seemed like an eternity, the first customs official returned the camera to the case and handed it back to Beth. "Is OK," he said.

Beth could feel her heart pounding, gasping inwardly with relief as the policemen turned and walked out of the compartment. "Nice breasts," said the first man loudly in English as they departed, obviously wanting Beth to hear him.

"Werrry niiizze," said the second as they both laughed their way raucously down the corridor.

Beth exhaled deeply. She was relieved and angry at the same time, but mostly she was thankful that holiday drinks had probably saved her and everyone else from a great deal of further aggravation.

Ambassador Pendergraph was standing on the platform when the train pulled into Bucharest at 8:20 the next morning. He looked rested and poised compared to the weary band of college students that slowly emerged from the railway coaches. Despite the ordeal of the previous two days, Dr. Wolfe had somehow managed to maintain his composure and dignity. Whatever the problem, regardless of how simple or complex, he was one of those people who always seemed in control of the situation. Durwood Hobson, on the other hand, was completely disheveled, though even under the best of circumstances, he carried his 6 foot 4 inch frame in some form of disarray. At this point, it didn't matter how Hobson, or anyone else for that matter, looked. They were all just happy to be off the train and finally where they were supposed to be. And now that they were in the very heart of Romania, seeing the ambassador produced a welcome sense of relief, real or imagined though it might be.

The necessary greetings and introductions were dispensed with including a detailed discussion about the difficulties encountered in getting everyone to Romania. Fortunately, the delay had not caused a major readjustment of the schedule. There had been a city tour planned for the previous day, followed by a briefing at the embassy, but those events were easily changed. The most significant pieces of the program, which included a lavish dinner at the ambassador's residence and a visit to a Baptist church for worship services were luckily not affected by the lost time.

The first order of business was to check into the hotel before embarking on the sightseeing excursion of Bucharest. Dr. Wolfe declined an offer by the ambassador to ride with him in his limousine by deferring the invitation to Beth. It was an opportunity she was not going pass up. Here she was thousands of miles from home, behind the "Iron Curtain" in the most Stalinistic country in Eastern Europe, and she was being given the chance to ride through the streets of Bucharest with the United States Ambassador to Romania. This was one for her scrapbook. It was an experience to be catalogued in a special category reserved for travel writer's small-talk when she and her travel writing colleagues compared adventures. This one was dripping with status.

The ambassador was tall and professorial in his demeanor. He had a diplomatic air about him, but at the same time he exuded great personal warmth and boyish magnetism. He was a graduate of Wake Forest University in Winston-Salem, thereby adding further credence to Beth's articles. If Pendergraph had any regrets about his Balkan outpost, it was primarily the difficulty of getting Atlantic Coast Conference basketball scores in a timely fashion. Other than that he was content in his position, and by now, reasonably adjusted to his environment. After leaving the university, Pendergraph had taken a teaching position at Campbell College, a small Baptist institution of higher learning outside of Raleigh, North Carolina. He had intended to return to the world of academia after his tour of duty as ambassador, but that possibility had become increasingly remote as a result of his indoctrination into the intriguing world of global politics and international diplomacy.

Electricity surged through Beth's veins as she rode behind the tinted glass of the huge black limo through the boulevards of Bucharest. She could see the American flag on the left and the ambassador's flag waving on the right side of the hood as she looked out beyond the driver. For a moment a sense of power swelled deep inside her. Not so much as an individual, but more from the feeling of being encapsulated within a vehicle that in some way represented the essence of the strength of her country as it rolled silently through the dismal gray of the Romanian winter morning. She felt proud to be an American, as if she was now a personal goodwill ambassador for the United States, bringing the message of two hundred years of democracy to others. She was going to tell the story of the grand experiment that had made her homeland the most powerful country on the face of the earth.

Beth knew that much of what she was feeling was a matter of being caught up in the moment, but she also had a keen sense of self-awareness that was unlike anything she had ever experienced. It was the aphrodisiac of power, brief though it was, which was undeniable, despite the fact that the journey from the railway station to the hotel took less than fifteen minutes.

It was almost 9:30 when the limousine parked in front of the hotel. The day was just beginning to brighten through the overcast skies. Oppressive, barren looking buildings made the entire city look bleak and uninviting.

Wolfe and Hobson were already at the desk going through the process of checking in when Beth and the ambassador walked into the lobby.

Watching them work together, with such a contrast in the size of the two men, combined with the difference in their personalities, at times conjured images for Beth of Laurel and Hardy or Mutt and Jeff. Not that they were inefficient or buffoons by any means, but the sheer difference in physical characteristics, and the manner in which they each approached a problem, was frequently amusing to observe.

The students were scattered throughout the lobby, some sitting on their luggage, others standing patiently talking to one another and still others curled up in lounge chairs trying to prolong any remaining moments of sleep they could grasp. Because of the trip from Vienna, followed by the sudden change in the itinerary, Beth had spent most of her time working out problems with Drs. Wolfe and Hobson rather than getting acquainted with the students. Now that she would be settled for a few days, she would have a better opportunity to get to know them.

Like everything Beth had seen in Bucharest so far, the hotel was minimalist at best. The main lobby was austere, but functional. There was an eerie atmosphere in the room, which Beth assumed was just an imaginary carry-over from the previous night. At first she thought it had been the full moon casting ominous patterns upon the inky Romanian landscape that had caused the sensation, but now, standing there in the lobby, the light of day altered nothing. In some ways, in fact, the daylight made everything even more mysterious. There was still a lack of color everywhere, as if everyone and everything had somehow been transported into a scene from one of those old World War II espionage films with Edward G. Robinson. Beth was certain there had to be a sinister character lurking somewhere nearby in a hidden hallway, dressed in a beige trench coat with his collar pulled up around the back of his neck and his hands stuffed into the pockets. Half of a cigarette would be dangling from the corner of his mouth with an ash that arched toward the floor, defying gravity, and he would have a black fedora on his head, tilted from the back so as to slightly cover one eye.

Though the figure never appeared, Beth was constantly looking for him anyway, especially after becoming unnerved by another incident during her check-in. It wasn't a big thing really, but it was enough to instill a sense of uneasiness in her that would not go away until she left the country.

Beth and the ambassador weaved through the students making their way to the front desk where Wolfe and Hobson were completing the arrangements. She had only been at the counter for a couple of minutes when the receptionist handed a fistful of keys to Dr. Wolfe, along with the rooming list.

"Everything is OK now, yes?" said the desk clerk. "Have single rooms for, ummm, Meester Wooolfe and, ummm, Meester Hahhbzen, yes. Annd ten rooms for to put students, yes. Is OK?"

"That's correct," replied Dr. Wolfe. "And there's another single room for Ms. Jacobsen."

"Ahh, yes. Bet Jaakobzen, yes. One moment."

The receptionist disappeared into an office behind the counter for a few minutes. When she returned she was smiling, but it was not a friendly smile so much as it was devious.

"Vee have werrry niize room for Bet Jaakobzen in this place, yes, but vould like to know if journalist in party vould liike perhaps a leetle bedder room in another hotel. Vee can prowide perhaps bedder accommodation in that place, yes?"

Wolfe and Hobson were caught completely off guard. Beth was stunned. She had had no contact with anyone that could even remotely identify her as being a journalist except during that horrible incident at the border during the night. That was it! Those drunken bastards! The customs officials had called ahead to inform the authorities in Bucharest that they suspected a journalist was traveling with the group. This was their way of intimidating everyone to let them know they were aware of Beth's status, and that they were going to keep an eye on her.

After Beth got over the initial shock of the receptionist's offer, she was momentarily torn between the idea of accepting the proposition or staying with the group. On the one hand she was intrigued by the opportunity to see just exactly what lengths the Romanians would go to in order to accommodate her. Would they be ultra-nice, or did they want to isolate her so they could be even more menacing? The alternative was to remain with the Wingate students, which was what Beth ultimately decided to do. Her reasoning was simple. She was on an assignment to document the *Winternational* program, and therefore she needed to be in the proximity of the group at all times in order to tell their story completely. Beth's professional curiosity had been aroused by the other option however, and it was something she would wonder about for years afterwards. Everything had happened quickly, but it seemed to have taken place in slow motion, and in another place far away. Wolfe suddenly regained his composure and spoke up.

"You must be mistaken," he said in a positive, unflinching tone. "We have no journalist traveling with us. We are a group from Wingate College doing historic research about your country. Therefore we must insist that Ms. Jacobsen remain with us. She is our administrator who takes care of all our traveling documents, and she cannot be separated from our group."

Wolfe was calm but firm. When he concluded his response, Ambassador Pendergraph moved forward to reinforce his colleague's reply in Romanian. Pendergraph's fluency in the native language was disarming to the receptionist, proving to be the perfect squelch to the incident. It not only gave the Americans the upper hand, it also let the Romanians know up front that they were dealing with someone who was familiar with their system of doing things.

The keys were passed around with instructions from Hobson that everyone should freshen up and then reconvene on the main floor in thirty minutes.

Like the hotel lobby, Beth's room provided the basic necessities and little else. In fairness, she realized that there were better hotels in the city and that this was primarily a low budget accommodation catering to groups such as

Wingate's. Still, the space was small with only a tiny closet and a single bed. It would not take long to acquaint herself with her environment. There was a dresser with a mirror against the opposite wall from the door. The cramped bathroom featured a toilet, shower only, and a sink with a mirror above it. Paint chips peeled from the walls, and the floor was damp and musty from the steady daily overflow of the shower, but it was not intolerable. Hanging from the abnormally high ceiling was a single naked light bulb that provided minimal illumination upon entering the room. There was no phone, no television, no radio, although Beth did manage to locate some writing paper in the drawer of the bedside table.

Under the regime of Nicolae Ceauseseu, who was elected in 1974 as the first president of Romania, it had become the most heavily surveilled country in Eastern Europe. More even than Russia. After the events at the border, and later the hotel desk, Beth could not dismiss the idea from her mind that she was constantly being watched, even if it wasn't necessarily true. During the ride to the hotel, Ambassador Pendergraph had mentioned to her that one out of every three people in Bucharest was an informant, and now alone in her room, she could feel the paranoia beginning to sweep over her. She even felt uncomfortable at the idea of changing her clothes because of the intense premonition that she was being observed by unseen eyes. She couldn't believe what she was feeling. Here she was standing alone in her room afraid to undress out of fear that she was being spied upon. How silly, she thought, to have the sensation of being violated while she was standing in an empty room. Furthermore, she was equally convinced that the moment she left the room it would be thoroughly searched, though she was comforted by the fact that there was nothing of consequence for anyone to discover. At least nothing they didn't already know about.

The city tour was a typical motorcoach excursion with a local guide offering trivia, as well as propaganda, in broken English about the various sights in the city. It was a good opportunity for Beth to finally begin meeting some of the Wingate students, and to gather their impressions of a world so far removed from their own.

Beth did find it interesting that Romania had no national history or identity until after the American Civil War. She was also increasingly aware of the despair in the faces of the people she saw out on the streets with their looks of sheer hopelessness. Everywhere she turned there were pictures of Ceauseseu. Nearly every shop window featured his likeness in one way or another, almost as a constant reminder to the people that he must be revered, but also to never let them forget that "Big Brother" had control of their lives.

Romania was blessed with an abundance of natural resources, but the president had misused them to such a degree that brownouts were now frequently the result of energy rationing throughout the city. A harsh reality during the bitter cold of winter that added to the aura of depression pervading Bucharest.

Now and then Beth could see remnants of the decorations on the trees that had been festively adorned for New Year's. They were the only signs of color anywhere in the city, and she thought to herself how much a dash of sunshine, combined with a touch of blue sky and a burst of spring flowers, would radically improve her perspective, and her mood. Decorations were forbidden until after Christmas since Christmas was a religious holiday and, therefore, not officially recognized by the state. New Year's, on the other hand, was nonpolitical, so once the trimmings were in place, the people let them remain as long as they possibly could.

After 45 minutes of riding, the driver made a brief stop at the State Council Palace to let everyone stretch their legs. Beth began taking pictures of the building with the students in the foreground, and then walked across the huge square to get a quick shot of one of the guards standing out front. She crouched down to get a better angle that would include the guard as well as some of the building behind him. The soldier had been standing motionless at attention with his rifle at his side, but the moment he saw Beth out of the corner of his eye, he instantly pulled his rifle diagonally across his chest and cocked it. The guide raced over, putting her hand on Beth's shoulder, waving a finger in her face, and scolding her by screaming, "Don't take pictures!"

Beth didn't need a second warning. When she rejoined her companions, she tried to recall a time when she had taken a picture that was worth getting shot over. To the best of her recollection there wasn't one. Most likely there would never be one either, but she did register the event as another example of a way of life that was totally alien to anything she had ever known before.

The tour concluded with a visit to the embassy. Ambassador Pendergraph was waiting in his office with a fresh supply of doughnuts, coffee and soft drinks for his guests. His desk featured, among other things, a large jar of jelly beans in honor of President Reagan, who had appointed him to his position. There was also a picture of Reagan prominently displayed on a side wall.

Pendergraph's office was sizable, but by no means designed to accommodate 23 people, and it quickly became claustrophobic with everyone moving around trying to get pictures. First there were the obligatory photos of the ambassador himself as he welcomed everyone and gave them a quick profile of his background, his career and what it was like to be a diplomat in a foreign country. That was followed by several group shots for which Beth assumed the responsibility of documenting for the college archives. Then she snapped numerous pictures with the student's personal cameras so they could all be included in the scene. Afterward, there was another series of pictures featuring Dr. Wolfe and Ambassador Pendergraph together, followed by individual photos of the ambassador with each student. Under normal circumstances Beth did not like having her picture taken, but this was not a normal circumstance, and even she got into the act before it was finally over.

When the photo session came to an end, Beth was under the impression that the visit had concluded, but there was still another surprise in store. Each member of the party began filing out of the room though it seemed to be taking an unusually long time for everyone to leave. Beth made the assumption that there must be a conversation taking place at the head of the line that was delaying the exit. She assumed incorrectly.

The door from Pendergraph's office opened into a hallway, which led to another office directly opposite. The line was moving across the hall into the next office and then, from what Beth could see from her location at the rear, through another door, which was actually a secret passageway built into the wall. At first Beth thought she was imagining things, but as she got closer she realized that her initial observation was accurate. Everyone was indeed filing into a hidden corridor beyond the office walls.

The reason for the delay soon became known. On each side of the entrance there was an official handing out a one-page document to every person who went through the secret panel. When Beth finally reached the doorway she took the letter and read it silently.

"You are about to enter a room that few Americans, and no Romanians, have ever seen. It is an isolated capsule, which is suspended within our embassy. This capsule is protected by many layers of metal and by numerous detection devices. These precautions keep it free from various types of surveillance equipment. It is also insulated and soundproof. The cell hangs from the ceiling of this building as further protection from infiltration from the outside."

"Since some members of the housekeeping staff within the embassy are Romanian, or of other ethnic backgrounds, they may be informers. This capsule is the only room where we can be absolutely certain that we are free to discuss matters of high level national importance without fear of being monitored."

"You are among a privileged few who have been granted access to this facility. We request that you respect the need for discretion. Please do not openly discuss the existence of this conference room with other members of your party and especially with strangers. We thank you for your understanding, and we appreciate your cooperation."

Beth handed the paper back to the aide and made her way through the hidden doorway onto a catwalk that surrounded the capsule. There was a separation of four or five feet between the outer wall and the cell. The walkway extended around the perimeter of the chamber and was not connected to either the wall or the capsule. There was only one entrance, which was located on the opposite side of the secret opening. Cosmetically the structure was sinister and ugly with all its layers of metal and electronic devices, but from its outward appearance it certainly seemed to be functional for its purpose.

Beth entered the room and found a seat at the huge conference table. The heavily padded door, which looked to be about two feet thick, closed with a dull thud, and for a moment the room fell silent with the hush of respectful anticipation. For the next forty-five minutes three military men, headed by a Marine colonel, briefed the Wingate contingent on the realities of life in Romania under the regime of Nicolae Ceauseseu. They made it clear that the chamber was the only place where they felt free to converse openly, and that often if they had important things to discuss with their wives or family, be they political or personal, they would come to the hidden conference room to ensure their privacy.

The meeting had a strange feeling about it. It was the kind of situation that takes on a life all its own when it is over. The type of occurrence that, upon reflection, makes a person wonder if it really happened, or whether it was part of some elaborate dream, or a scene recalled from an Alfred Hitchcock movie.

It was a sobering lesson. The students listened in awe at the engrossing details of daily life in the dreary Soviet satellite where the sheer act of existence was in itself a kind of harsh punishment. Much of what the students heard was already obvious from simple observation, but getting the specifics from informed military personnel while sitting within the confines of a secret room somewhere in the American embassy thousands of miles from home had a chilling effect. It was a hands-on experience they would not soon forget. It was an indoctrination into another society that came as a total shock to everyone. A stern taste of reality for a group of young students from the sticks of North Carolina, some of whom had just a few days before flown in a plane for the first time in their lives.

Hushed discussions about what they had just heard in the embassy briefing room were the only topic of conversation as the group strolled up the street toward their motorcoach. Though the conference had ended only moments earlier, and though the information was freshly, and indelibly, imprinted on the minds of the Wingate students, none of them was prepared for the scene that was about to transpire. If nothing else, it served to reinforce what they had just learned, though no one really expected to come face to face with such a graphic example during their visit. Not only was it disconcerting, but it was terrifying at the same time. Little wonder that the citizens of Romania felt so helpless in their plight.

The ambassador and his wife had said their good-byes until later in the evening when there would be a gala reception and dinner at their residence. Drs. Wolfe and Hobson brought up the rear of the entourage as they walked a few blocks up the street to where the motorcoach was waiting. When the first group of students reached the corner, they paused briefly to allow the others to catch up and to be certain they were headed in the right direction. About halfway down the cross street to the left, a shopkeeper opened his doors for business, and within minutes, a long line formed to the end of the block and around the corner. People came out of nowhere and from everywhere, running as quickly as they could to get a position in the queue. Almost simultaneously there came the high pitched uneven whine of police sirens rushing to the scene, and in a matter of seconds, there were fully armed policemen with automatic weapons stationed outside the store and on each street corner ready to put down any uprising that might occur.

The Wingate group watched in fearful fascination as the drama unfolded before their eyes. Soon people began leaving the store carrying grocery bags in their arms as they exited. As one old man rushed away from the building, he hurried to cross the street and slipped off the curb, sprawling forward in a spread eagle position onto the road. The contents of his bag spilled out onto the tarmac, but no one came to his aid or tried to assist in any manner. He looked around anxiously, panic stricken as though he had done something horribly wrong. Then he got to his feet, more embarrassed than hurt, and hastily brushed himself off before retrieving his purchases. One by one the man picked up his spilled merchandise from the street. Quickly. Nervously. As if fearful that he had committed some horrible crime. From their vantage point up the street the students easily recognized what the man had dropped. It was toilet paper. Four rolls. And for that, policemen stood armed and ready to guarantee that there would be no disturbances.

Beth knew better than to take pictures in her normal rapid-fire fashion, especially after what had taken place a few hours earlier at the State Council Palace. But neither could she resist having some sort of visual documentation of what was taking place. Without bringing the camera up to her eye, she began snapping shots by pointing the lens in the direction of the incident, shooting from her chest with the camera hanging from her neck. The police were preoccupied with what they were doing and did not see her. Beth had no idea whether she was getting anything worthwhile or not, but it was the only way to function without attracting attention to herself or to the group.

Wolfe and Hobson watched with disbelieving curiosity for a while longer, then for safety reasons urged everyone to resume their walk to the bus without further delay.

Dinner at the ambassador's residence was a festive occasion with dignitaries from several countries on hand to greet the American visitors. It also afforded Beth another opportunity to acquaint herself in greater detail with several more students and to obtain their perspectives on the events of the day.

An elaborate dinner followed the reception with traditional Romanian folk dancing afterward. As Beth watched the colorful display of lively footwork, she reflected upon the day's activities with its dramatic contrasts. In the warmth and comfort of the ambassador's residence, the *Winternational* group was being entertained by carefree, happy Romanian folk music, while beyond its walls, much of Bucharest shivered in bitter cold and darkness.

Beth thought about the early days of her career and recalled the comments of friends or acquaintances who always returned home from their travels with the same theme. "Oh yes, it was a wonderful, inspirational trip. Simply marvelous. You should go sometime. We enjoyed it thoroughly, but you know it sure is good to be home. There's just no place like the good old United States."

Beth often wondered if people from other countries felt the same way when they returned to their homes. Or did they have the opposite reaction and hate to leave the States by virtue of what they had seen? From time to time Beth felt a little unpatriotic because she had never totally subscribed to the philosophy that everything in the United States was necessarily better purely by default. Not that she didn't appreciate and love her country. It wasn't that at all. Rather it was more that she felt that sometimes her fellow Americans failed to appreciate the riches of what other destinations had to offer. She believed in her heart that she had become a citizen of the world, and she felt that it was wise to recognize the achievements of other cultures as well as those of her own. She had long ago learned that she must embrace those perspectives in a way that now made her complete. It always made Beth a little sad when Americans had to think of themselves as being the best at everything rather than accepting the contributions of other nations in creating the global community in which we now live. As if being "best" was some sort of validation in the eyes of other countries. To Beth that notion reflected a kind of deep seeded insecurity within the American people that had to be expressed aloud in order to make us feel better about ourselves. Beth was proud to be an American and the heritage that it represented. She saw no need to apologize for that. By the same token, neither did she feel compelled to aggrandize the fact that she was an American by attempting to diminish or criticize the lifestyles, cultures or quality of life of the peoples of other countries. There was much to be gained through the knowledge and experience of those cultures, and just because she was an American did not mean that Beth, or any other countryman, was better than the citizens of any other part of the world community. It was a foolish comparison to begin with.

Romania was different. Though she was only a guest in the country, Beth could feel the same oppression of the heavy hand that controlled the lives of the Romanian people. Control that suppressed them in such dire circumstances. She had felt it from the moment she encountered the gypsy woman on the train, and less than 24 hours later, the cancer of that desperation had grown within her to unbearable proportions. Beth wondered what it must be like to have to deal with such a situation for a lifetime, and worse, to never have known anything better.

Beth's thoughts continued to haunt her as she walked out of the hotel around midnight for a short stroll before going to bed. She didn't feel like going to the room anyway. Magnificent as the ambassador's dinner had been, she needed some time to herself. Time to reflect upon all that had taken place since arriving in Romania. Beth was exhausted, but she was too tired to sleep, and she didn't want to deal with the specter of unseen eyes lurking beyond her walls. At least not right now. Strangely enough she had no sense of fear while walking alone so late at night on the sidewalks of Bucharest. There was nothing ominous or foreboding at all. Not on these streets. Not in this city. What a paradox.

When she reached the corner Beth received her final shock of the day. A day which had already been filled with surprises. By then it shouldn't have caught her off guard, but it did nevertheless. There in the dull, washed out glow of a streetlight were women cleaning the streets. Eight of them! Two on each corner! They were slumped over, going about their business, oblivious to anything other than the task at hand. There was no traffic. No pedestrians. There was hardly any trash to speak of. After all, it was midnight. The women worked as teams. One swept with a broom made of branches and twigs, while another would follow behind placing whatever refuse she found into a large barrel on wheels. It was all very methodical and plodding. There was no enthusiasm for the futile chore, and little wonder. What little trash there was could have easily been handled by a single person, much less eight.

"Full employment," thought Beth. "Ceauseseu's way of making certain that everyone has a job. I wonder what he's doing tonight while his slaves sweep the street?" These were women. Mothers and grandmothers who should have been at home with their families. The thought sickened her. Beth returned to her room saddened by what she had just witnessed. Disheartened by the way the day had concluded.

Ambassador Pendergraph met the *Winternational* group at the church at 5:30 the next evening. He was waiting with Reverend Ilie Ionescu who was the pastor at a small Baptist church in the eastern part of the city. Prior to the service, which was scheduled for six o'clock, the group was treated to tea and cookies in a room off the right side of the sanctuary.

The reverend welcomed everyone and thanked them for coming such a great distance. "You must know that my members will appreciate your visit very much. For them you represent hope. Freedom. They know little of your country, but they know enough. Do you have questions, perhaps?"

The minister spoke excellent English with only a slight trace of an accent. Dr. Wolfe hesitated for a few seconds to see if any of his contingent would ask a question. After an uncomfortable pause, he was ready to pose one of his own when Karla Johnson spoke up. "How many members do you have in your church, and how are they able to worship under such difficult conditions?"

"We have more than 400 members. For most of them it is very difficult to get here so we have three services each Sunday. This makes it easier because some are able to come in the morning and others in the afternoon or evening. We have no young people. You will see. Everyone who joins us is very elderly. Young people cannot afford to come. They must register with the government if they want to attend services, and the government does not like it when they go to church. They make it very hard for people to get decent jobs if they worship. So the young people stay away. For the old people it does not matter so much. There is little that can be done to them. They come, and they pass along the messages they hear to their families. Only in the choir will you see young people. This is regarded as a cultural program, not a religious program, so some of the young people come to sing because this is not counted against them."

Elisa McSwain had another question. "Why is it so difficult for them to get here?"

"Most have no means of transportation so they must walk. There is no other way. Some walk a couple of miles in both directions. But their faith is strong. They believe. This is a place of hope. Sometimes there is no heat in the church, or we have no light. There are brownouts you see. But we do our best. We try very hard."

There was sadness in Reverend Ionescu's voice, but he was as open and matter of fact as he could be under the circumstances. His answers were deeply meaningful to the students who found it incomprehensible that people would be denied the right to worship. Or, at the very least, given a reasonable opportunity to do so.

"So now we must go, I think," said the reverend. "Dr. Wolfe, Dr. Hobson and Ambassador Pendergraph will go with me into the sanctuary, and I believe you have selected one of your students for the prayer, yes?"

"That's correct. The students have taken a vote and chosen Brent Walker for that honor," answered Dr. Wolfe.

"Very good then. If you don't mind we will seat the rest of you upstairs in the balcony so that you may have a better view. You will also be able to remain together there. The church is not so big you see. Is this acceptable?"

The group responded with a unanimous, "Yes."

"Good. Then we go. Please." The reverend led the way with the two faculty members, the ambassador and Brent Walker close behind. The others followed, then walked up the stairs to the balcony.

Just as Reverend Ionescu had said, the sanctuary was filled with senior citizens. Only the choir showed any signs of youth, as the reverend had also pointed out, but the surprising thing was that the choir was 100% young people. That fact alone gave Beth a positive feeling inside because she knew that the older members saw them as a link to the future, if for no other reason than their mere presence.

The service was lengthy by American standards. Beth surmised that if these people had to endure such extreme hardships to attend services, then the church was probably making every effort to ensure that the congregation was ministered to thoroughly through words, music and prayer.

Judging from the number of people in attendance, Beth would never have guessed what they had been through for the privilege of worship. The sanctuary was filled to capacity. As Beth looked down she noticed that all the women were seated on the left side of the aisle and all the men sat on the right. No one removed their coats despite the length of the program. Aside from a small stained glass window at the front of the sanctuary, the only other color to be seen was in the babushkas the ladies wore on their heads. Those who were not wearing the vivid scarves had fur hats on instead.

Shortly after the service began, Reverend Ionescu rose to introduce Dr. Wolfe, Dr. Hobson and the ambassador. He explained the reason for the visit by the Wingate students and their interest in the Romanian people. After brief welcoming remarks, Dr. Wolfe went to the podium to greet the Romanians personally. He thanked them for their hospitality, then praised them for their courage and strength in continuing to find a way to maintain their beliefs regardless of the barriers to do so. Ionescu handled the translation duties for Wolfe, as he did for Hobson and Brent Walker. To the delight of the congregation Ambassador Pendergraph said a few words in their own language, which naturally endeared him to the audience.

The reverend's comments only further aroused the curiosity among the members of the church. Throughout the service they kept turning toward the balcony, particularly when everyone rose to sing. It was unusual for them to have visitors of any kind, especially so many and so young. To see youthful faces that were not members of the choir was difficult for them to comprehend, but the message resonated loud and clear. Americans too. Rarely did they see Americans. For the next couple of hours the Romanians down below continuously turned and gazed upward toward the balcony, communicating only with their eyes as they reached out to touch the Wingate students with their hearts.

It was a powerful study in subliminal exchange, as if the Romanians were making a plea to have their story told to someone beyond the barriers of their borders. When the service finished the Wingate students walked down the balcony stairs into the vestibule to greet the Romanian people who were leaving the sanctuary. Since Ambassador Pendergraph spoke the language, he took the first position by the door. Wolfe and Hobson placed themselves at the head of the line on the opposite side, and without instructions the students formed a semicircle from the door down through the narthex, shaking hands with people and smiling as they departed.

Beth began taking pictures as rapidly as she could. It was one of those serendipitous occasions that sometimes caught her unprepared, but she quickly adjusted to the situation.

The Romanians looked tired. Weary. Yet they were deeply appreciative, and thankful that these young Americans had journeyed such a great distance to visit with them. It was a quiet scene filled with hushed voices. The mixture of languages was somehow comprehended, though neither group spoke the other's tongue. Soft words. Muted tones. A silence of sharing the moment.

As one old woman passed the ambassador she caught the eye of Elisa McSwain. Elisa had become one of Beth's favorite people on the trip. She was poised beyond her years with an uncanny ability to interpret other people's personalities. Her slender frame, combined with a rosy complexion, bubbly personality and long flowing pony tail gave her an even younger appearance than she was, yet she was dynamic and outspoken in a manner that drew people to her.

She had an infectious charm that often caused others to confide in her because they knew she could be trusted with even the most intimate of secrets.

Perhaps the old Romanian woman recognized that trait in Elisa too, for as she passed before her she quietly uttered the word, "Pace."

Bewildered, Elisa looked to Ambassador Pendergraph, who was standing next to her, for an answer. He grinned and said, "Pace. In Romanian it means "Peace."

Elisa turned back to the Romanian woman with a sincere smile and repeated the word, "Pace."

A classmate standing to the left of Elisa overheard the exchange and immediately spoke to another woman in front of him. "Pace," he said.

An uncontrollable smile spread across the woman's face as she returned the wish by again saying, "Pace."

Soon the vestibule was filled with the soft sounds of Romanian and American voices, all echoing the same simple word, "Pace." No other word could have been more appropriate. It was the only word that was necessary.

They repeated it over and over again, "Pace. Pace. Pace."

Then in the dim light of the room, Elisa reached into her purse and removed one of the small Bibles she had brought with her from home. She gave it to the old woman, placing it in the palm of her hand and covering it with her own. The woman gazed intently at Elisa for a long moment before looking down at the treasure she gripped within her ancient fingers. And then she began to cry.

As the tears made silent trails down her cheeks, the Romanian woman looked at Ambassasor Pendergraph and said something to him in her native language. The ambassador listened carefully to be sure that he understood precisely what the woman was saying. When she had finished, Pendergraph translated for Elisa. She says, "All of my life I have dreamed of having a Bible written in English. For me it is a symbol. Today, you have answered my prayers."

Beth had been snapping pictures furiously, trying to document what was happening in front of her, but now she stopped. She was spellbound by the words of the little Romanian woman who had but one simple wish; to possess a book written in a language she could neither read nor understand, yet one that symbolized all of her hopes, dreams and aspirations for a life she would never know. A book that was her bridge to a world she would never see.

But the old Romanian woman wasn't finished. Not just yet. Again she spoke to Ambassador Pendergraph, only this time the interpreter translated her words simultaneously as she spoke them. Pendergraph cast his eyes toward Elisa while the old woman slowly uttered her message to the young college student. "She says, "I only know three words in English," the ambassador told her. At that moment the Romanian woman moved forward to Elisa and hugged the young Wingate student. When she pulled away she smiled gently, then leaned forward and whispered into Elisa's ear the words, "I love you."

Beth had been standing close enough to hear the conversation, but when the Romanian woman spoke those three little words she was overcome with emotion.

Three words. Three simple words. "I love you." The message was universal. Now Beth knew for sure that even in that bleak corner of the world there was indeed hope, there was faith, and yes, there was love.

The cold no longer mattered. It had been nullified by something far greater. In a few brief, spontaneous moments, Beth had come to realize that these people had warmth enough for everyone nestled deep within their hearts. And she also knew that there would always be candles to brighten the darkness, flickering with their silent, gentle flames of hope, for these people still believed in miracles.

Beth felt spiritually uplifted. She was joyful and gratified. Now she understood how the Romanian people had managed to persevere for so long under such impossible living conditions. Through it all their faith had kept them going, and perhaps better than anyone else, they knew the true meaning of the word, "Pace."

THE ROCKS OF CORFU

The pier was bustling with people. It was always an active place anyway, but on days when a cruise ship was in port, it was especially busy. Though it was only 7:45, the bright morning sun was already intense, burning its way through a cloudless blue Grecian sky.

It was impossible for Beth Jacobsen to contain her anticipation and excitement. First-time assignments were always that way for her, and this project had been an entire series of "firsts." For one thing, this was the first time she would be doing an article for a major travel magazine. She had met one of the editors of *Leisure Holidays* at a Society of American Travel Writers luncheon over the winter, sent him some tear sheets from her most recent newspaper features, and the next thing she knew she was cruising the Greek islands.

This was also the first cruise for Beth. For some unexplained reason, throughout her years of travel writing, the opportunity for a cruise had never arisen, so this was a totally new travel experience to write about. And finally, it was the first time she had ever been to Greece, so as she walked away from the ship along the wide concrete slab that would dead-end into the road leading to town, she had to keep reminding herself that she was really in Corfu.

Rather than doing her usual abundance of research and preparation, Beth had decided to let this adventure be completely serendipitous. She was going to let the "place" come to her fresh and untouched by preconceived ideas or the writings of others. At least she intended to start out that way. Maybe later she would study the words of those who had preceded her, but for now, this project would be Beth Jacobsen's personal discoveries and perspectives, nothing more.

The pier ended, and Beth turned left to walk toward town. She had long ago made it part of her traveling strategy to walk whenever possible, especially in a new destination. For one thing there was much to be learned by traveling on foot. Besides, she enjoyed the exercise, and the Mediterranean sun was seductive as it splashed across her face. There was independence in Beth's step and optimism in her soul as she soaked in the surroundings and absorbed the colorful ambience of Corfu.

Before long the city of Corfu began to open up in front of Beth as she ambled along the main street leading toward the capital of the island. Even at that hour the city was a lively scene filled with the activity of morning rituals. Shopkeepers washing windows. Merchants sweeping in front of their stores. Leather goods and clothing displays multiplying at storefronts. Tables and chairs being set out at restaurants and tavernas for tourists and visitors. Soon the perpetual flow of locals would begin with the same daily routines that had taken place for centuries. Echos of time. Rhythms of life. Sequences of events that remained the same as they had for hundreds of years. A timelessness where only the faces were different and everything else went unchanged.

There were morning smells, too. Delicate pastries, rich coffees and other food preparations wafting irresistible aromas into the air. Here and there freshly cut flowers occasionally provided other pockets of sweet fragrances along the streets. Over the years Beth had also learned to smell a place as well as to walk it. She had come to know that each district of a destination has distinct aromas that define the area, and set it apart from anyplace else. By now Beth had assimilated herself into the hub of the community. It was time for further discovery and exploration.

Corfu is an old town. There is an ancientness to it where remnants of civilizations past mingle with the present-day myriad of streets, alleyways and squares. Like so much of the Mediterranean it has a crumbling atmosphere, as if the layers of history are gradually peeling away from its buildings with the passage of time. It made Beth wonder what had happened to the great Greek civilization that spawned the likes of Socrates and Aristotle and Plato. How had the culture that created the Parthenon, Delphi and the Palace of Knossos evolved to this run-down state? How could a Golden Age of philosophy and literature and drama and architecture deteriorate to a place where thoughts and ideas seemed to be dictated by little more than the changes in the weather, the movement of the sun or whatever might be taking place in the moment?

It was more a matter of speculation for Beth than a critique. She was curious about what had occurred over thirty odd centuries to create such a dramatic metamorphosis. Maybe the country just got tired. Perhaps it had suffered some kind of civilization burnout, and now Greece was simply content to exist in the deep blue of the sea and the golden rays of the Mediterranean sun. Still, Corfu had more than its share of character and charisma. It was filled with fascinating architecture; Italian, Byzantine, French. Even English and Russian.

Beth became quickly aware of a strong Italian influence mixed throughout the language. Perhaps because she had spent a fair amount of time in Italy during her travels, the linguistic mixture was pleasing to her ears. It gave her a strong sense of confidence. It made the place seem friendlier than she might have otherwise expected.

As she continued to wander through the maze of streets, Beth thought about the others she was traveling with and wondered where they were on such a spectacular morning. Travel writers often moved about the world in packs of eight or ten. At least when they were observing their obligations to whomever was hosting a trip. But this was a free day, and that meant freedom from the herd. It felt good to get away from them, to be on her own even though it was only the third day of a ten-day excursion. By now in her career, Beth usually knew one or two of the people in any given group, but not this time. The manifest was composed of five women and three men, plus a male public relations person and a woman from the tourist board.

As a rule, most of the writers Beth traveled with were older than she. She could usually count on being the youngest member of the party. But one of the guys on this trip was, as near as she could tell, relatively close to her age. He was a photographer with a writing assignment for the *Houston Chronicle*. Beth hadn't spoken to him much, other than to exchange a few pleasantries now and then. The rest of the crowd was pretty salty, and opinionated. One thing travel writers never lacked for was opinions about anything and everything. In no way did they feel the necessity to restrict their points of view to travel either. Still, most of the writers Beth had met over the years were very nice. There were a few however, who were just downright tedious. To put it in even the politest of terms, some of them were terminal pains in the ass.

On any given trip, Beth had learned that there were three phases of psychological interaction. The first always came at the airport where the group mustered for the long international flight across the Atlantic. This was the "One-Upsmanship Phase." It was the time when everyone gathered for the first time, when new acquaintances were made and old ones renewed. It was also the time when, old or new, the conversations became verbal wrestling matches. The purpose was to make certain that everyone in the group knew the status of each writer's most recent adventure and, of course, what the next destination would be following the particular trip at hand. The immediate itinerary was of no consequence because there was absolutely no prestige in sharing common territory.

There were a couple of different layers to this stage. Veteran writers who knew each other wanted to be sure that past traveling companions were aware that they had been selected from an elite list. They also liked to believe, whether it was true or not, that they had been chosen for specific trips that had been organized by PR firms with the most impressive and influential credentials. The competition at this level was fierce.

Beth was always amused by these little tests of geographical dodgeball. Especially when she overheard comments like "how lousy the service was at the *Oriental* in Bangkok. Why does everyone always rate it among the best hotels in the world?" Or, "how dreadful the food was at high tea at the *Empress* in Victoria." Or, "the gall of that airline not to give me an upgrade to first class. Don't they know who I write for and how much free publicity I give them? Why I'm read by every travel editor on the face of the earth, yadda, yadda, yadda."

As time went on, and she had become more experienced, these little scenes were just part of a necessary game for Beth. But she also came to realize that these people were only talking shop, regardless of how pretentious it might sound, and that, for them at least, the whole world really was quite literally their office. So in some ways, the conversations did become less elitist with the passing of time, but there was still an air about them that Beth found amusing.

The second phase was the most awkward. Beth thought of it as the "Politeness Phase" of travel writing. This was the time when the sparring stopped and the trip began to unfold. The overnight flight to a destination was always an intermediate stage in this process because the writers were more or less isolated from each other and therefore, less able maintain any sort of real contact. Not only that, much of the time was taken up with matters of survival. Such things included availing oneself of all the first class amenities, eating and drinking, studying the itinerary, trying to sleep, eating and drinking, trying to figure out how to use the in-flight communications system, eating and drinking, stepping over people to wait in line to use the restroom, reading the in-flight magazine, eating and drinking some more, making sure they had all their documents with them, trying to freshen up so they wouldn't look as if they had been up all night, and generally, killing time until the arrival. In short, this was not a time that was conducive to an abundance of socializing.

The "Politeness Phase" didn't really kick in until the group reached the baggage claim area at the destination. From that point on, approximately the next two days would be filled with courtesies and helpfulness that would long be forgotten by trip's end. This was the period when everyone tried to remember names, made observations about the other personalities and learned about the various backgrounds of their fellow writers. It was the time when friendships were made, or when an enemy's list was created, and it was also the time when the "character" of the group began to be fully determined.

Usually somewhere during the middle of the third day the "All-Hell-Breaks-Loose Phase" would commence. That's when politeness was thrown to the winds, only to reappear again sporadically as individual situations dictated. Alliances had been made. Individual personality traits were now well established and known to everyone. It was at this point that the host and/or the PR person would grit their collective teeth, hold their breath and stand back to pray that their cluster of prima donna wordsmiths had reached some element of compatibility. It was also when each person knew exactly which members of the group he or she could tolerate and, more importantly, which ones to avoid.

As Beth casually made her way around the streets of Corfu, she was still in the process of evaluating to herself the eclectic blend of people with whom she was traveling. After a brief stop to look in the window of a shop, she turned to move on and was surprised to see another member of the group up ahead. It was Tyler Scott, the photographer on assignment from Texas. He was alone and deeply engrossed in his work, darting among the people, and the shops, and the congestion as he snapped pictures of the tableau of life that was unfolding before him.

Beth was intrigued by his concentration. She was drawn to the intensity of his routine. Tyler wasn't just clicking off photo after photo. Rather he was studying the people, the architecture, the culture. He was soaking in the richness of his surroundings. He was immersed in his environment, and for all intents, he had himself become part of the scene.

Beth was fascinated. She followed Tyler at a distance watching him work. Here was someone who had obviously traveled to Greece to learn something. Someone attempting to grow beyond his personal boundaries, trying to comprehend in some small way the dance of life that was taking place all around him. Beth liked that. She was infatuated by his dedication, turned on by his unassuming manner and his care to capture the vignettes of life as they really existed without infringing upon the rights of those he was documenting. In just those few brief moments, Beth felt she had learned more about this individual than she had in any of the conversations with him during the previous two days. She made up her mind to follow Tyler a little while longer. Then she would interrupt his concentration and speak to him. Perhaps they could explore Corfu together. Perhaps they could learn from each other.

For the next ten minutes Beth became an amateur stalker as she sneaked around watching Tyler doing his work. Finally, at one point when Tyler went down on one knee trying to get an angle on a clothesline stretching between two second-story windows, Beth inched her way up behind him and spoke. "I think the light's better over there," she said in a playful tone as she pointed down the street.

Tyler fell back on his heels, stunned to hear an English speaking voice, but he quickly recovered when he recognized Beth. "Just trying to capture some of the local color. This whole place looks like every picture I've ever seen from this part of the world. So you really think there's better light down there?" Tyler was eyeing a spot where three little roads converged.

Beth looked at him with a broad smile and the magnetic twinkle in her eyes that captivated people immediately. "How would I know, I'm a writer, not a photographer. Looks like there's some nice contrast though."

"Let's go see," Tyler responded, secretly thrilled at his good fortune of being discovered by Beth while he was alone. He had wanted to speak with her further, but he was uncomfortable with everyone else always around. Besides that only made for the usual chitchat which he didn't really want to get into anyway. This was the perfect opportunity to get to know Beth better. A whole day to discover a new place with a beautiful woman. Perhaps there were gods in Greece after all.

"You know I could really help you with your pictures," Beth volunteered.

"How so?" asked Tyler.

"Well, you could probably use some people to pose for you. Especially when you can't catch people in the act of being natural. I used to do a lot of fashion shoots before I started travel writing. Maybe I could recruit people to be in your pictures."

Tyler thought for a moment and said, "But can't I do that myself?"

"You could try, " Beth replied, "but I'll bet people will cooperate with me quicker than you because I'm a woman. They won't be as intimidated by me as they will you. Not only that, if you need any females for your pictures, I'll bet I can get them to say 'yes' twice as fast as you can."

Tyler knew she was right. He always had difficulty asking people to let him take their pictures. Naturally he preferred to get shots that captured life as it was in the moment, but that wasn't always possible. Besides, he liked the idea of having Beth assist him. "OK, let's try it. We'll make a pretty awesome team," Tyler beamed.

For the two writers the next several hours in Corfu took on the appearance of one of those montage scenes from the movies. Everything was a blur, a series of vignettes all meshing together. One gigantic photo essay. Beth and Tyler became lost in their own little world, and they could almost hear the musical score in the background.

The shots were classic. Craggy, weather-beaten faces. A pair of old Greeks sitting in front of a taverna playing checkers as if they hadn't moved in decades. Women carrying bundles of food and laundry on their heads. The stereotypical scene of an elderly woman peering into the cluttered streets from an upstairs window. Donkeys laden with bundles standing near dilapidated walls. There were markets. Shops. Flower stalls. In one place a Greek man was sitting outside a small restaurant playing a homemade stringed instrument while two of his buddies drank and occasionally sang along with him. In another, a haggard sailor stood in front of a fish market smoking a cigarette. His hands were huge. Maybe three times larger than normal. Beth guessed he was probably a fisherman by trade, and the size of his hands was the result of a lifetime of reeling in his nets filled with fish. And there were churches, too. Wonderful scenes of silver-haired Greek women dressed entirely in black sitting in the darkness of cathedrals illuminated only by the flickering of candlelight.

Beth and Tyler were indeed a good team. Beth managed to get several people to pose for pictures that Tyler would never have been able to obtain on his own. In fact, she even found two stunningly beautiful young Greek women to model for a couple of shots. With their classic midnight black hair and smooth olive skin, they were ravishing subjects for the camera, and they were flattered to think that they were pretty enough to be included in the photos. It would not have been flattering had Tyler approached them by himself, however. In the end, the contrasts of the radiant beauty of his two youthful subjects, combined with the marvelous character of the other faces he had seen, provided Tyler with a nice selection of shots that, to him at least, captured the essence of Corfu.

The time passed quickly. Too quickly. Brief though it was, it had certainly been rich and fulfilling. Tyler and Beth had become friends, though there had been little conversation between them because they had become so deeply involved in their "project." The lack of discussion didn't matter, however. There was a subliminal inner communication that was far greater than any verbal conversation could possibly have been, and both Beth and Tyler sensed it.

In the flurry of documenting centuries of culture on film in a matter of hours, Tyler became so wrapped up in his work that he lost track of the time. As he and Beth rested briefly at the edge of a fountain, splashing water on their faces to refresh themselves, Tyler realized that he was hungry. "Let's get something to eat," he said.

"I'm starving," replied Beth, "let's go." Droplets of water glistened upon her face, making her radiant in the sunlight. Tyler was staring at her, mesmerized by the lovely vision before him when Beth broke his trance by jumping to her feet to begin the quest for something to eat. The fountain had not only provided a cool liquid respite that washed away a layer of grime, it had also established a renewed burst of energy. As the clock approached 1:20 in the afternoon, it was time to utilize that spirit to seek out a tiny bit of refreshment to take the edge off their hunger.

"I just remembered, it's the middle of siesta, or whatever they call it in Greece," said Tyler. "We may have a little trouble finding a place to eat at this time of day."

"Not to worry," answered Beth with confidence. "It's all part of the adventure."

The pair of explorers searched through town for fifteen or twenty minutes before they found a place they thought might be suitable. There had been a couple of other spots that were open, but they didn't look very appealing, so they had carried on with their mission.

"Leave it to a couple of Americans to choose a place called *ZORBA'S*. How trite is that?" asked Beth glancing at the sign as they entered. The small taverna featured ten or twelve tables scattered around a cluttered room, and also a bar with eight stools lined up in front of it.

Two men were sitting at one of the tables. They were talking when Beth and Tyler walked in, but their conversation wasn't engrossing enough to keep them from stopping to stare at the tourists who had just entered the establishment. Tyler noticed a rough looking man behind the counter and smiled. The Greek had a dark face that was made even darker by his scruffy two-day old growth of beard. A cigarette dangled from the left corner of his mouth with the ash hanging precariously from the end of it. On his head he was wearing the typical black Greek cap with the short bill. A red and white striped T-shirt strained over his muscular torso. His ebony eyes were piercing, giving him a sinister appearance as he glared at the Americans.

"Do you speak English?" Tyler asked with a friendly grin.

The Greek nodded and in a broken accent said, "Leetle."

Tyler paused for a moment and then spoke again. "Are you Zorba," he asked, amused at himself for being so clever.

"Si." replied the bartender in a gruff tone.

It really wasn't the answer Tyler expected, and even if it had been, this guy could never have been as congenial as Anthony Quinn. Tyler looked at Beth with questioning eyes. Beth glanced back without an answer. They were uncertain as to whether to stay or to go, and the ominous countenance of Zorba wasn't making the decision any easier. In its own way, the restaurant did have a certain charm and atmosphere to it. Gentle breezes wafted through the open doorways, and the desire for some type of sustenance was rapidly overtaking any apprehensions. After a few moments of hesitation and soul searching, Tyler and Beth gave each other a nod, and shrugged their shoulders as if to say, "OK, why not."

"Let's get a drink and something to munch on, and then we can decide what to do from there," suggested Tyler.

"Suits me," said Beth. "Why don't we just sit at the bar and see how it goes."

Tyler ordered a beer while Beth had a glass of wine. Between them they deciphered the menu,which had been translated into something that looked like Italian, and pointed to what they believed to be seafood appetizers. Neither of them could read the menu, but Beth guessed that they had ordered calamari and prawns. Just to be safe, they also ordered some bread and cheese, and all things considered, it turned out to be a decent little meal.

After the hectic activities of the morning, time now became suspended, as though the whole world had come to a screeching halt during siesta. For Beth and Tyler, the good old U.S. of A. might as well have been on another planet. There was no rush. No schedule to meet. No common friendships to be discussed. In a way it was better than beginning a relationship at home, because there in that remote corner of the world everything was different and undiscovered. Everything grew from an equal reference point, and whatever happened to either of them was happening for the first time, to them only, and to no one else. It was joyous. Satisfying. Uncluttered.

As the couple sat munching their seafood, Tyler told Beth of his days as a football player at Baylor University before an injury forced him to quit the team. After college he had tried a stint at broadcasting before going into newspaper work. Even though Tyler was sporting a bit of a middle age paunch, Beth figured that he had once been an athlete of some kind. Maybe it was his broad shoulders or the way Tyler's buns sat up so high on his legs. Beth was into butts anyway, and Tyler definitely had an athlete's rear end. A dead giveaway that he had played sports somewhere.

At 41, Tyler had a full head of sandy brown hair that was cut a little too short for the high cheekbones of his face, which narrowed at the chin. He wasn't what Beth would describe as handsome, but he was ruggedly charming, and he became increasingly appealing the more she knew about him. There was a surprising depth to his personality. From that perspective she never would have guessed he had once been into sports. Beth had thought that all athletes could do was grunt and eat raw meat when it was thrown into their cage. But Tyler seemed to have a caring sensitivity about his personality that was inconsistent with most other athletes she had ever known. He was also more intelligent than his past might have indicated. A literate jock? No way. That seemed like an oxymoron to Beth.

For the better part of an hour, the two journalists laughed and giggled and talked about travel and movies and books and art. By the time Tyler had ordered two more rounds of drinks for each of them, the heat of the day, and the alcohol, took their toll, and the discussion turned philosophical by moving on to subjects such as hopes, dreams, aspirations and the future.

There was magic in the Greek air. Beth had read stories of young people who had been caught up in the sensuality and spontaneity of the Greek islands only to become lost for a while. Now she was aware of how easily it could happen. The atmosphere was addictive. People were friendly and carefree. The breezes refreshing. The tempo of time languid.

The days lingered in limbo. Credit card payments and bills suddenly became nonexistent. Telephones were unnecessary. CNN was little more than an odd series of letters. All that mattered was the all-consuming present. But even in her blissful state of intoxication Beth was keenly aware that none of what she was feeling was real. It was only temporary. Still, for the moment it felt wonderful, exhilarating, uplifting. Most of all, for that microsecond of time extracted from the overall context of her life, there was complete freedom. Personal space to be whomever she wanted or needed to be. That alone was a mental and emotional high that in its own way, in that time, and in that place, was highly erotic.

There was a lull in the conversation as both Tyler and Beth drifted away into their own private thoughts. Then suddenly Tyler perked up and said, "You know what we haven't had yet? Ouzo! You can't come to Greece without having ouzo. Opa, Zorba, opa!" Tyler clapped his hands in self-approval and promptly ordered two glasses of the infamous lethal liquid.

In a matter of seconds the two writers had downed round one and were well on their way toward finishing off another. Whatever opportunity there might have been for sobriety before Tyler and Beth left Zorba's was no longer within the realm of possibility. The two men in the corner were now ready to consider these foreigners as one of them, and as his patrons polished off their drinks, Zorba beamed a broad smile of approval.

Tyler and Beth were each sporting a hefty buzz as they walked out of the taverna. Though it wasn't a state of staggering inebriation, it had clearly affected their moods, and they were in the process of taking full advantage of the situation. In truth, it was probably as much of a natural high as anything else, fueled by feelings of satisfaction and relaxation and calm. When combined with the alcohol however, it exuded a momentary interlude of happiness, which required immediate attention, because Beth and Tyler both knew it was not permanent.

Rather than attempt any more work, they decided to walk off the side effects of their wicked lunch by heading back to the ship. They were still about three-quarters of a mile from the pier. Plenty of time to allow their intoxicating exploits to diminish.

Under normal circumstances they could have walked the distance much faster than they did, but there was no hurry. For the next fifteen minutes Beth and Tyler passed the time with idle conversation that was dictated, for the most part, by the various curiosities they observed along their route. One subject led to another, recalling a personal travel experience or some event back home, but generally there was no probing for the intimate details about either of their lives. This was not going be an intrusive kind of relationship. They had both traveled enough to realize that in less than a week their lives would once again go in separate directions, and the odds were likely that they would rarely, and probably never, see each other again. So the thought of relating their personal odysseys to one another wasn't even a consideration.

As they made their way to the open span of dock that led to the ship, Tyler noticed another pier running parallel to theirs. It appeared to be a breakwater of some type, and several hundred yards away, Tyler could see fishermen casting their lines into the sea, idling away what was left of the splendid afternoon.

"Let's walk out there for a while," he said to Beth, not wanting to return to the ship right away, hoping to avoid the inevitable for as long as possible.

Beth nodded in agreement. There was an unwritten travel writer's rule about relationships being forbidden on a trip. In Beth's case, it had never even been a consideration to break the rule because no one had ever been appealing enough to challenge the idea. Now that this was happening to her, she tried to rationalize to herself that this situation was different. It wasn't. Nevertheless, both Beth and Tyler were savvy enough to know that the entire adventure was merely a fleeting moment in their lives. Neither of them said anything to the other, but there was an unspoken understanding between them that their newfound relationship couldn't go much further. They liked each other. A lot. It wasn't a remorseful idea that they would never be together, just something they both accepted. Perhaps it was because there was a keen sense within them both that time and distance, and especially the patterns of their individual lives simply wouldn't allow it to happen. If nothing else Beth had learned that lesson when she broke off her engagement with Todd Harper. Even though she seemed to have more in common with Tyler than with Todd, the logistics of having any kind of meaningful relationship were totally against them. Besides, right now the ouzo was probably making most of the decisions.

One really special aspect of Beth's friendship with Tyler was that they were able to communicate without saying very much at all. The conversations were fun and insightful, but there had been reflective moments as well. That was really nice, and strangely enough, now that she thought about it, it was during those quiet times that the synergy between them was the strongest. As if they could hear each other's thoughts. As if they could touch the other person's heart. As if they could reach into the other's soul. Those were the feelings that had been missing from each of their lives for so long. Feelings that intensified this particular situation. That made everything about these particular emotions so magical.

There was one final element to the equation, and that was the place. Not that Corfu was necessarily more special than dozens of other romantic spots in the world. It just happened to be that it was the backdrop for this particular event in their lives. Nothing could ever duplicate that, and therefore, Corfu would remain forever in their hearts as a destination filled with a story that neither of them would ever write, and a poignancy that no one else would ever experience.

Tyler and Beth came close to the end of the pier. This time it was her turn to make a suggestion. A foot or two below the wall there was a pile of large rocks extending the full length of the dock and about 15 or 20 feet out into the water. "Why don't we jump down there and sit on the rocks?" said Beth.

"OK," came Tyler's enthusiastic reply.

Soon the pair were easing their way among the boulders, stepping carefully onto the slippery rocks trying to find a suitable resting spot. After a couple of minutes they found a good place, settling in among the crevices and contours to gaze at the timeless expanse of the sea.

The Adriatic Sea was bluer than it was in pictures they had seen. There were a few strands of wispy clouds crisscrossing the heavens like vapor trails, but for the most part, the sky was clear and deep blue. Along the horizon, where the blues of the sea and the sky merged, there was enough of a contrast to define where one element of nature ended and the other began, but it was difficult to decide which shade of the color was the richest. Perhaps the scene was merely an illusion, for it too was only a fleeting moment in time, a metaphor for the two people who stared out at its vast panorama. Two people, represented by two shades of blue, converging in a far away place for a brief moment in infinity.

Peaceful sounds enveloped Beth and Tyler amid their pervasive cocoon of solitude. The lapping of the water upon the rocks. The occasional whirrrrr of a fishing line being cast into the sea. The high pitched squeal of a gull gliding upon unseen currents of air. There was an infectious serenity that even the sea understood. On days like this there was nothing more beguiling than the ocean when it decided to rest, to remain gentle and slumbering. The late summer air was mild and full of sea smells, and the brine from the Adriatic swirled lovingly around the boulders with liquid caresses. It was the time of day, and the kind of scene, that made Beth want to sigh deeply, to reflect upon the glorious omnipotent tableau that spread out across the panorama of the Adriatic. She closed her eyes and listened to the soothing silence all around her.

When Beth reopened her eyes, she noticed the water inching higher and higher upon the rocks. She pulled her feet back so they wouldn't get wet from the incoming tide. Otherwise she didn't move. She didn't say anything to Tyler, but she wondered if he had noticed the rising water too.

Then something strange and wonderful happened. One of those lovely, unspoken moments when each of them knew precisely what was going to happen next. Without a word, they leaned down at the same time and removed their shoes and socks. Tyler turned around and placed his footwear on the edge of the pier. Then Beth handed her shoes over to him, and he put them up next to his. Afterwards, Tyler bent down to roll up the legs of his pants.

It was a useless exercise. As the two friends splashed their toes in the water, they realized it had now risen up to their ankles. But still they refused to move back higher on the rocks. Moments later the water was midway up the calves of their legs, yet neither of them ventured to climb higher. Eventually the sway of the water began to slosh around their thighs, and within minutes they were waist-deep in the slowly surging ocean. Tyler splashed some of the seawater at Beth, and she playfully splashed back.

Before long they were nearly immersed. The fishermen had long ago given up their quest, and now Tyler and Beth were alone on the rocks. They looked at each and laughed at the silliness of what they had done. At last the buoyancy of the water lifted their bodies higher on to the rocks until they were forced to climb back up on the dock. Soaked to the skin, they reached down, picked up their shoes and socks, and began to stroll back to the ship.

"If we take our time, I bet we'll almost be dry by the time we get to the boat," remarked Tyler with a grin.

"All we need now is for one of the others to see us," laughed Beth.

Tyler was right. They were wrinkled and disheveled when they got to the ship, but for the most part they had drip-dried in the sun and the sea air. Best of all, nobody they knew had seen them arrive.

Quickly they raced up the gangplank and on to the ship. When they entered the main lobby, the rush of the air conditioning felt especially cool on their damp clothes and bodies after coming from the extreme heat outside. The pair hastened through the lobby to the main stairway and walked as quickly as possible to the stateroom where Beth was staying. She fumbled with her key as she tried to get into the room as fast as she could without being seen by anyone else in the group.

When they finally found themselves within the safety of the tiny cabin, Tyler and Beth breathed a collective sigh of relief. Once inside, Beth shut the door with lightening speed, and the moment it closed behind them, they burst into laughter like a couple of children who had just gotten away with something. It had been a marvelous day. A day filled with adventure, and a day that had become an all too brief memory in the making. Tyler rubbed his hands together to ward off the chill as Beth hopped up and down to keep her circulation moving.

"We'd better get out of these clothes before we catch cold," said Tyler without thinking. Though his utterance was completely innocent in a moment of spontaneity, he realized as soon as he spoke that Beth might misinterpret his meaning. Dread quickly overcame Tyler, fearing he had said something offensive that might inadvertently spoil what had been a perfect day in that split second when those words rolled off his tongue.

There was a momentary pause at Beth's end of the room, but it seemed like an eternity. Then she said, "I'll get some towels."

Tyler was stunned. He had meant what he said, but he didn't intend for it to come out as it did. It was simply an instinctive outburst. And he certainly didn't expect the response that he got from Beth. Tyler stood in the center of the cabin, dripping tiny pools of the Adriatic on the floor, freezing and trying to decide what to do next as he waited for Beth to come back.

He was unbuttoning his shirt when Beth returned with the towels. She put them on the tiny dresser by the bed, and began removing her clothes too. As they stripped away each soggy layer, they looked around for places to hang their things out to dry, momentarily oblivious to each other's stage of undress. Their skin was still damp and cool as they reached for the towels and wiped away the moisture from their bodies. The thick dry cloth made them feel immediately warmer as they blotted away the salty residue. And then they were finished, standing at each end of room with their backs to each other, and nothing but their towels in their hands.

It wasn't as if they didn't realize what they were doing. They just hadn't given a single moment of thought to the aftermath of the process. In the effort to get out of their damp clothes and to warm themselves up, Beth and Tyler had simply gone about their business, engrossed only in their own personal tasks at hand. But now they were finished, and slowly they turned to face one another. Reality finally dawned on them. They knew what to expect, or thought that they did, but they still didn't really believe it was happening. Beth and Tyler stood facing each other. Neither uttered a sound. Neither blinked. Neither knew what to do next. They were naked. Stark, bare-assed, buck-naked, and all they could do was stare at each other without saying a word.

The awkward pause continued for several long seconds. Then both of them looked down at the floor, as if that might change something, as if the damage could somehow be undone. It wasn't an uncomfortable situation really. Odd maybe, and certainly a bit of a strange sensation to explain, but it wasn't uncomfortable. Neither Beth nor Tyler felt compelled to look away, but neither felt any need to continue to gaze at the other either. Nor was there any feeling of vulnerability. More silence. Beth glanced to her right and then sidled over to the bed where she sat down and leaned back against the bulkhead.

Following her lead, Tyler did the same resting his back against the side of the dresser. They continued to sit quietly for a while longer at opposite ends of the bed, before Beth broke the silence. "Well this is a first for me," she said matter of factly.

"Oh, not me," said Tyler sarcastically, "I do it all the time."

Beth knew he was joking. "You know I've always been kind of shy about taking my clothes off in front of a man, but for some reason I don't feel that way now."

"How DO you feel?" asked Tyler.

"I don't know really. Content, I suppose. Alive. Pretty. I feel happy," said Beth softly.

Tyler smiled. "You're more than pretty, you're beautiful. It's always been hard for me to imagine how beautiful people can ever be unhappy."

"You're sweet. Misinformed, but sweet," said Beth.

It was a gentle conversation. Another unexpected moment in a day filled with unexpected moments. They continued to talk. Softly. Poignantly. Almost poetically. Both of them knew that this could never have happened back home. There was too much clutter and inhibition. Too much baggage back there. But here, at this moment it seemed right. It seemed more than right. It was perfect.

If Tyler was embarrassed at all it was because he wasn't more fit. Especially sitting there across from Beth who was a vision. Her breasts were stunning to behold, her stomach smooth and flat. The mound of her femininity formed a triangle that nestled between two magnificent thighs and extended to exquisitely shaped calves. Watching Beth in front of him, Tyler began making mental excuses for all the years of inactivity after his football days were over, rationalizing to himself that he could never have anticipated an occasion such as this. This was Hollywood stuff, the product of some screenwriter's imagination.

The conversation droned on in hushed tones as early evening approached. In the waning moments of the afternoon the room had taken on the ambience of womb-like protection, as if it was isolated from the rest of the ship. Though they were naked, Beth and Tyler felt strangely euphoric in each other other's presence, an unexpectedly natural sensation of total enchantment as a feeling of sublime serenity surrounded the stateroom. Tyler tucked his right leg under the left, extending his free leg along Beth's right side so that their extremities touched. At the same time, Beth raised her outer leg, resting her chin on her knee while running her left hand along the thickness of Tyler's thigh, tenderly manipulating it with a series of soft squeezes. Tyler responded by guiding the crest of his fingers to the base of Beth's calves before stroking her ankles and the tops of her feet.

They stopped talking. Tyler and Beth just sat there staring at each other as their eyes darted subtle messages back and forth. Tyler moved forward and began kissing her. Gentle soft kisses. Sweet kisses. Succulent kisses. He put his hand on Beth's shoulder, then slid it down along her arm and over to her breast in a single continuous motion, coming to rest beneath the curvature of her bosom, cupping its weight with his palm in a bowl of loving caress.

Tyler moved his hand down along Beth's side and across the top of her thigh wiping the back of the hand across her stomach, causing Beth to let out an involuntary gasp as she momentarily lost her breath.

The fondling was gentle and kind and loving, with kisses that never went beyond being anything more than a slow sensual touching of lips. Despite the extremes of their stimulation there was no exchange of saliva, no swallowing of tongues, no sucking of faces. It was more delicious than that. It was sentimental, sweet and caring.

Tyler and Beth knew that the touching would be the extent of their sexual activity. They didn't know why really, but like all the other events of the day, it just seemed to be the most appropriate conclusion. Everything that had already taken place had happened naturally without need for explanation, and this was no different. There would be no sweating bodies, or pressing of flesh. No penetration followed by violent thrusting. Nor would there be any scratching or clawing. No howls of orgasmic pleasure. Instead they were content to kiss each other gently in their glorious matinee session of prolonged foreplay.

There was joy in their hearts and peace in their souls. They had shared each other in the most intimate way without ever reaching the ultimate act of lovemaking. That in itself was probably a first in the annals of sexual history, but in a way, they had given to each other without taking from each other. That was a comforting feeling for both of them. Two people who had each lost their way for a while, now had suddenly found themselves again through the giving of another. In another week the situation would change from one of incredible passion to the realm of the impossible. They both knew it, and so they stopped, for they knew that if the passion continued now, the pain that followed would be unbearable later on. This way was better.

Rather than frustration there was a poetic beauty to it all. A comforting feeling. It was an experience to savor and enjoy. There had been a sense of discovery. There was a powerful mutual bond between them that neither had ever known before. Tyler and Beth had in some small, unplanned way proven to themselves that their search, whatever it meant to each of them, was worthwhile after all. Whatever their individual dreams were, whatever their personal aspirations were, whatever their own unique desires were, did indeed exist, and could indeed be found. They had drawn it out of each other. It wasn't merely the sex. No, it was bigger than that. It was the cumulative effect of all that had taken place in one marvelous day on a bright, sunny island in Greece.

In truth it came at a different level for each of them. The process didn't have quite the same meaning for either of them. But that didn't matter, because their bond was unique. It was shared in a way that only they could understand. The fact that the physical act of love had never been consummated seemed to each of them to be even more meaningful than if it had.

Tyler looked at his watch. "I've got to get dressed," he said. There was more urgency in his voice than Beth had heard all day. It was now close to 7:30. Dinner was at 8:00. He got off the bed and went over to his clothes to see if they were dry. They were still cool to the touch, and a bit damp, but he didn't have far to go anyway. Beth leaned back on the bed and watched Tyler dress. She made no attempt to cover herself.

Tyler pulled on his shoes without putting on his socks. Then he looked up and over toward Beth. They smiled at each other. Tyler walked over to the bed. He leaned down and kissed Beth on the mouth. "What do we do for an encore?" he asked smiling.

"I don't know," Beth replied. "But we've still got a week. Let's just see what happens."

Beth gave Tyler a warm, friendly, satisfied smile.

Tyler kissed her again and moved to the door. He wanted one final look at Beth as she was. He wanted to memorize her sitting there in total natural freedom, as if she were some artist's model, in a state of reflection upon the events of the day. He walked out of the room, closing the door gently behind him. The day had ended as quietly as it had begun.

* * * * *

Tyler arrived for dinner just a few minutes before Beth. There was a seat next to him, but Beth chose to sit diagonally across instead. All of the other writers were already there, ready to detail their exploits of the day. Everyone greeted each other with the usual flurry and great excitement of their newest adventures. Tyler and Beth remained quiet. This would be a night for listening rather than talking. When the question came around to Beth about what she had done for that day, she simply answered, "Oh, shopping, browsing, just looking around. I took a few pictures. That's about it."

Tyler had a similar nondescript answer. As far as the veteran writers were concerned, Tyler and Beth may have been the youngest among them, but they were also the most boring.

Occasionally Tyler looked at Beth. Now and then she would catch his eye as well. Tyler could see the sparkle he had come to know so well over the past several hours. For the rest of the group, the "Politeness Phase" was temporarily back in full force, but as Beth and Tyler listened to all the idle dinner chatter, it was difficult to contain their amusement, because none of them would ever know the secret they held in their hearts.

The ship was at sea now. There was a gentle rocking as it made its way through the darkening sky to the next port of call. Outside the large picture windows of the dining room the sun was slipping into the Adriatic as it pushed golden pink rays up into the cool blue of night.

The rocks of Corfu were a thing of the past now. But the memory would live on. And for Tyler and Beth so would the knowledge that dreams really can happen in the brief span of time between sunrise and sunset.

Beth planned to be up on the main deck early the next morning. And so did Tyler.

ENCOUNTER IN MOSCOW

The square was immense. Vast. Startling. The perimeter that formed the massive rectangle was comprised of four distinctive structures. On the eastern side there was the mammoth red wall surrounding the Kremlin. Directly opposite, to the west was *GUM*, the huge state department store that extended more than 2,000 feet along the length of the square. To the north was the *State History Museum*, the oldest museum in Moscow. The southern end was bounded by the magnificent symbol of the city, *St. Basil's Cathedral*, with its multicolored onion domes. And down at the southeast quadrant, between *St. Basil's* and *GUM*, was the circular platform known as Lobnoye Mesto, which was once the designated site for the reading of official decrees. Russians knew it better as the location where high profile death sentences were carried out, because Lobnoye Mesto translated to mean "place of execution."

For decades the two primary Soviet festivals, May Day on May 1st, and Revolution Memorial Day on November 7th, have taken place in that square. Like everyone else, Beth Jacobsen had seen the films of those periodic Russian celebrations of pretentious flag waving and military might. But like so many things one sees when reduced to the frame of a television screen or a photograph, the awesome proportions of the square had never registered with her until she was actually standing there.

It was midmorning on a Wednesday, and the square was filled with people. It didn't matter that the late December temperatures were below freezing under a steel gray sky that made everything appear even larger and more ominous than it already was. Most of the people had come to visit the *Lenin Mausoleum*, and to view the remains of the man who founded Bolshevism in the early portion of the century. The body of V.I. Lenin is proudly, and grotesquely, displayed in a glass sarcophagus located at the center of the Kremlin wall in Red Square. Every hour there was an impressive changing of the guard ceremony. Another pompous display of military prowess. Apparently, the bitter cold had no impact, because hundreds of people were patiently standing in the snaky line that meandered through the square. That part of the process was nothing new. Standing in line was a common practice, a way of life. Merely part of a daily ritual that took place at virtually every undertaking.

Beth watched the procession for a little while and then moved to the end of the square to view the cathedral. *St. Basil's* is a landmark in Moscow. Whenever a news item is televised from Russia, *St. Basil's* is almost always the building that reporters use as a backdrop to make their presence undeniable.

Ivan the Terrible commissioned the project in the middle of the 16th century, and when it was finished, the structure encompassed nine churches. The central building stands more than a hundred feet high with eight surrounding domed chapels. Each dome is a different size featuring a variety of colors and patterns. According to legend, upon completion of *St. Basil's*, Ivan asked the architects if it would be possible for them to create an even more beautiful cathedral. Flattered that another grand opportunity might be in the offing, the architects replied, "Of course." But the prospects of such an idea were unthinkable to Ivan, so the architects were blinded in order that such a project would never be undertaken.

Beth was enjoying a morning of free time away from her group. It was the second year that she had been asked to participate in the international studies program known as *Winternational* with Wingate College. It was also the second time in as many years that Beth had accompanied Dr. Paul Wolfe, the president of the college, and the founder of the *Winternational* program. Wolfe had developed the idea out of his belief that every college student should have an international experience before they graduated. Now the tours had become an annual event, open to every Wingate student during their junior year.

The Russian trip was extremely special however, far exceeding anything Wingate had ever attempted before as part of the *Winternational* curriculum. It was the first time the college had ventured into the Soviet Union, so interest throughout the campus was unusually high. Because of that, the group was considerably larger than usual. As she had on her previous *Winternational* mission, Beth was asked to document the trip for the school, as well as her newspaper.

Over the years Beth had learned that no matter how enjoyable or enriching her traveling companions were, it was important to find time of her own for a while. This particular tour made it more difficult than usual to accomplish that goal, however. The Russian hosts were not keen on the idea of allowing individual exploration. In fact, the method that was used to organize the itinerary was an eye-opening insight into the Soviet mindset. All tours began and ended at the hotel, regardless of the distance required for a particular excursion. There was little opportunity for any flexibility in the schedule, even though the guides insisted that there was plenty of room for changes, if desired. All they needed to do was to ask, they had said. None of that was true, of course, but it sounded good. Such a structure meant that even if the schedule called for an all day outing, lunch would be served at the hotel, so the group had to return to their point of origin rather than continue their sightseeing.

The meals themselves were particularly interesting. Each table was set for a prescribed number of people. If there were to be twelve people for breakfast, then there would be exactly twelve hard-boiled eggs at that table. No more, no less. There would be twenty-four slices of bread. Two for each person. Everything neatly counted out and itemized. There was no choice of beverage. Sometimes there was coffee, sometimes tea, but never both.

And drinks didn't necessarily bare any logical relationship to a particular meal or time of day. Often there were bottles of some sort of Russian-style soft drink at the table. Precisely one bottle per person, of course, containing juice that tasted like an odd blend of fruits and vegetables such as mangoes and celery, or kiwis and spinach. Whatever it was, it wasn't a flavor that anyone could recognize. Or wanted to.

Despite the inefficiency, Beth was enjoying the experience of it all. It was part of her personal understanding of the culture, providing her with another interlocking piece in the gigantic puzzle she had created for herself when she began to explore the world so many years before. Occasionally in her travels there were times when minor inconveniences had a way of becoming major hassles rather than merely quaint local idiosyncrasies being imposed upon a foreigner. But in this particular instance, the entire process was amusing to her. Part of it was the fact that she was traveling with a large group, and there was comfort in having so many fellow travelers share the struggles with her. Frequently, when Beth had to travel alone, the difficulties become magnified, causing major anxiety attacks, but this time she simply put it down as another page in her diary of traveling philosophy. A diary that she liked to call *The Essence of Travel*.

Getting away from the guides for the morning had been tricky. They were equally as adept at counting heads as hard-boiled eggs and slices of bread. It was especially tough for Beth because, being a journalist, she was always the first person they looked for. She had already informed Dr. Wolfe of her calculated attempt to slip away at the first opportunity, advising him that she would be sure to return in time for the afternoon outing. One thing that was good about the Russian travel system, it was easy to locate the group before, during or after a tour, because they always came back to where they started. Wolfe was highly supportive of Beth's curiosity, so they agreed that if anyone should happen to get suspicious of her whereabouts, he would just plead ignorance, and assure them that she would show up eventually.

Beth knew that she couldn't escape often. In the first place, her job was to record the activities of the trip for her paper and for the school. Secondly, she realized that she had an obligation to the school not to create a problem in an already difficult environment. Still, Beth rationalized that to give the story the proper impact, she needed to do some personal exploration.

The golden moment came during a tour of the *Central V.I. Lenin Museum*. Everyone gathered at a large sculpture of the one-time revolutionary leader, and it was there that they chose to take the traditional group picture. Beth was not among them. In the confusion and preparation for the photo, she slipped through a side door and never looked back. For one brief moment she felt like Steve McQueen, sans motorcycle, when he made his daring dash for freedom in *The Great Escape*. The getaway made her feel clever. After all, wasn't it part of the American psyche to find new and creative ways to succeed at a goal? This was nothing more than an exercise in exerting her independence, which was enough to bring a smile to Beth's face.

Her first stop was *St. Basil's Cathedral*. The frescoes and icons inside the building were not of particular interest to Beth. It was the exterior of the structure that was so stunning. The multitude and variety of the domes was magnificent, especially against the bleak canvas of the Soviet sky. At first, she began snapping pictures of individual domes, followed by combinations of the bulb-like structures from as many diverse angles as possible.

Remembering that her time was limited, Beth worked quickly to get as many photos as she could before moving on to capture whatever else she could document. She considered returning to the Kremlin, but there was really no need to go back. The group had visited there the day before, and though some closer study would have been worthwhile, Beth decided she should see something new and different.

One thing Beth learned during the tour on the previous day was that there were many "kremlins" in Russia. The translation of the word "kremlin" simply means "fortress." and many places throughout the country had "fortresses" which were built as a source of protection. Though Beth found the information to be noteworthy and interesting, she was also a bit disappointed. Somehow the idea of *THE KREMLIN* had a kind of power and majesty to it. *THE KREMLIN* always struck a note of intrigue and mystery in Beth's heart when she saw it in the movies or heard about it on the news. But it was different now that she had learned that there were dozens of other "kremlins" scattered all across the country, even if they weren't as vast as the one looming behind the gigantic red walls in Moscow.

It wasn't the first time Beth had been disillusioned by an item of trivia regarding the origin of a word. She had the same reaction when she discovered that "acropolis" was nothing more than a Greek word referring to "the upper fortified portion of a city." Damn! Beth wanted the Parthenon to be rising majestically from *THE ACROPOLIS*, not just a pretty building on top of AN acropolis. Of course, everyone called it the *THE ACROPOLIS*, but somehow knowing there were other "acropolises," or "acropoli," or whatever you called them, all over Greece only diminished the image. Now the Kremlin had lost some of its magic too.

Beth decided to take a quick look around *GUM* to get an idea of what people were shopping for. If in fact anyone was shopping at all. As she walked up the center of Red Square to the entrance of the department store, she began taking more pictures of the long lines of people waiting to view Lenin. It was an eerie scene. Except for the huge red wall in front of the Kremlin, there was virtually no color. The Russians were dressed entirely in black, standing beneath a dreary, overcast sky. The ground was frosted with a dusting of white from snow flurries that had begun in the early hours of the morning. At that time of year, in that part of the world, it didn't become daylight until nearly 10 a.m., and it was dark again by 2:30. So the buildings were mere silhouettes, creating little more than massive shapes that defined the parameters of the square.

Beth was preoccupied with her picture taking when she was startled by the muffled pressure of a gloved hand pushing down on her shoulder. The unexpected weight interrupted her concentration. Beth turned quickly to find herself looking up at a menacing Russian policeman. With the bulk of his winter clothing, the fullness of his black fur hat and the unfriendly scowl on his face, the officer was an imposing figure. He was also frightening. There was no trace of hospitality in either his countenance or his demeanor. He never spoke a word. Instead, the policeman used a short series of gestures to point first to the lines of people, then to the camera. Finally, he concluded his pantomime by waving his finger back and forth at Beth, and shaking his head to indicate "no".

Beth wanted to protest, but thought better of it. Everything had happened so quickly that she didn't have time to be scared. She did have the presence of mind to know that creating a scene would be pointless, and might even result in having her film confiscated. So she nodded humbly in agreement and shrugged her shoulders as if to say, "I'm sorry, no harm intended." Besides, she already had some pretty good pictures anyway. Why risk losing them now?

It was the first encounter of its kind during the trip. In every other situation Beth had been part of a group with Russian guides, and this had been her only opportunity to be on her own. To be honest, she had expected more events of a similar nature than what she had experienced thus far. On her first trip with the college the previous year, she went to Hungary and Romania. For some reason, Beth figured that the Soviet Union would be significantly more severe in its paranoia than either of those countries. Perhaps it was all the propaganda she had accumulated over the years from newspapers and television. Hungary turned out to be fairly tame, and in many respects, very much like a western European country. She quickly discovered that Romania however, under the regime of Nicolae Ceausescu, was the most Stalinistic of all the Communist bloc countries, including the Soviet Union. By comparison, Russia, with Yuri Andropov in power, seemed to have mellowed from the days of Leonid Breshnev. As a result, after the first few days in Moscow, Beth began to get a false sense of security that Russia wasn't nearly as intimidating as she initially expected. The incident with the policeman quickly snapped her back to reality and instilled in her a greater need for caution, respect and awareness of her surroundings.

Beth didn't intend to spend a lot of time browsing around *GUM*. Unlike most women, she had little personal interest in shopping as part of her travel experiences. Still, she was keenly aware that most of her female readers did not share that philosophy, and indeed, wanted to know about bargains and local specialties. With that in mind, she always made it a point to research at least some aspect of shopping for her articles. In this case however, *GUM* was more of a tourist attraction. It was more of an opportunity to observe an aspect of Russian lifestyle than a place to write about any great shopping ideas. Almost everything she would find would be of inferior quality, except for a few traditional arts and crafts that could just as easily be purchased out on the street.

The square footage of *GUM* was enormous. At first glance there was plenty of merchandise available even though the shopping areas had a starkness that was cold and uninviting. Closer inspection revealed that, in fact, there was not an abundance of products. To be sure there were plenty of boxes on display, which gave the illusion of shelves full of products, but the boxes were an empty façade. In reality, there was little to buy. In many places there were only one or two items of a particular commodity, and in the clothing and shoe departments, there was usually just a single unit of a certain size or color. There wasn't much variety in styles either. And very few, if any, products from western countries. When there was something of quality to be found, it was so glaringly superior next to the Russian-made merchandise on display that there was absolutely no comparison for the discerning shopper to make. Such items were rare however, because any time a first-rate product appeared on the shelves, it was usually gone in mere minutes. Often consumers would buy two or three quality items when they became available and take them home to their friends. The rationale being that the best things would be long gone before their friends could possibly return to make the purchase.

One thing Russians were experts at was adapting to their plight in order to make the best of a bad situation. For example, on any given day, since it was impossible to tell when there might be something of value to buy, friends would form shopping pools and take turns going to the store in the hope of being on the premises whenever any superior goods appeared.

Another trick was to make friends with someone who worked at the store. Having inside information was valuable because the store clerk could frequently provide advance notice about the availability of the quality products.

By virtue of their positions, clerks had a huge advantage over the general public. They could hold things back long enough to inform providers of other necessary services that the best merchandise was in stock. In this way, store personnel were often able to barter with doctors, automobile mechanics, repairmen or the like to arrange for assistance at a time when they were needed. It was a neat little system to avoid waiting for days or weeks for an appointment.

What fascinated Beth most were the lines. Lines everywhere. For several minutes she surveyed the situation, and it wasn't long before she understood what was taking place, the hard way. In an effort to provide employment for everyone, the Russian system for making a purchase was a masterpiece of inefficiency. A complete and total quagmire that staggered the imagination. The lines were not so much the result of a lack of something to buy, though that fact certainly added to the situation. Rather, they were caused mainly by the process itself.

To test the system, Beth decided to buy something. She looked around and spotted a small Russian-made transistor radio sitting on a shelf. Beth got into line and inched her way toward the counter. Knowing that when she finally arrived at the register the salesperson would speak no English, Beth simply pointed to the radio she wanted. Then, following the normal routine of conducting a purchase, she took out her Russian money to pay for it. For some reason the clerk wouldn't accept the rubles. Instead she began writing a page full of information on a large printed form. When the form was completed, the clerk tore the sheet off the pad, handed it to Beth and pointed to another line nearly halfway down the length of the store.

At first Beth didn't understand what the clerk was telling her, but eventually she realized that she was only at the first stop. It was merely the means of selecting the item she wanted to buy. There was another stage in the process. Beth moved to the next location and got into another line. More waiting. At long last she arrived at the counter, gave the saleswoman the chit and paid for the radio. The lady took the rubles and disappeared. Several minutes passed. The clerk wasn't gone very long, but the waiting period was uncomfortable, and to Beth it seemed interminable.

Beth fully expected the lady to have the radio with her when she came back. Instead the saleswoman gave her another voucher. Beth couldn't believe it. She stared down at the piece of paper trying to figure out what the Russian information said.

"Is there," came an unexpected voice from behind. Beth turned to see a large, blond Russian woman who was next in line. The woman looked to be in her mid-30s. She had a fair complexion and bright red cheeks, which were all the rosier from being indoors after braving the icy weather out in the square.

At first Beth was startled. She didn't expect to hear any English, especially in this place. "You go there," said the woman pointing to yet another line in the same approximate location where Beth had been in the first place. The woman seemed gruff at first, but it was obvious that she was trying to help. It was mostly her broken English that gave the impression of abruptness.

"But I don't understand," Beth replied in a bewildered tone.

"This line only for to pay. That line for radio."

Then it became clear. Beth would have to wait in yet another line! The paper she held in her hand was nothing more than a receipt verifying her purchase. It was only an authorization to pick up the radio. Three transactions. Three lines. All to make one simple purchase of a small pocket radio. The Russian mentality was an exercise in patience that defied description. Beth wondered how such a system would ever survive in the U.S. where attention spans were such that microwave ovens couldn't heat water fast enough, where fast food was a daily ritual and where television programs lasted only as long as it took to click the remote button.

"Come. I show you," said the woman.

Beth followed reluctantly. As they walked down through the aisle, the Russian woman did her best to make conversation. "You are American. I am Olga. Why you come to Soviet Union?"

"My name is Beth Jacobsen. I'm a writer," Beth replied. "I'm traveling with a group of university students who are visiting here to study in your country."

Beth spoke slowly and more deliberately than normal, and louder too. For some reason, when she was trying to be understood, she raised her voice. The strange thing was that it seemed to work. Nevertheless, she had a gut feeling that loud or not, Olga comprehended more than her limited vocabulary suggested. Being monolingual, Beth was always impressed by people who could communicate, even to the slightest degree, in a language other than their own.

Olga seemed pleased with Beth's response to her question. Then she learned why. "Is nice to meet you Beth Jacobsen. My brother is also writer. You would like to meet brother? Maybe you talk about work."

Beth was taken aback. She didn't know what to say. On the one hand, her journalistic curiosity was increasing with every step. Even so, her instincts told her to take Olga's proposal with caution. After all, she had only met this woman three minutes ago, and suddenly she was inviting her to meet her brother. If the brother was indeed a journalist, or a writer of some sort, it might be a worthwhile encounter to share ideas and to get some really good insights into a Russian point of view. But this could just as easily be something that Beth had no business getting involved in. There was a natural, and obvious, hesitation in her voice as she thought about the best way to approach the situation.

The two women reached the third line and stood at the rear creeping their way forward. Olga continued the conversation. "We get radio now. Very soon. Not much longer wait. My brother, you will meet him? You talk together?"

Beth kept trying to delay. "Yes, but ahhh, I cannot meet him today. I must be with my group. Perhaps tomorrow. Is that possible?"

"Is possible, yes," answered Olga without hesitation. She seemed determined to arrange the meeting. Beth kept trying to stall. "Tomorrow. You meet tomorrow."

Beth nodded. "OK. Yes we can get together tomorrow afternoon if you like. Where should I meet you?"

Beth chose to set up the meeting for the next afternoon so as to allow her time to decide exactly what she wanted to do. Her first thought was to see if Dr. Wolfe, or one of the other professors in the group, would go along out of academic curiosity. At the very minimum that would provide Beth with some protection. By setting a time for the next day Beth figured she could also be a "no show" and never have to see Olga again. It would be rude, but at least it would give her a way out if she concluded that something wasn't quite right.

"This is big square. You see church over there?" Olga was pointing to Red Square and the cathedral.

"You mean *St. Basil's*? The cathedral? Yes, I know it," answered Beth.

"We meet behind church. On corner. Is big square there also."

Beth thought for a moment and said, "All right. Is two o'clock OK?"

"Is good. Two o'clock. Yes. Tomorrow," said Olga in agreement. "Now we get radio. Why you buy Russia radio? Japan best. You get Japan radio easy in your country, no? Why you need Russia radio?"

Beth tried to be diplomatic. "Oh, it's just a souvenir. Something to bring back from the Soviet Union." It was a weak excuse. Beth knew that Olga knew that an American wouldn't take a Russian radio home as a souvenir. She smiled meekly and shrugged her shoulders. She could tell that Olga was ignoring the answer anyway.

At long last the radio arrived. Beth took the package from the clerk and then turned to her new acquaintance. "OK. We meet tomorrow. Two o'clock," said Olga.

"Yes. On the square behind the cathedral."

"Behind church, yes. Goodbye." Olga smiled and stuck out her right hand, which Beth shook. She smiled back, but it lacked confidence.

"Thank you," said Beth.

"Welcome," replied Olga, and then she turned and disappeared out the door of *GUM* into the sobering brutality of the Russian winter.

The more Beth thought about the strange events of the morning in *GUM* with Olga, the more she believed the incident wasn't totally accidental. She didn't know why Olga had spoken to her, but Beth felt certain there was more to it than simply helping her get a radio or meeting Olga's brother. It was entirely possible that there was no such person as Olga's brother, that he was an imaginary figure. As she mulled the encounter over in her mind however, Beth felt strongly that Olga's mysterious sibling really did exist. Furthermore, she also sensed that Olga was not up to something sinister. Though she couldn't quite put her finger on it, she knew that Olga hadn't given her the entire story. One thing was certain, if she did show up for the meeting, Beth would find out for sure the next day.

On the following morning Beth made her decision. If one of the professors would go along with her, she would meet Olga at the appointed time. If not, she would remain with the group and carry out her assigned duties. It was a perplexing problem because Beth knew that the arrangement could turn out to be a complete waste of time, or that it might also become a most enlightening experience. At this point there was just no way to tell which it might be.

The other aspect of the dilemma was trying to figure out another way to disappear again for a few hours. It didn't take long for Beth to come up with a solution for that situation. During the morning outing she would pretend to be ill. When the group returned to the hotel for lunch, she would explain that she didn't feel well enough to eat, and that she'd like to rest in her room for the remainder of the afternoon. She promised that a few hours of sleep would be enough to revive her so that she could rejoin everyone in the evening to attend a performance of the Moscow Circus.

At breakfast Beth asked Dr. Wolfe if anyone might want to go along with her that afternoon. She explained the reason for her request to Wolfe, with the hope that during the sightseeing excursion one of the professors might volunteer. At first Beth thought the president might object to a second departure in two days, but to the contrary. He was intrigued by the possibility of someone in the party getting closer access to the Russian people. In fact, he was fascinated enough by the prospects of the adventure that he almost decided to go himself. Further consideration told him that he needed to remain with the group. As a substitute, he got a positive response from Dr. Keene who was delighted to be able to tag along. Keene now had his own logistical problem of getting away, but Beth left that to his creativity, and never gave it another thought.

Beth and Professor Keene arrived at the square about fifteen minutes before two. Since they were unfamiliar with Moscow, they wanted to allow plenty of time to be sure they had their bearings correct. They went to the square by way of the subway, which was fast and efficient. On the way from the hotel to the area of Red Square and *St. Basil's*, Beth was impressed by the extreme depth of the metro stations. But the most notable thing was that each station was different and uniquely designed. They were beautiful, filled with chandeliers, mosaics and stunning works of art. In their own way, the metro stations of Moscow were miniature museums.

Once Beth and Dr. Keene emerged from the underground, they located the site where they were to meet Olga. Beth decided to take advantage of the extra time and look around. During the night the skies had cleared, and the overcast of the day before had been pushed back by a sheet of stunning blue. Even so, it was becoming increasingly darker as the sun was beginning to set. Temperatures were falling too, dipping even lower than they had been on the previous day.

Just down the block Beth noticed some street vendors selling goods from tiny covered stalls. She quickly scanned the scene to make sure there were no police around. When she was satisfied that she was momentarily safe from the watchful eyes of the law, Beth took out her camera and went to work. At one location a man was selling hot tea. Patrons exchanged their money for a token, which was then inserted into a vending machine. Rather than having Styrofoam or paper cups for the customers, the containers for the tea were glass mugs, which were used by everyone who purchased a drink. There were four or five of these communal tea mugs which always found their way back to the vending machine without ever being washed or cleaned in any manner.

Other stands were selling fruits and vegetables. The produce didn't look particularly appetizing, but it was available in relative abundance. Another vendor had various kinds of meat for sale. With the bitterly cold temperature, there was no need for refrigeration, so the merchant was able to display his wares right out in the open.

The ultimate surprise came when Beth spotted a stall that had more people around it than any other. The size of the crowd alone indicated that this had to be something special. Special it was, but Beth couldn't believe it when she discovered that the item creating such a throng was ice cream. Ice cream! On the streets of Moscow with temperatures well below freezing, these people were eating ice cream as if it was summertime in the park. It made Beth even colder just thinking about the idea. She knew that she had to take a picture because no one back home would believe it unless she brought back some kind of proof.

When Beth returned to the corner she was still shaking her head in bewilderment over the ice cream stall. It was nearly 2 p.m. now, and so far there was no sign of Olga. Dr. Keene was hopping up and down, alternating from one foot to the other to keep his circulation going. In the meantime, both he and Beth kept looking in all directions to see if they could locate their missing contact.

"How long do you think we should wait?" asked Beth.

"Well it's just two o'clock now," answered Keene. "We should give her a few minutes just because we don't know where she's coming from or how she's getting here. You never know what her situation might be."

"OK. But I think if she isn't here by 2:30 we should find someplace warm and get a hot drink."

"I'm all for that. A half-hour is fair." The professor smiled. It was comforting for Beth to have him along. Not only for the security he provided, but also just to have another opinion if decisions needed to be made.

At that particular moment Beth envied Dr. Keene's full growth of beard for the warmth it must be providing him. He had a moderate build and a pleasant professorial face. His black hair had just a twinge of gray at the temples giving him an air of dignity and wisdom. Though she had been traveling with the college group for several days now, Beth still did not know everyone in the party by name. It was nice to have a chance to get to know Dr. Keene better and to learn more about his career.

The professor had his doctorate degree in literature. His original plan for *Winternational* that year was to take a group of students to England to trace the footsteps of Shakespeare. A good portion of the program would have been centered in Stratford upon Avon, with additional research on Charles Dickens and Henry James in London, since all three had spent time there during their lives. But when Dr. Wolfe announced that he was taking a group to Russia, Keene scrapped his own proposal and decided to go to the Soviet Union instead. His theory being that England would be an easier target than Russia for a future study course, so why not take advantage of the immediate opportunity when it presented itself.

It was nearly twenty past two when Olga finally arrived. She apologized for her tardiness, but explained that she could not get away as early as she had planned. Expecting Olga's brother to be with her, Beth and Dr. Keene were surprised that she was alone.

"Olga, this is Dr. Keene. I asked him if he would like to join us. I didn't think you would mind," said Beth.

"No. Is good. I am Olga," replied the Russian woman.

"But where is your brother? I thought he was coming too?"

"We take taxi. We meet at home. Is still working. Will be there soon."

The story sounded suspicious to both Beth and Dr. Keene, but their interest was intensified by the idea of visiting a Russian family in their home. The two Americans figured that between them they could handle the situation, so they agreed to press on.

"Where do you live?" asked the professor trying to get an idea of which direction they would be going.

"Not far. There," said Olga pointing toward the eastern sector of the city. "Will not take long."

By now the city was dark though it was only 2:30. The streetlights were lit and Moscow was enveloped in a cocoon of midnight blackness in the middle of the day. Olga spent the next several minutes trying to hail a cab. Eventually she was successful, and she and Beth climbed into the back while Dr. Keene got up front. Olga said something to the driver in Russian, and the taxi lurched forward heading in a westerly direction. Keene realized right away that the car was not going where Olga said she lived. Almost as quickly he heard Beth speak up from the back.

"Are you sure this is the right way, Olga? I thought you lived in the other direction."

Olga was ready with an answer however. "Must go other place first. You help. Then we go to house."

"Help?" asked Beth. "Help do what? Is there a problem?"

"No problem," smiled Olga. "I get radio for you yesterday. You get radio for me today.

Beth still wasn't sure what was going on so she continued asking questions. "But how can I help you. I don't understand. Can't you buy a radio at *GUM*?"

"*GUM* no good. Only Russian radio in *GUM*. Need Japan radio. Japan is best. SONY. We go to *beriozka*."

"*Beriozka*? What is *beriozka*?" asked Beth.

"I think I know what it is," said Dr. Keene who was beginning to see what was happening. "I read a little about them before we left. It's a hard currency store where you can buy imported goods. Russians aren't allowed to shop in them, but they can go in with visitors. It's part of the government propaganda."

A light bulb suddenly went on in Beth's head. "I see. So Olga wants us to go in and find a SONY radio. We pay for it in dollars, she gives us rubles later in exchange and she gets the radio."

The professor nodded in agreement. "You help?" asked Olga. "We buy radio, OK?"

"OK," said Beth. Now she understood what had happened the day before in *GUM*. Olga wasn't really trying to help a confused American decipher the Russian shopping system. After all, Olga was in line right behind her when she spoke to Beth. When Olga realized that she could possibly get Beth to take her to the *beriozka* store, she got out of line and decided it was worth the gamble to meet an American. Then she'd try to figure out a way to get what she wanted.

It still wasn't clear to Beth why Olga didn't just explain the system to her in the first place. Perhaps Olga thought it was easier to do it this way than to confuse matters by trying to communicate in a series of fractured English sentences. But then what about the story of Olga's brother? Was it true? Did the brother really exist or was there more to this strange scenario that was yet to unfold?

The purchase of the radio in the *beriozka* store didn't take long, though it surprised Beth that they used the same system as the day before at *GUM*. She still had to make three separate transactions in order to buy the radio. The difference was that there were no lines, and Olga didn't waste any time making her decision. She knew exactly what she wanted.

When they returned to the taxi Olga paid Beth for the radio with roughly the dollar equivalent in rubles. Beth wasn't really concerned about the money, figuring it was worth the expense to see how this little drama played out. The only real problem now was that she had a purse full of rubles for which she had little or no use.

Olga leaned forward in the cab and gave the driver some instructions. "We go now to house. Is OK?"

Beth and Dr. Keene responded with a quick and emphatic, "Yes." At last they were on their way to accomplishing the original purpose of the trip.

Twenty minutes later the cab stopped in front of a high rise apartment building in the eastern part of Moscow. The building looked to be about fifteen stories high. Throughout the area there were similar buildings clustered about, all the same height, all the same architecture, all with the same cold, unwelcome outward appearance. Every one of them could have been built from the same blueprint. Beth looked around to take in the surroundings and made the observation that even on a sunny day, in the middle of spring, the buildings would still look threatening and ugly.

After paying for the cab, Olga moved rapidly to the front door of the building. Her demeanor changed almost as soon as they arrived. She seemed apprehensive and flustered, as if she was in a hurry to get away from the cab, to move off the street and into the building.

Once inside the small lobby of the apartment complex, Olga went hastily to the elevator and pushed the button. A few moments later the doors parted, and the threesome entered the tiny box that was barely large enough to accommodate them. Olga pressed the button for the sixth floor.

When the doors opened again at the sixth level, the trio got out and walked down the hallway to one of the apartments. A single light bulb provided the only illumination in the hall, making it feel dingier than it really was. Olga knocked. No one answered at first, but soon they heard a woman's voice from behind the door. Olga spoke to the woman for a few seconds, then came the sound of a chain lock sliding to one side and the door finally opened.

The woman inside clearly was not expecting company. She was dressed in a flimsy transparent robe which she wore over a black bra and white panties. On her feet she wore a pair of ragged, well-worn slippers. Her hair was in curlers, and though obviously embarrassed by the presence of Beth and Dr. Keene, she did her best to make their acquaintance while shielding herself from their inquisitive gaze.

Beth was even more confused now. Who was this woman? Why didn't she know they were coming? What had made Olga become so paranoid within the last five minutes? And where was this elusive brother who was yet to make an appearance?

The four of them were standing in a small entranceway to the apartment. To the left was a tiny kitchen, and off to the right was the living area. Other than that, there didn't seem to be any more rooms. There was a closet in the entrance hall where they were standing, but as far as Beth could tell, the only purpose for the area they were in was to serve as a connecting point for the other two rooms. Most of the space in the kitchen was taken up by an ironing board, which had obviously been in use by the mysterious female resident just prior to the unexpected visit. The remainder of the room was taken up by the bulk of a large German shepherd that sat quietly panting and drooling on the floor.

The main room of the apartment was approximately twelve feet wide and twenty feet long. At the far end of the room a large picture window looked out to the street and some of the other apartment buildings in the block. On the near wall there was a sofa which served a dual purpose as a bed at night. There was a small coffee table in front of the sofa and two chairs in front of that. The right hand wall was taken up by a tattered easy chair and another cot-like piece of furniture that extended to the back wall. Above the cot were a series of cabinets that resembled the overhead bins of an airplane, and the left side of the room featured a makeshift bookshelf with a few knickknacks and pictures plus a record player. There was only one visible sign of any recordings and that was an album jacket printed with the name "Chicago" on it. Finally, sitting in the far corner of the room on a small table was a television set with rabbit ears.

"Come," said Olga motioning to the right hand room. "You sit. I call brother. We talk. Then he come."

As the group moved to the living area Beth spoke up. "But isn't your brother here? Doesn't he know we are coming?"

"Yes. Brother knows. He say he come when you get here. I call. He come soon. You sit."

As Olga escorted Beth and Dr. Keene into the room, the other Russian woman went back to the kitchen. Olga made a motion to indicate that the two Americans should sit down while she made the phone call.

"I call now. Come right back."

"Is it all right if I take some pictures?" asked Beth as Olga started out of the room.

Olga nodded. "Is OK. Yes, you take."

For the next several minutes Beth flashed as many pictures as possible to document the interior of the room. She then moved to the picture window to see if she could get some shots of the apartment area, but it was already too dark outside. As she snapped her photos, she made small talk with Dr. Keene, occasionally looking at him with a perplexed expression as if to say "what have we gotten ourselves into?" They knew they couldn't talk out loud about anything important because whatever they said would easily be heard in the next room. Beth figured it was best to get her pictures quickly since there was no way to tell what might take place next, or whether another opportunity would arise.

From the kitchen came the sounds of a spirited discussion. The two Russian women were keeping their voices purposely low, and though it didn't sound like an argument, there was a definite edge to the conversation.

Beth finished her picture taking and moved to the sofa where she could speak with Dr. Keene in whispered tones. At first the chatter in the kitchen subsided, and then it became distinctly different. Olga's voice was louder now. She was using the telephone. As Olga continued to speak, the other woman entered the room and smiled sheepishly as she went to one of the cabinets. She reached up and pulled down a neatly folded dress and a pair of shoes. Then she backed out of the room as quickly as she could, trying to be as polite as possible, having no other way to make a graceful exit.

When Beth and Dr. Keene were alone in the room again, Beth spoke to him in a hushed voice. "What do you think is going on?" she asked.

"I'm not sure. This isn't Olga's apartment. That's pretty clear. But I don't know why we are here, and I don't understand why Olga is being so secretive with us."

"Should we ask her or is it better to wait? And who is this other woman? She was really surprised to see us."

"I think we should ask Olga to explain who the woman is and where we are, but maybe we should hold off about the secrecy. We don't want to make her less committal than she already is, and maybe she'll open up on her own," said the professor.

Time, or the lack of it, was becoming a factor. It was now after 4 p.m., and if the brother didn't show up soon, Beth and Dr. Keene would have to leave in order to get back to the hotel in time to meet the group. Finally Olga returned and sat down in one of the chairs across from the sofa.

"Brother coming. Little time. Very soon," said Olga. She sensed that Beth and Dr. Keene were growing impatient and might decide to leave. She seemed flustered at that possibility. At the very least, Olga's frustration was an indication that her brother would show up eventually, but the question was when, and whether there would be time enough to visit with him.

"Olga, who is the woman in this apartment?" asked Keene. He decided to be direct, thinking he might as well get some explanations while they waited.

"Brother's wife. Is his house. Three people in house. Brother. Wife. Sister of wife. Wife make food. You hungry? You drink wodka?" The words were barely out of her mouth when Olga's sister-in-law left the apartment on a mission to find refreshments.

"Vodka? Oh sure. Certainly. We love vodka." Dr. Keene glanced over at Beth. He didn't have a clue whether or not Beth drank vodka, but he took the initiative and spoke for them both. When their eyes met, he could tell that Beth wasn't any more thrilled about the idea of drinking straight vodka than he was. Nevertheless, they both knew that if this was a sincere attempt at Russian hospitality, then it was worth a try to go ahead and participate.

At the same time, Beth and Dr. Keene were relieved to get answers to some for their questions. Olga and her brother hadn't told anyone about the meeting, which explained why the wife was caught off guard by their sudden appearance at the door. Beth reasoned that Olga and her brother didn't say anything because the fewer people that knew about the visit the better. Beth had heard that Russians would sometimes attempt to meet people from beyond the Iron Curtain, but it was only now that she was beginning to understand the extremes of their efforts in order to make such contacts. It also explained Olga's sudden change of personality when the taxi dropped them off at the building. She trusted no one, and if possible, she wanted to be sure there were no witnesses to her covert maneuver of getting Beth and the professor into the building.

The reason the brother wasn't at home when they arrived now seemed simple. Olga was no more certain that Beth would show up for their meeting than Beth had been about Olga. How intriguing Beth thought to herself. Here in miniature was a perfect example of the same mistrust that existed between the governments of their two countries. The only difference was a matter of scale and magnitude. How sad that the lives of these people had come to this level of desperation to learn the truth, yet how encouraging that they even dared to make the attempt. How awful it must have been to live every day of their lives not knowing who to trust or where to draw the line between fact and fiction. How frustrating must it be to live in a world where everything they did was an adjustment, not to obtain luxuries mind you, but merely to achieve life's basic necessities of food, shelter and clothing.

As the threesome continued the process of getting acquainted, the front door opened and a man and young woman walked into the room. The man was about 6 feet tall with dark hair and a solid frame. He looked to be in his early 40s. The woman was 20, or thereabout, and she was a vision of loveliness. At roughly 5-feet-5 with medium length black hair and deep brown eyes, she could have easily been a model.

Everyone rose to their feet. Olga exhaled a deep sigh of relief that at long last her brother had arrived. With her limited English, Olga attempted to make introductions.

"Please. This brother. Name of Roslin. And this, Tanya. Tanya also live here with brother and wife."

Dr. Keene moved forward to shake hands and to introduce himself and Beth in order to make it easier for Olga. "I'm Dr. Paul Keene, and this is Beth Jacobsen." Beth nodded and then moved closer to offer her greetings.

Roslin appeared shy and uncomfortable, but Tanya was brimming with poise, confidence and an infectious smile. "Roslin and I are very pleased to meet you. Thank you for coming. Roslin does not speak any English, but I will translate for him," said Tanya in nearly perfect English tinged with a slight British accent.

"Your English is excellent. Where did you learn to speak so well?" asked Beth.

"At the university. I am studying English there," replied Tanya. "Let's sit down so we can talk. Roslin has many questions to ask you."

Tanya moved to the easy chair by the wall as Keene and Beth returned to the sofa. Roslin and Olga sat across from the coffee table. Olga was relieved to have Tanya do most of the talking. It was tiring for her to think and speak with her basic knowledge of English. Especially since she did not use it very often.

Except for the navy blue sweater with "Adidas" embroidered upon the left breast, Roslin's clothing looked Russian-made. By contrast, Tanya was wearing a black "Land's End" jacket over a light gray sweater. She also had on black jeans, giving her entire ensemble a "westernized" appearance. A stranger walking into the room would never assume that she was Russian. In fact, Beth and Dr. Keene were having a difficult time believing it themselves.

For the first ten or fifteen minutes the conversation centered on general chitchat. Roslin was indeed a writer, but purely as a hobby. He was a factory worker by trade. With Tanya's assistance, Roslin had taken to writing essays and poetry about life in the Soviet Union. He had long been curious about the freedom of expression that Beth had in her profession in the United States, and knowing this, Olga had made the effort to establish contact when she learned that Beth was a writer.

Both Roslin and Olga had been chain smoking Russian cigarettes from the moment they sat down, but Tanya did not participate. Not only was she not smoking, neither was she drinking. It didn't take long for Beth and Keene to realize that they were in the presence of a significant philosophical shift between Soviet generations just within that single family unit. There was no way to determine how long it might take to complete the transition, but Tanya clearly represented a bold new outlook for the future of the country.

Moments later, Roslin's wife returned with a selection of small pastries, which she brought into the living room, along with a bottle of vodka and some glasses. While Tanya drank tea, Beth and Dr. Keene accepted the vodka so as not risk offending their hosts.

As the discussion continued, it gradually focused upon the political perspectives of the two countries. There was great interest in obtaining direct knowledge from each other. The probing from both sides became increasingly deeper and more profound as everyone became more comfortable with each other. It was soon obvious that each side had been dramatically influenced by the propaganda of their respective governments. Despite the fact that the Americans had far greater access to news and information about the Soviet Union, the Russians were astonished by the amount of misinformation they were hearing from their guests regarding their country. By the same token, Beth and the professor were not at all surprised by the fearful points of view the Russians had of Americans, though they were amazed at the intensity of their ideas.

Tanya had an explanation about the Russian viewpoint that made sense. "We get information in many ways," she said, "but most of it is indirect. Almost always the news we hear is distorted. For us there is no way to know exactly where the lies end and where the truth begins. Russians know that what we see on television and read in our newspapers is what our government wants us to know. We understand that they are telling us what they want us to hear, but what we don't know is how much of what they have told us is true."

"Like everything else in our country, we must struggle for the information we want and need, and we try to find it in many ways. Sometimes we talk to friends who have met with people from the west such as yourselves. If they have conversations as we are having now, they will tell us what they have learned from such meetings. But you must understand that often there is a language problem during this sharing of information, and therefore, the details are not always translated correctly."

"Sometimes the information we receive does not come directly from our friends, but instead from friends of our friends. So the stories often change before we hear them. Then we must try to sort out the truth from those details as well."

Tanya continued with her insightful commentary. "When we have the chance, we try to meet people from the west, but even when we have direct contact, we cannot know for certain how much of what they are telling us is true either. We believe that Americans are very honest. We also have learned that Americans are open and friendly, and wish Russians no harm in the way that we are often told by our government. We can see that people are much the same all over the world, except for cultural differences, of course. But still we must be careful not to believe everything we see or hear, because Americans have so many of their own opinions and ideas about things, and much of what we learn comes from a very different way of life and outlook upon the world. So we never seem to have a very clear picture of what is true or right for us. Whether what we learn is good or whether it is bad does not matter, because it is always distorted."

"Do you have contact with Americans often?" asked Beth.

"No," Tanya answered, "this is very unusual. It can be quite dangerous for us. We are never certain if anyone is watching us. Officials say that if we talk with outsiders they will only tell us lies. They explain that they are protecting us from the lies, and only our government can give us the truth. They can punish us severely if they think we are getting too close to foreigners. A meeting such as this is very risky for us, but we know that sometimes we must do it."

The discussion went on for another half-hour with several toasts in between. Roslin was only able to listen and nod during most of the conversation, but he did venture forth some questions through Tanya in Russian. As time moved along the vodka began to take effect, and Roslin became less shy and more at ease. With the passage of time the whole group grew less formal. They liked each other, and there were genuinely good feelings that they were being open and sincere in expressing their opinions.

The only time Beth felt on the spot came when Roslin asked the question, "What about Reagan? Why is he so much against the Soviet Union?"

Beth hesitated in her response. She knew what her personal beliefs were, but she was not familiar with the professor's politics since she had really only gotten to know him within the past few hours. While it was entirely possible that they agreed on the subject, it was also likely that they didn't. Beth could see what was happening. Just as Tanya had explained a few minutes before, there was conflict in trying to describe what she thought was true and what was not.

Fortunately for Beth, Keene spoke up and gave a detailed answer of his own. As she suspected, the professor's ideas were vastly different from hers. Beth decided it was best to let it pass. She was not here to discuss American politics from an adversarial framework, nor did she desire to create a controversy with a fellow American when she had an opportunity to learn more about the lifestyles and the feelings of the Russian people. Besides, the vodka was having its effect on her too, and though Beth was still absorbing all that was happening, she was beginning to get a slight buzz which could seriously effect her ability to communicate coherently.

She glanced down at her watch. Almost 5:30. Time to go. It had been a worthwhile and rewarding afternoon. It was an experience forever etched in Beth's memory. She had taken a number of pictures of Roslin, Olga and Tanya during the course of the visit, and now as the session was winding down everyone began exchanging addresses and phone numbers.

"Roslin will call for a cab," said Tanya. "Your hotel is only fifteen minutes away."

Roslin went to the kitchen and made the call. Tanya explained that they knew a driver who lived in another building, and that he would be ready in a few minutes.

"We will be here for two more days," said Beth as they began the general process of parting ways. "If there is time, perhaps I can call you again, and we can talk more."

"Yes. That would be fine. We can arrange it," responded Tanya.

Roslin was at the window at the far end of the room. He looked out and saw the cab, and signaled to the driver that Beth and Keene were on their way.

Tanya looked at Beth and said, "It is better if you can go down alone. The taxi will just be to the left at the corner of the building. I hope you don't mind going down by yourselves."

"Not at all. Thank you for all of your gracious hospitality," said the professor.

"I will write to you when I return to the United States," added Beth.

"Good," said Tanya. With that everyone said goodbye and hugged each other as if they had been friends for decades rather than only a few hours.

Outside in the darkness, the temperature seemed to have dropped even further. Beth and Dr. Keene climbed into the taxi, and shortly after 6 o'clock they were safely back at their hotel.

*   *   *   *   *

The activity for the next evening was to attend a performance of the *Bolshoi Ballet*. When two members of the Wingate group didn't feel up to it and requested to remain behind to rest, Beth immediately asked Dr.

Wolfe if she could offer the tickets to Tanya and Olga or Roslin. She thought it would be an ideal way to establish further contact, as well as a nice gesture to afford their new Russian friends the opportunity to experience their own world famous ballet.

Early the following afternoon, on the day of the performance, Beth made a call to Roslin's apartment but there was no answer. A couple of hours later she tried again. This time Beth recognized Tanya's voice when she answered the phone in Russian. "Tanya, this is Beth Jacobsen."

There was a long pause at the other end of the line.

"Tanya, I've been given a couple of tickets to the *Bolshoi* for tonight. I was wondering if you and Roslin or Olga might like to join us."

Another long pause. Then the voice said something in Russian, and finally, there was a click. Without warning or any inkling that she understood a word of what Beth said, Tanya hung up.

After another day of sightseeing in Moscow, the *Winternationals* traveled on to Leningrad for several days before flying back to the United States. As promised, when Beth returned home she wrote a long letter to Olga, Roslin and Tanya thanking them for taking time during that dark January afternoon to allow her and Dr. Keene to visit them in their home. She told them about the remainder of the trip with the Wingate group, and concluded with an offer to be sure to visit if they ever had the opportunity to come to the United States.

Beth never received an answer. She never knew if the letter reached its destination or if her friends were just too afraid to reply. Whatever became of her three Russian acquaintances would remain a mystery. The photos she took were visual proof that the events of that day did indeed occur, but in those few short hours, Tanya had conveyed the same fears to Beth about life in the Soviet Union that she and her family had learned to deal with on a daily basis. Change was surely coming to the Soviet Union. It was inevitable. But the change would be painfully slow, and often it would be excruciatingly difficult.

In the end, Beth would always have questions about what she had witnessed and experienced during that brief time in the Soviet Union. But she also knew that the Russians would continue asking their questions too, and she prayed that one day they would find their way to the truth and get the answers they were so desperately seeking.

TREASURES OF LUCERNE

Lucerne, Switzerland was beginning to feel like a second home for Beth Jacobsen as her train pulled along the platform of the recently renovated railway station. There was a time when everything in her travels had been new and fresh, but now Beth's career had enough mileage behind it that she was periodically returning to certain destinations, and they were becoming comfortable, like old friends. She often recalled the words of one of her earliest traveling companions, Doris Blackstone, who had boldly proclaimed that "I want to go every place once before I see any place twice." That comment still resonated with Beth. At the time she had regarded Doris as a veteran journalist whose vast knowledge and sage acumen meant that she most assuredly had to be correct. Paul Fussell had a similar perspective in *The Norton Book of Travel* when he wrote, "the wise traveler learns not to repeat successes but tries new places all the time." Now that she considered herself a veteran globe-trotter, Beth had modified that philosophy. There was something to be said for returning to a destination from time to time, to relive special memories, and, more importantly, to establish some traveling roots. It was comforting to have two or three bases that she could count upon as safe havens when she was far from home. One of Beth's favorite writers, the well known adventurer Paul Theroux, echoed the idea of going back to certain places because it afforded him the chance to trace their evolution, to see how they had changed within the context of history. To Beth's way of thinking, that point of view only heightened her desire to explore new destinations, and certainly did nothing to diminish her wanderlust spirit.

Ever since she was a little girl, Beth had yearned to visit Switzerland. Maybe it was because her father had worked for a Swiss company, and he was forever bringing home pictures and souvenirs from his office. In her heart she knew it had to be more than that, though she really couldn't pinpoint the allure. Perhaps it was her childhood fondness for *Heidi*. Whatever it was, Beth had now traveled to Switzerland more than any other country. Her current trip was probably her eighth or ninth visit to Lucerne. She had lost count, and it worried her that she might be getting blasé about her good fortune to travel the world.

Like so many Swiss railway stations, Lucerne was bustling with people involved in the perpetual act of coming and going. It was the first time Beth had been there since the remodeling had been completed, though she did see it once or twice during the construction phase. It was now a state-of-the-art tri-level facility with the departure platforms on the middle floor at street level, and most of the services such as ticketing, information, lockers, fast food and rest rooms down below. There were even tunnels under the main streets that let passengers avoid the traffic above by providing easy access to the pedestrian areas, while also offering refuge during inclement weather.

On the upper level there was a sit down restaurant belonging to a franchise known throughout Switzerland as *Bahnhof Buffet*. The food in these establishments was always excellent, frequently serving some of the best meals in town. On any given day, it was not uncommon to see locals eating lunch or dinner at the railway station, even if they weren't traveling anywhere. In addition to the restaurant, the administrative offices were also located on the third floor.

From the upper two elevations of the station there were good views of the lake steamer docks directly across the street. A couple blocks away, diagonally to the left stood the famed Chapel Bridge with Lucerne's Old Town just beyond. The ancient wooden structure, which has been the symbol of the city for centuries, created international headlines when it burned in the early 90's. Anyone who travels to Lucerne is forever captivated by the bridge, so the fire was devastating to visitors from around the globe. The Chapel Bridge is such an important landmark to the heritage of the country that, after the fire, it was rebuilt in less than a year in time for the celebration of Switzerland's 700th birthday. During the restoration the decision was made to let it age naturally, and for the time being at least, the newness of the wood robbed it of much of its medieval charm. Beth had been in Lucerne only a few weeks after the fire, and the charred remains had left a far greater impression upon her than she expected they would. Now she was seeing the updated version for the first time, and her feelings were bittersweet. She was thrilled that the bridge was once again standing proudly, as it had for centuries, but she was melancholy that its proud history had been replaced by timbers that were not even trees when the original bridge was built.

This junket to Lucerne was the midpoint of a whirlwind tour of the country focusing upon Switzerland's artistic and cultural history. The idea came about as a result of a massive promotional survey by the Swiss government to learn more about why people travel to their country. In most cases the results were predictable. Scenery, transportation, small villages and towns, and the people were the responses that were readily anticipated. But there were two other categories that caught nearly everyone by surprise; cuisine and culture.

When Beth received a press release from the tourist office identifying the six primary reasons why travelers visited Switzerland, the concept of going there for its art and culture sounded like an intriguing angle for a story. Beth reveled in doing features with odd twists to them. They were among the best travel stories she had ever written. She had long ago made a solemn promise to herself that, whenever possible, she would take advantage of any story that uncovered some tantalizing off-the-beaten-path theme. Without hesitating, she had contacted the tourist office with a proposal. They were thrilled with the idea, and before she knew it, Beth found herself immersed in a world of museums, galleries, castles, artists and collectors, plus a host of other art related subjects she had never imagined before. From the outset Beth knew the project would be interesting, but she had no idea that it would evolve into one of the most provocative assignments she had ever undertaken.

Sylvia Elsner was waiting at the end of the railway platform when the train slowly came to a halt. The platform was a traditional place to greet arriving travelers, especially when meeting them for the first time. The only information Sylvia required was Beth's point of departure and the arrival time. The efficiency of the Swiss Travel System did the rest. Since she had never met Beth before, Sylvia stood at the end of the platform holding a small rectangular sign in front of her with Beth's name on it, just to be certain they wouldn't miss each other.

The itinerary had been a steady sequence of one new encounter after another. Beth would meet someone in one town, spend a few hours with them and then quickly move on. After a few days, the process had become exhausting. It was now day four of an eight-day journey, and already Beth had visited more than 15 museums. Trying to keep all the information and the minute details straight was overwhelming, but surprisingly she was beginning to notice that a picture was developing and a storyline was emerging.

Much of the difficulty in the itinerary was the task of constantly making new acquaintances. Some of the people were easy to deal with, others were more demanding. In this case, Beth could tell from the moment she arrived that Syvlia's enthusiasm would make this leg of the program a delightful experience.

As it turned out, Sylvia didn't even need her sign, she spotted Beth immediately as she walked up the platform, greeting her with a wave and a hospitable smile as though they were lifelong friends. When Beth finally drew near to her, the Swiss woman dispensed with the formality of the customary handshake, choosing to hug her instead.

"Hello Beth, I am Sylvia Elsner. Welcome to Lucerne. Anders says to tell you hello, and he apologizes that he could not be with you today."

Sylvia was referring to Anders Becker who had been head of the tourist board in Lucerne for years. Beth had met him on several occasions during previous visits, and the fact that he was still there in the same position reinforced a feeling of security in the time line of her travels. There was comfort in the knowledge that Anders had remained at the same post all those years. It gave continuity to things. The director was an interesting chap having served a tour in the Swiss Guard in Rome during his youth. The Swiss Guards are assigned as protection for the Pope at the Vatican. It is regarded as a great honor to be granted such an appointment, and Anders' tales about his duties were fascinating to listen to.

"Please tell Anders that I'm sorry I missed him as well, but that gives me a good reason to come back. Anyway, I know that you'll show me everything."

"Oh yes, I'm very excited about this. You know usually we take people around and just show them all the things in the guidebooks, but this is different. I think you will enjoy it very much. I know I will."

Sylvia had a bubbly personality. She was medium height with a slender frame but amply buxom for her size. Her short blond hair was ideal for her facial features, which gave her a youthful appearance though she was probably in her mid-forties. Outwardly she was enthusiastic and expressive with the type of charisma that often made things appear better than they really were. Even so, there was nothing phony or pretentious about her at all.

"We will make two stops. First we go to the *Picasso Museum* and later to the *Hans Erni Haus*. You know I have lived in Lucerne all of my life, and Hans Erni is the most well known artist in Switzerland, but I have never met him. So you see this will be a real treat for me as well as for you."

Sylvia could not contain her joy at the prospect of meeting Hans Erni. The two women crossed the river by way of the Chapel Bridge, then turned left and walked along the waterfront. After a couple of blocks they came to a series of steps leading up to the town hall and the main square of the Old Town.

"I have made arrangements for Lady Rosengart to join us at the *Picasso Museum,* if you don't mind," said Sylvia as they started up the stairs.

Beth felt a little foolish because she didn't always know or understand how each person related to a particular site. With her helter-skelter program, it was impossible to keep track of it all. Sometimes it made her uneasy that she was not able to speak with authority about a particular person or subject. "Now who is Lady Rosengart?" she asked in one of her moments of unpreparedness.

"She owns the *Picasso Museum.* I think you will find that she is most interesting," answered Sylvia. The two women reached the top of the steps and turned right down a narrow street just beyond the town hall.

A few houses down, on the right hand side of the alley, they came to a sign which simply read, *"Picasso Museum".* It was amazing to Beth that in all the times she had been to Lucerne, and as often as she had been down this walkway, she had never noticed either the sign or the museum. Now she wondered how many other people had done the same thing because they had been so engrossed in shopping or talking that they simply passed it by.

"Here we are," said Sylvia. "This is a very old building, dating to the 14th century. Isn't it a wonderful place for a museum?"

Sylvia was right about that. It was indeed a marvelous location. Because of the stone interior, the temperature inside was about ten degrees cooler than outside. There were wide, ancient steps leading to the second floor gallery where the main collection featured a priceless selection of Picasso's paintings, etchings and woodcuts. The stairs to the third floor, and the upper gallery, were lined with the black and white photographs of American photographer David Douglas Duncan. Over the years Duncan became a close friend of Picasso by highlighting much of the artist's life in pictures. Now his photographs were the lifeblood of the little museum by providing insights into the soul of Picasso. Insights that gave further depth to his art. The photos were works of art in their own right, for they breathed with the essence of the artist. Though Picasso's paintings had been created by one of the great masters of artistic history, it was the photographs by Duncan that brought the museum together. They fleshed out the space so that Picasso's work became more than a series of paintings hanging on walls. What Duncan's photographs did so masterfully was to capture the process of creative genius in progress, and to brilliantly freeze that process in time.

"Frau Rosengart will be here shortly," said the lady at the reception desk who had been expecting Sylvia and Beth. "Perhaps you would like to go across the hall to her apartment for some hot tea and berliners? Yes?"

"That would be lovely," replied Sylvia, giving her approval while nodding to Beth at the same time to see if she agreed.

There was an empty space of approximately 20 feet between the museum and the Rosengart apartment, as if there had long ago been a road between the two buildings which were now combined into a single structure.

"Lady Rosengart loves to entertain in this apartment because it has such a wonderful view of our city," said Sylvia as they entered the elegant living room. "Come let me show you what I mean."

Beth followed Sylvia to a pair of glass doors that opened out to a balcony overlooking the street below with the River Reuss rushing beside it. Just to the left, the Chapel Bridge stood proudly surveying the waters of the Lake of Lucerne that spilled into the rapid flow of the river. From this perspective the bridge appeared even more dominating than it had from ground level, looming in such a way that Beth felt as though she could reach out and touch it.

The view was stunning. Because of its location in a bowl surrounded by mountains, Lucerne is often overcast, but on a clear day the Alps are breathtaking, peering over the lake and its ancient bridge. On this day the sky was bluer than Beth had seen it on any of her previous visits, and the bridge seemed like a centerpiece that was chiseled into the tableau of the living canvas of blue and green and white. The rushing river beneath the bridge reminded Beth that water is Switzerland's only natural resource, and that every major city in the country is situated on a lake or a river, or both. A delightful bit of trivia to recall as she stood transfixed by the familiar scene she was viewing for the first time from a balcony perspective.

The Lake of Lucerne snuggles within the cradle of Swiss history, which makes it a favorite resort that is popular with the Swiss as well as tourists. The Swiss Confederation was established at the far end of the lake in 1292, when three cantons declared their independence from Austria and formed a new nation. It was also in this region that the legendary William Tell shot an apple off his son's head. A deed for which he was immortalized in music by Rossini and poetry by Schiller, thereby placing the crossbow expert in the annals of folklore forever. At the same time, his feats of skill thrust him into the history books as Switzerland's national hero.

Perhaps it was merely the mood of the moment, but something powerful was overtaking Beth. The combination of the converging elements as she stood on the elevated landing was an awesome experience. The history, the art, the music, the literature and the stunning beauty of the setting were almost too much to comprehend in a single fleeting moment of time. In a matter of hours it would be catalogued as little more than a memory among Beth's growing list of treasured occasions. She tried to memorize every detail, to savor every second, realizing that one day when she returned, she would only be able to tell others that she had been in this spot without being able to bring them there. She knew this was a rare opportunity that had been granted to her purely by virtue of her job description. One of those magical moments that made travel her passion and drove her to constantly seek equally rewarding life experiences. Events that breathed texture into her own character just as each loving stroke of an artist's brush caressed life into the fabric of a canvas.

When she returned to reality Beth could hear Sylvia's voice getting louder from the far end of the room. "Would you care for some tea, Beth? Beth, tea? Berliner?"

Beth awoke from her reverie and finally responded. "Oh yes, please. No milk thank you."

"These berliners are wonderful. Have one. They come fresh every day from the bakery down in the village."

Sylvia was right, as usual. Berliners are, in the most basic terms, nothing more than jelly doughnuts, but these had a distinctive, delicate flavor that Beth found irresistible. For the next quarter of an hour, the two women became acquainted with each other, detailing the stories of their lives, talking about their families and sharing other personal background information.

After two berliners, a cup of tea and several good laughs, Angela Rosengart arrived and entered the room. She was a tall woman, in her early 70s, with graying hair that was pulled back into a tight bun. Despite her gaunt features, her movements were elegant and poised. She possessed a flair that was immediately noticeable, and her stylish clothing left little doubt that she was also a woman of independent means.

"Frau Rosengart, this is Beth Jacobsen. She is a journalist from North Carolina in the United States doing some newspaper articles about Swiss culture, and she would like to interview you for a few minutes," said Sylvia. "I have been telling Beth about your museum, and a little bit about how you became interested in Picasso, but I am sure I don't know the whole story. I explained to Beth that one of the portraits downstairs is a picture of you that Picasso did when you were a young woman."

The elderly collector smiled at Beth before responding to Sylvia's introduction. Then she shook hands and said, "Yes, that was many years ago I am afraid. It is so nice to meet you, Miss Jacobsen. Thank you for coming to see us in Lucerne. I must say that I am honored that you would visit our little museum."

Beth could sense that Lady Rosengart was unusually shy for a woman of her stature. There was a lack of confidence in her English causing her to speak hesitantly though she possessed an excellent vocabulary. Beth knew that Rosengart was truly humbled by the idea of being included in her articles. "I too am honored Frau Rosengart. It is such a great pleasure to actually meet someone who knew Senor Picasso. This is a wonderful opportunity. And you're apartment is simply beautiful. You must be very happy living in such a lovely setting."

"Yes, I am most fortunate to be surrounded by so much beauty. Manmade and also natural."

"How did you come to meet Picasso?" asked Beth.

"Oh I was very young. Only nineteen, I think. My father was a collector, and he had a little gallery here in Lucerne. He was a proud man. He wanted all of his customers to think that he was the personal friend of all the great masters of art in that era, so he did a lot of, how do you say it, name dropping."

"And did he really know all of those great artists personally?"

"Well, yes and no. In many cases he had met them, but only at exhibitions and auctions. They were not what you would call his friends, or even acquaintances, though he had been introduced to many of them at one time or another."

Sylvia was listening as intently as Beth. She had heard bits and pieces of the story from time to time, but never from Lady Rosengart herself.

"One day my father decided to take me along to an exhibition where Picasso was showing many of his most important paintings. He had met Picasso once or twice, so to hear my father tell it, they were the very best of friends, but that was only in my father's mind. At that time I was very naive about the world. My father very much wanted me to make the acquaintance of the great artist himself, to impress me I suppose, at how well they knew each other. When we were introduced, Picasso looked at my father and told him right away that he must allow me to pose for him. He said that I was the most beautiful woman he had ever seen, and that it would be a sin not to capture my image upon the canvas."

"Wow," exclaimed Beth with glee, "You must have been thrilled. How did you react to such a compliment from such a famous person?"

"Well of course, I was very flattered," answered Rosengart. "But I also knew in my heart that Picasso thought every woman he met was the most beautiful. At that moment however, it didn't matter. His adulation was most charming. I could not resist him, even if he had not been such a wonderful painter. Naturally, my father was also delighted. It was even more important for him because he believed it would allow him to be closer to Picasso than ever before."

"So what happened next? I know that you sat for him because I've seen the portraits in your gallery, but how did it take place?" asked Beth with increasing interest.

"Picasso asked my father when it might be possible to schedule an appointment for the sitting. He was a most demanding person. Of course, my father would have agreed anyway, but Picasso didn't even wait for the answer. They made the arrangement, and two weeks later I was posing for him. I sat for Picasso on three separate occasions, but over the years I met him more than fifty times, and each time, I wrote the encounter down in my diary. Naturally, my father was now granted the privilege of knowing Picasso better than he would have otherwise, so it made him very happy to live out his fantasies thinking he was the artist's very best friend in the world."

"What a thrilling story. Imagine being so captivating to Pablo Picasso that he insisted you pose for him, not once, but three times."

"What was it like sitting for him?" asked Sylvia who was now sitting on the edge of her seat waiting for more details.

"I must say that at first I was quite scared because I knew of his work, and I thought that perhaps I would come out looking like one of those abstracts that made him so famous. But in the end, it was wonderful because, as you can see from the works in the gallery, he captured my likeness as a young woman with his own special interpretation. I was ecstatic about the finished work. That's when I decided to collect more of his paintings and to have a museum of my own."

"Was it intimidating for you?" asked Beth.

"Oh yes, very much so. Of course, I had all of my clothes on for the sitting, but I did not know if he would leave them on in the picture. Not only did he have a fondness for the ladies, but also a great love of naked ladies. He was very intense. There was something hypnotic about him. I could not move. I dared not breathe. It was those Spanish eyes. Those deep, dark Spanish eyes. They went through me like arrows. I could feel his gaze piercing my soul, as if he was eating me with his eyes. But it was marvelous. I am a little embarrassed to say it, but it was a very sensual experience. And the best part was that he did not make me look funny or naked in the portrait." Lady Rosengart leaned back, laughing apologetically at her confession.

Beth and Sylvia joined her in the amusement of her disclosure, partly out of envy and partly for the refreshing candor of such a delightful person who was recalling the intimacy of events in her life over half a century ago. The spontaneity of the moment put everyone at ease. "Would you care for more tea," offered Lady Rosengart, still reacting to her sudden indiscretion. "Or perhaps a glass of wine."

"I'll have another cup of tea," said Sylvia.

"Thank you, no," answered Beth. "Tell me Frau Rosengart, how did you acquire these marvelous photographs?"

"When my father died, he left me his collection of paintings. I kept only the Picasso's and sold the rest so that I could acquire additional Picasso's of my own. One day I happened to meet David Duncan at an exhibition of his work, which documented the life of the artist in black and white photographs. I inquired about the possibility of purchasing his entire portfolio, and so I did. And now you may also view those pictures in my museum."

"It's a unique idea. The photographs really show Picasso as a person, as well as an artist, in a way that simply viewing the artwork alone does not. They are truly an insight into the man, and his genius.

"Yes, I think so as well. In this way, I feel you begin to know and to understand the man behind the art, and you come away with a sense of his dedication to his craft. I believe you can also see his complexity both as a person and also as an artist. This is what I wanted to show in the space of my gallery, but you know, I think perhaps it is even better than I had imagined."

Lady Rosengart handed Sylvia another cup of tea. "Oh it's fantastic what you have done," she said with great enthusiasm while taking the saucer from her hostess.

"You know, it's a very interesting story about Picasso and Duncan how they met. Unbelievable really," added Rosengart.

"What do you mean?" asked Beth.

"Well, Duncan was a wonderful photographer for *LIFE* magazine during the war, and he had a good friend who also knew Picasso quite well. During a casual conversation one day, Duncan asked his colleague if it might be possible to arrange an introduction for him with the artist. Well the friend felt a great imposition had been placed upon him, but a short time later he passed the message along to Picasso. To his surprise the artist responded by saying that any friend of his was welcome and that Duncan could stop by whenever he liked."

"No doubt Duncan jumped at the opportunity," said Beth.

"Oh yes, very much so. Picasso knew of Duncan's reputation, and he was apparently intrigued by his creativity as a famous photographer, so the two men had much in common, though they worked in entirely different disciplines."

"What happened after that?" asked Sylvia sipping her tea.

"One day, when he was on an assignment near the place where Picasso lived, Duncan took his first opportunity to call on the great master. However, like so many artistic people, Duncan was a little eccentric, and rather than calling ahead first, he just showed up at Picasso's door. He knocked but there was no answer. He waited a long time, but still no one came. Duncan banged loudly again, and he was almost ready to leave when Picasso's mistress opened the door to see who was causing the disturbance. "I am Jacqueline," she said, "Can I help you?" Duncan still had his cameras around his neck because he had been working in the area and had not even stopped to put away his equipment. He explained to Jacqueline who he was and why he was there. She excused herself for a moment, leaving Duncan standing in the doorway, and then a few minutes later she returned. "Pablo is upstairs taking a bath," she said, "But he says to tell you to come right up." Sure enough when Duncan walked into the room, there was Picasso sitting in the tub. Duncan could not resist. He began snapping photographs from the moment he arrived, and he never quit. From that day forward, Duncan spent years taking pictures of Picasso, telling the story of his life in those magnificent black and white images. You can see the photographs of that first meeting downstairs in the museum. They are on display. I think it says a great deal about the personalities of both men, and I think it also says much about the respect they had for each other."

"What a wonderful story. I'll be sure to look for those particular shots when we leave," said Beth. The three women continued to chat for another twenty minutes as Angela Rosengart added further details about her life and her encounters with Picasso. The conversation would likely have continued indefinitely, but Sylvia brought everything to a halt when she announced that she and Beth had another engagement at the *Hans Erni Haus* on the lake.

"Please give my best to Mr. Erni," said Lady Rosengart, "And thank you for coming to my little gallery. I shall look forward to seeing your articles." Beth and Sylvia thanked their hostess for her hospitality and promptly left the museum to catch a bus for the *Transportation Museum* and the *Hans Erni Haus*.

Like most Swiss cities the mass transit system of Lucerne is superb. Fast, efficient, frequent and on time. Sylvia was beaming with excitement as the two women came to the end of a narrow street which opened to the main thoroughfare that would take them to their next appointment. The grand five star *Hotel Sweitzerhof* dominated the left side of the boulevard while the lake shimmered in the afternoon sun to the right. Further down the avenue two more deluxe 19th century hotels dominated the shoreline, proudly facing the majestic Alps far in the distance.

There was an unusually happy bounce in Sylvia's step on this day. "You must come to Lucerne more often Beth Jacobsen. That way I will meet all of the most interesting people in our village."

"Lady Rosengart was charming wasn't she," added Beth. "Do you think we will be so fortunate with Hans Erni?"

"Oh yes. Of that I am sure. I am told that he is also a most engaging individual. Can you believe it, that I am meeting him for the first time today?"

They were at the bus stop now. Sylvia was bursting with anticipation at having the chance to talk with Hans Erni personally. "Please forgive my ignorance," said Beth, "But just exactly who is Hans Erni? If I understood you correctly, you mentioned that he's Switzerland's most prominent living artist, but I haven't been able to do proper research on every aspect of this trip, and sometimes it has been so fast that I'm losing track of everything."

A bright blue bus arrived and Beth and Sylvia got on. As they boarded Sylvia answered Beth's question. "This is a short ride. The museum is just outside of town. Not too far, but a little too long for walking. We could have gone there by lake steamer, by the way, but this is faster, and we don't want to be late. It's lovely to visit that way, though. Now, about Mr. Erni. He also knew Picasso. In the days of their youth they were, in fact, studying together. But Picasso went in one direction and Erni another. Hans Erni had very little money at that time. Like so many artists, I suppose. Why is it, I wonder, that so many of them must struggle? Anyway, the only way he could make a living was by doing commercial art. Posters and advertisements and such. He was very good at it, and in the end, he became financially secure. Unfortunately, he was also criticized quite heavily because many people said that he was not a true artist. So he has spent much of the remainder of his career proving his skills as a painter and a sculptor. As I told you before, he is indeed the best known artist living in Switzerland today. He never stops working, and he is very much in demand throughout the country. Erni is quite old, however. I imagine him to be about 86 now. So you see this will be very special because we do not know for sure how much longer we will have him.

"Is he ill?" questioned Beth.

"Oh no, quite the opposite. He is extremely healthy and youthful look-ing, and he's a most positive person. You will never believe that he is as old as he is."

The bus came to a stop beside a wooded park. Just ahead a lake steamer was docking to let people disembark for the *Transportation Museum* which was a couple of short blocks away. "If this is the *Transportation Museum*, then what exactly is the *Hans Erni Haus*?" asked Beth who was now thor-oughly confused.

The two women began walking toward the *Transportation Museum* by way of the park. "It's really part of the same facility, but it is a building dedicated only to the works of Hans Erni. He provides everything from his own collection. They call it the *Hans Erni Haus* because it does not really belong in the same category as transportation. They had the land available here, and so they added on to it in order to honor his work."

Erni was standing at the glass door waiting for his guests to arrive. Just as Sylvia had described, he was far younger in appearance than his actual age. He could have easily been in his late 50s or 60s. "Welcome to my dis-play," said the artist as the two women greeted him. "I hope you don't mind if I am your tour guide today."

"Mind? Not at all, not at all," replied Beth with a broad smile. "We are honored that you would take the time from your work to show us around. Mr. Erni, I'm Beth Jacobsen from North Carolina in the United States, and this is my guide while I'm here in Lucerne, Sylvia Elsner."

Sylvia greeted Erni with an adoring handshake, "I am delighted to know you at last after all of these years. I cannot believe that our paths have not crossed at some time, but now we meet and I am thrilled."

"The pleasure is all mine," answered Erni. "You understand that I could not consider having someone else escort you through my gallery. After all, this work is my own. How could I allow someone else to describe my thoughts and emotions to you. No, of this I could not approve. It will be great fun for me to show you around."

The museum was spacious with floor to ceiling windows that allowed natural light to wash throughout the exhibition area. There were two floors with a wide stairway in the center leading to the second level. It was a positive space filled with the essence of the artist himself, yet it was uncluttered, allowing room to breathe, and to absorb the work. Hundreds of paintings, etchings, posters and sculptures were displayed throughout the two large halls with no visible indication that they represented any particular theme or period in the artist's life. Rather it appeared that the presentations had been made in such a way as to draw patrons into the exhibition, almost as if they were leading the viewer through a predetermined path designed by the artist himself.

Beth and Sylvia pivoted slowly in awe around the lower level as Erni began describing the fulfillment of his lifelong dream to have a museum dedicated entirely to his work. "Are these permanent exhibits?" asked Beth.

"Oh no my dear. Art is constantly changing, and I must change with it. It keeps me young. We put some new things in and take some old things out every four months. That way the museum is always something new, something fresh. It is better that way, don't you think?" asked Erni without expecting an answer. "You see I am always creating. My mind is never empty. There is always something to explore. So I must continue to make new things to display. God gave me the talent to create. It would be a sin not to continue to find new methods of expressing myself."

It was easy to see why the artist was so youthful in appearance. There wasn't an old thought in his mind. In just those few initial minutes of meeting the man, Beth could see that his world was always alive with ideas. That was also evident in just the few pieces she had focused upon. Erni's strength was his ability to capture the nostalgia of the past while, at the same time, incorporating the future into his work. It was obvious that he could see the benefits of both worlds, and that he was not intimidated by the pursuit of knowledge. He had not allowed himself to become lost within the timeline of his own generation.

Erni was medium height with a solid frame. Especially, for a man of his years. He was not stooped or slumped over, nor did he have difficulty walking or getting about. In fact, he was extremely spry. His curly hair still showed traces of its original umber color, though gray was now dominant. He was in no way balding, however. His physique was sturdy, almost muscular. Most of all, his eyes were bright with enthusiasm, and the same was true of his voice. His exuberance for living was surpassed only by his enthusiasm for his craft, and the same powerful philosophy that he revealed through conversation was also displayed in whichever medium he chose to create a particular work of art.

"Shall I show you around?" asked Erni.

"By all means," replied Sylvia.

"How special to have a private showing by the person who created such magnificent things," added Beth.

"Ahh, but you see, I have the pleasure of escorting two beautiful women through my gallery. What could be better?" said Erni in a devilish tone.

"Flattery will get you everywhere," laughed Beth before she became serious for a moment. "Mr. Erni, before we begin, I must warn you that I am not terribly knowledgeable about art, so I hope you will forgive me if I ask some stupid questions."

"No one is ever totally understanding of art. That is what makes it so exciting. Art is what you feel. It is a purely personal experience whether you create it or whether you view it. Make no apologies, my dear, for even I am not an expert, and I never will be. So you see, there can be no silly questions."

Erni had put Beth completely at ease. He had a gentle personality that exuded kindness. It was easy to see why he had been so successful, because his outlook on life transformed those traits into his art.

The tour lasted more than an hour and a half. Erni explained what was happening in his life when certain works were produced, bringing sharply into focus his creative process by offering a window into his motivation for any given piece. Beth could sense by the enthusiasm of Erni's responses that, even if she didn't fully comprehend a particular piece, he was aware that she had a keen interest in his work and the subject matter surrounding it.

Beth and Sylvia were correct in their assessment that there was no special theme to the displays. There were sections of work however, focusing upon periods of the artist's life where it was obvious that his mind was occupied with specific world events, or that he was experimenting with a particular style or medium or materials.

"I see that you have included Albert Einstein in many of your paintings. Was he important to you for some reason?" asked Beth.

He was important to the world, don't you think? You are most observant." Beth could tell that Erni was pleased that she had noticed his interest in the famous mathematician. She also sensed that he was flirting with her at the same time. A couple of times she had noticed him concentrating upon her breasts rather than her face. In his defense however, Beth was well aware that the robin's egg blue sweater she was wearing was genuinely flattering to her figure.

"Einstein lived in Switzerland, you know, in Bern. So I was able to visit with him on several occasions," Erni continued.

"And why did he have such an impact on your life?" asked Beth.

"Because, like myself, he was a dreamer. You see reality is in many ways nothing more than the fulfillment of dreams. You must first have the dream, and then you must turn it into reality. The reality of what you believe. Whether it is art, or writing, or music, or dance, or even physics. You do not have to be brave to dream, but you must be brave to make it become real. Einstein was a very brave man. I admire that."

"I see that you incorporate aspects of technology into your work. Especially your paintings. Is that what you mean?"

"Very much so. We must look to the future. No matter what we do the future will come, and with it will also come change. We cannot ignore that, even if we do not like it. But we must also be aware of our past, because the past provides the map. It tells us how we must go forward. It shows us where the mistakes were made so that we can improve upon them. It gives us the answers even if we don't always see them at first. Here let me show you."

Erni led Beth and Sylvia to a section of the museum that obviously dealt with conflict. Conflict between man and himself, and conflict between nations. "The last world war made a great difference in my life," said the artist. "Switzerland was not involved because we are a neutral country. So I was able to view the destruction from a distance. The destruction of lives. The destruction of families. The destruction of architecture and art and history and the environment. As you can see, my paintings reflect the way I felt about all that was going on at that time. Picasso did the same thing when he painted his masterpiece, *Guernica*. It was his reaction to the destruction of the Basque town of Guernica during the Spanish Civil War in 1937. If you look at it you see the distortions of war, and you then begin to understand the process in his mind that led him toward cubism and the abstracts which later evolved. You see that is part of the dream which became reality. My paintings are different, because I am a different person, so I have a different interpretation, but the emotions are the same. Go to Berlin and view the paintings that have been done on the remains of the wall. You will see many, many different points of view, but the feelings are almost always the same. That is why art is so important. There is no right or wrong."

Beth and Sylvia were fascinated by the descriptions of the artist and his work and how it related to the messages he was trying to convey. "What about color? Is it important? I see that your colors are vibrant," said Beth.

"Color is very important. Especially for me. It is as important as the strokes of the brush or the composition of the frame. Colors are emotion. They evoke certain feelings. I like to use brilliant shades because I am a happy person. I see the world in bright textures, therefore I must express myself in those tones. It is part of who I am. Come upstairs. I will show you what I mean."

The two women followed their guide to the next level and entered an auditorium. The room, which had been created for lectures and seminars with a capacity of about 300 people, occupied a sizable portion of the upstairs space. Covering the length of the two side walls were frescoes by Erni detailing the history of man's journey through technology from the beginning of time to the present day. The colors followed the layers of the spectrum around the perimeter of the room blending in such a way as to create a vibrant rainbow-like backdrop for the figures depicted in Erni's timeline. Copernicus. Galileo. Da Vinci. Michelangelo. Edison. Newton. Einstein. A stunning representation of mankind's achievements down through the ages.

"You see. Not only are you affected by the people in these frescoes, but you are also influenced by the colors," said the artist. "Sometimes artists take advantage. Sometimes they attempt to evoke ideas that do not seem to make sense. That is when we have controversy. Disagreement is often a good thing, but trying to make an argument merely for the sake of argument is not so good. Today there are too many artists with too much freedom. The barriers have come down, and as a result, it becomes quite difficult sometimes to tell what is good and meaningful, and important, and what is nothing more than junk. But still we cannot suppress the creative artistic process, because if we do, we stifle civilization, for you see, art is a footnote to history."

Erni's last sentence had a profound impact upon Beth. "Art is a footnote to history." How true. She had never thought of it in quite that way, but those six words seemed to bring everything together in the proper context.

"So that concludes my tour," said Erni. "Shall we go downstairs again, and I will give you some materials about the museum."

The threesome walked down to the first floor to a display case in the center of the gallery. Erni looked over at a clerk behind the souvenir counter and requested brochures and books featuring his art for Beth and Sylvia. She returned momentarily and handed them to the two visitors. As soon as Sylvia received the booklet featuring numerous selections of Erni's paintings she made a request by handing the document to him and asking for his autograph. "You know it took me quite a long time to have this opportunity. I'm not going to allow it to pass without getting your signature, just in case our paths do not cross again."

Erni was amused by Sylvia's determination and endorsed the thin volume with pleasure. Then he turned to Beth and asked, "Do you have a business card perhaps?"

Beth reached into her purse, located her wallet and removed a card. She handed it to him without thinking for a second that he might want it for something other than the usual reason for requesting a card. Beth continued to speak with Sylvia and Erni, not realizing that Erni was now busily sketching a line drawing on the inside cover of his brochure. In less than two minutes the artist had pencilled in a likeness of Beth. It was only as he was completing the drawing that she took full notice of what he had done. Erni handed the booklet back to Beth and said, "I hope you will not be offended that I have taken some liberties, but you see I am quite fond of beautiful women, and I believe they must be seen naturally, and unadorned."

Beth opened the brochure. On the inside cover Erni had drawn a fully standing nude portrait of her with an inscription along the left side which read, "Cordially for Beth Jacobsen". Underneath the sketch, he had signed his name and dated it. The reason for obtaining Beth's business card now became clear. Erni wanted to be certain that he spelled her name correctly.

Without realizing it Beth had been posing for Hans Erni as she stood in front of him. She wasn't offended by any means, but she was momentarily taken aback by the sudden spontaneity of events. At first glance, she didn't know how to react because of her surprise at what the artist had drawn. On the one hand Beth was flattered that she had in some way been a source of inspiration for Erni. From another perspective however, she was uncomfortable that his vision of her went beneath her clothing, exposing her in his mind. From that point of view, she even felt somewhat violated, but only momentarily. Not that being naked was an embarrassment to her, but that a total stranger had perceived her in such a way, and that he was so unabashedly willing to express it. And so accurately too!

Beth knew that she had to respond, but she didn't quite know what to say. All she could do was tell herself that she needed to say something. It was as though Erni had x-ray vision, and that was slightly unnerving. Still, the drawing was exquisite. Particularly when she considered the brief amount of time in which it had been executed. "Mr. Erni this is fabulous! I am very proud. What a great honor you do me. I shall cherish this for the rest of my life."

"Beauty is my business. It is my job to depict the beautiful things that I see, and you are very beautiful. I have done nothing more than to represent what stands before me. I have merely exhibited your spirit upon a piece of paper." Erni was pleased by Beth's acceptance of his gift.

"Let me see. Let me see," said Sylvia curiously. "I must see what Mr. Erni has done." Beth passed the booklet to her guide and awaited her reaction. "Marvelous! Simply marvelous. Beth you should be thrilled to have this. What a treasure for you."

"Just remember one thing," concluded the artist, "Don't ever stop dreaming. Dream. You must always do so. For if a person does not dream, they are in a way already dead. No, you must never forget to make your dreams become reality."

With that parting thought Beth and Sylvia left the *Hans Erni Haus* and the man for whom the museum was named. Beth returned to the railway station and said goodbye to her newfound friend from Lucerne. Then she boarded the train, and continued her whirlwind, marathon tour of the art and culture of Switzerland.

During the next several days Beth accumulated six bags full of brochures, magazines, books, posters and postcards. At each remaining stop along her epic journey, she mentioned her encounter with Hans Erni, and each time the reaction was always the same, as if she had met the most famous celebrity in the world. At that point Beth would produce her booklet and open the cover to the pencil sketch of her that was drawn and signed by the artist himself. No one could believe her good fortune.

Everyone expressed how excited she must be to have been immortalized in that simple series of elegant lines.

When she was alone on the trains traveling from village to village, Beth would open the booklet now and then, and reflect upon the drawing for long contemplative moments. She recalled the details of her interview with Angela Rosengart, of what it had been like for her to pose for Pablo Picasso so very long ago, and the impact it had had upon the rest of her life. Now in her own unique way, Beth was also the subject of a small piece of art. It would never be seen in the *Louvre* or the *Prado* or the *Hermitage*, but it did make its way to a prominent place on a wall in Beth's home. And it became a conversation piece to say the least. A one of a kind treasure with a wonderful story behind it, for it represented the most intimate gift that an artist can bestow upon another person, a personal creation, signed by its creator, identifying it as one of a kind from a singular moment in time. A moment unlike any other.

Now Beth knew exactly how Angela Rosengart had felt for more than fifty years, and she was thoroughly convinced that the wisdom of Hans Erni was an undeniable truth, that personal dreams should never ever die.

ANGELS IN BERLIN

"Berlin is a city in transition. In fact, it has become the crane capital of Europe. Especially at Potsdamer Platz where the Germans and several international corporations are rebuilding it to once again become the focal point of the city. When it is completed in about 2010, it will be an ultra modern version of what was once regarded as Europe's busiest thorough-fare, standing as a contemporary symbol of the city which was so tragically divided by a wall for nearly thirty years."

Beth Jacobsen was standing in the lobby of a snazzy new East Berlin hotel providing background information to her tour group prior to embarking upon a three-hour excursion of the city. Most of the 52 people she was addressing were members of a Presbyterian church choir from Charlotte, North Carolina, but there were also 13 non-singers who had joined the tour simply for the chance to visit Berlin and other parts of Germany.

Escorting a trip was something new for Beth. It was an idea she had considered pursuing when her journalistic career was over, but when this opportunity arose she decided to accept the challenge just to see if she could make it all come together.

The adventure had begun more than a year before when Jean Palmer approached Beth about serving as the escort for a European choir tour. Palmer was the committee chairman for the trip. She had been in Winston-Salem visiting relatives one weekend and was captivated by Beth's travel column that appeared every Sunday in the *Winston-Salem Journal*. Upon initial contact, Beth quickly informed Palmer that she was a travel writer, not a tour guide, but to no avail. Jean Palmer was delightfully insistent, and Beth was intrigued. "This will the third tour of Europe our choir has undertaken in the past six years," Jean explained, "But the first two programs had lots of problems. Especially the last trip. It was a nightmare."

"But I don't understand where I fit into all of this?" Beth replied, somewhat perplexed by her role in the project.

"You're a travel writer. Travel writers travel. You've been everywhere and done everything. That's what we need, a traveler. For some strange reason the *Charlotte Observer* doesn't have anybody of your caliber writing for them. Don't ask me why. To be honest, they don't even have a good travel section. You'd think the largest city in the state of North Carolina, with all the growth it's had in the past fifteen years, would have a first rate travel section, or at least a top notch travel writer, but it doesn't. Can you believe that?"

"Hold on a second. Whoa. Slow down a minute," answered Beth. "Now I really don't understand. What does the *Charlotte Observer's* travel section, or lack of it, have to do with your choir trip?"

"I'm sorry to be so disorganized. Let me back up and try to explain from the beginning," said Jean.

"Next year our church will celebrate its 50th anniversary, and our choir director and his wife have been with the church for most of that time. Over the years they have developed a music program which is regarded as one of the best in the city. It may even be the finest in the state. Six years ago, partly as a tribute to their contribution to the music of our church, the adult choir went to Great Britain, starting in London and singing their way north, tracing their Presbyterian roots to Edinburgh, Scotland."

"Sounds grand to me," said Beth.

"In many ways it was very successful, but in other ways it was a disaster. Whatever else it was, it was extremely ambitious. The main problem was that despite the difficulties, it was popular enough among most of the participants that three years later they decided to do another concert tour."

"Well, based upon your previous comments, I'm beginning to see what happened," said Beth anticipating the rest of Jean's story.

"I know what you're thinking, and you're exactly right," replied Palmer.

"So where did you decide to go next."

"We went to Rome. In July! The hottest month of the year in a city where many of the hotels don't have air conditioning. Eighty-four of us! Can you imagine?"

"OK, so your choice of destinations was good, but the timing was bad, and the group was way to big, but there must be more to it than that."

"Oh there was. We didn't just go to Rome, that was only where we started. Then we went to Florence."

"Well that's fairly typical. Rome, Florence, Venice. Everybody seems to do those three places," Beth replied.

"Yes, but then from Florence we went to Vienna."

"Vienna?" questioned Beth. "You did say Vienna? Not Venice, but Vienna?"

"Vienna. As in Austria. Gateway to the Alps. Vienna."

"Well that certainly is a strange combination of destinations. I mean, Vienna is incredibly far from Venice. Who planned the trip, the Marquis de Sade?" joked Beth.

"You haven't heard the end of it."

"You mean there's more?"

"From Vienna we went to Salzburg to sing at a music festival."

"You're kidding! You took 84 people from Vienna to itty-bitty Salzburg during the middle of a music festival? That's insane," said Beth in amazement.

"Oh yes. We did it. You talk about hot, angry, tired, frustrated travelers, we were the hottest, the angriest, most tired and most frustrated group you've ever seen."

"No wonder. This is incredible. Didn't your travel agent warn you against putting together such a strange itinerary?"

"We didn't use a travel agent. Our committee planned it themselves. All we had the travel agency do was the ticketing for the airlines."

"Ahhh, now I'm beginning to see my role in all of this," said Beth.

"Precisely. You travel for a living. You understand the logistics of a destination. You know what is possible and what isn't. So our idea is to have a professional traveler help us eliminate the mistakes before we make them. I thought perhaps I could talk you into designing our next itinerary for us so that we don't repeat the same problems again."

"Well I'm flattered that you think I can be of assistance, or that I could make a difference, but you have to understand that the way I travel is quite different from the way a group travels," said Beth firmly.

"I'm well aware of that," answered Jean, "But who better to know the pitfalls of traveling, plus you also know the destinations and how to get around them, and all that inside knowledge has to make a difference. The way I see it, you are actually better than a travel agent."

The conversation continued for another half-hour. When Beth hung up, she was officially in charge of coordinating a choir trip to Germany. For the better part of the next year Beth and Jean worked hand in hand to create the best possible workable blueprint for the journey. Now slightly more than 12 months later, the preparations were over, and the implementation phase of their epic plan was in high gear in Berlin.

It would have been unthinkable to accommodate the choir in a modern, air-conditioned hotel in East Berlin during the days when the wall divided the city. No one would have even considered the idea of staying in the east. Times change however, and in an odd sort of way, it was rather exciting to be comfortably housed in a part of the city that was now undergoing rapid revitalization. To be sure it wasn't as convenient as being located on the Kurfurstendamm, or Ku'damm as the locals call it, where all the glitzy West Berlin hotels line the avenue amid elegant shops and lively cafes. Still there was a U-bahn station less than two minutes from the hotel, and the mass transit system in the city is superb. Population-wise Berlin is huge, but it is also a sprawling metropolis that demands fast, efficient mass transit in order to survive. In addition to the subway, there is also an excellent above ground S-bahn, plus a well-established bus system, all of which can be accessed for unlimited travel by a single daily ticket.

While the group awaited the arrival of their motorcoach and guide, Beth looked around to see if she could locate Harry Briggs. Everyone was concerned about Harry. In fact, he and his wife, Joan, were last minute additions to the manifest after Harry had been given the OK from his doctor to participate in the trip. When Beth and Jean Palmer agreed to their partnership, Jean had requested that Harry be included as a member of the planning committee. He accepted at first, but later recused himself after just two meetings upon learning that he had been diagnosed with terminal prostate cancer. Miraculously, Harry had heroically, and victoriously, battled his unseen enemy with chemotherapy to the extent that his physician had told him that it might even be good for him to make the trip, within certain guidelines and precautionary measures.

For most people the arduous endeavor of traveling to another country while they were in such a condition would have been out of the question. Traveling is a tough business under the best of circumstances when you're healthy. Beth knew. She had been at it for nearly fifteen years, and it was not an easy process. But Harry was not the typical traveler. In the first place, he had been a highly successful urologist in Charlotte for many years, and it was his prominence as a physician that had afforded him the freedom to travel the world. Not only did he travel extensively for lectures, seminars, conferences and professional symposiums, he also traveled purely for personal enjoyment. So Harry knew the logistics of moving around the world, and what he was getting into. Even without his globe-trotting expertise, Briggs was considered by most of his friends and colleagues to be a Renaissance man. He was a writer of elegant prose and poetry. He was also a historian, a philosopher and a humorist. But most of all, he was an accomplished musician with the ability not only to sing, but to play a variety of instruments as well. Music was his passion, so singing for one final time with his own church choir in a foreign land to honor the church's 50th birthday was an event he could not deny himself. In retrospect, if there was one thing that was confounding to everyone, it was that he, of all people, with his medical background, would be stricken by that particular illness. That made everything seem all the more contradictory and ironic.

Harry and Joan were the original "odd couple". Despite his affluence, Harry possessed an infectious sense of humor, humility and graciousness that made him popular with the other choir members. By contrast, Joan was completely different. The old expression that "opposites attract" was an accurate description of these two people, because their personalities were 180-degrees apart. Considering Harry's condition however, there was a great deal of empathy for Joan among her fellow travelers.

Beth found Joan and inquired about Harry's status. "How's he doing today? Is he going on the tour with us?" she asked.

"I don't think so. He has good days and bad days, and today isn't so good. He knows he has to pace himself so that he can be as strong as possible to sing. I left him in the room to rest. He has all of his medicine beside the bed. He'll be all right while we're gone."

Nobody had said anything, but it was the consensus among the choir that Harry and Joan had reached an agreement before leaving on the trip that she would participate in all the group activities, and he would stay back to rest whenever possible.

The motorcoach pulled up outside the hotel. Everyone was ready for the tour when Anja Wuertz entered the lobby and introduced herself as the guide. Early in the planning process Beth and Jean agreed to a few basic ground rules that would be strictly adhered to, without exception, throughout the trip. Because the size of the group was by its very nature unwieldy, rule #1 was that the "times were the times". If the bus was scheduled to depart at 8 a.m., then it would leave at 8 a.m. and any stragglers would be left behind. Thus far no one had challenged the edict, so when Anja walked through the front door, everyone was gathered and ready for immediate departure.

Anja introduced herself to Beth and Jean who in turn made a mass introduction to the choir. Then everyone filed on to the bus with Beth and Jean taking the front seats across the aisle from the guide.

"How're we doing?" Beth asked Jean as the bus pulled away from the curb.

"So far so good. They all seem to be more relaxed and rested than on any of the other trips we've done. That's why I called you. I knew you'd keep us straight."

Beth laughed. "Well I think it was a good idea to stay in one spot for several nights and do day trips from there, rather than being constantly on the move, changing hotels, unpacking and packing every night," said Beth.

"Oh I agree one hundred percent. They've all settled in and they're getting oriented to one particular location instead of having to learn a new place every day," Jean replied.

"Actually, I got the idea from reading cruise brochures. They're always promoting that you only have to unpack your suitcase once because the ship is your hotel. I know Anja's company thought we were crazy to do it this way, but when you think about it, a two hour bus ride when you're traveling with friends is much better than constantly being uprooted from place to place and never having a chance to get comfortable."

"That was one of the problems we had on the first two trips. We were always on the go. People were completely exhausted by the third day. No, I think this is by far the best way to do it," said Jean.

It would be impossible to see all of Berlin in a single three-hour tour, but the program did provide an excellent overall orientation to the city, allowing everyone to get their bearings and to figure out what they might want to explore in depth later on their own. There were all the usual stops at the Brandenburg Gate, Checkpoint Charlie, the Gendarme Market, the Nikolai Quarter, Alexanderplatz, the Dom, Charlottenburg Palace, the famed boulevard known as Unter den Linden, and finally, a brief pause at the East Side Gallery to view the remains of the wall. Two of the most famous churches in the city were excluded because the choir would be singing at both places on the following day. Anja didn't even attempt to include any museums during the outing, figuring that most people could pursue personal preferences during their free time. Berlin was a cultural showcase, and Anja knew better than to highlight one or two museums or galleries at the expense of others. Particularly when she was trying to satisfy over 50 different personalities.

The afternoon was set aside as leisure time for everyone to pursue individual interests. Beth announced that the group would muster in the lobby promptly at 6:15 to catch the bus for a performance by the world famous *Cirque de Soleil.* At first Beth thought she might have allowed too much travel time to the circus since the program didn't begin until 7:30, but crossing town in a bus through the fringes of rush hour was a tedious process, and her estimate ultimately proved to be right on the money.

Beth had seen the *Cirque de Soleil* on several occasions on television back home, and to tell the truth, she had never really been impressed. As a result, she had no burning desire to see the show. It was a single-ring affair under a huge tent with a seating capacity for perhaps three thousand people. While the tent was enormous, the venue itself was quite intimate which dramatically added to the power of the performance.

In the end, the circus turned out be one of the highlights of the trip. Even Beth had to admit that she had been captivated by the combination of costumes, lighting, music, dance, characters and, of course, the performers. For some reason the inherent limitations of television had never quite captured the full spectrum of the charm of the live performance. It became another of those unexpected gems that Beth had come to love in her travels, where diminished expectations often were suddenly transformed into an overwhelming sense of elation and discovery. It was this serendipitous nature of travel that made Beth's wanderlust so keen. At the same time, it was also the most difficult aspect of her enthusiasm for world exploration to convey to others.

Everyone was still buzzing with excitement when the bus returned to the hotel around eleven. Most of the older members of the traveling party retired for the night, but others found their way downstairs to an Irish pub for a nightcap in the atrium adjacent to the hotel.

There were two choir performances scheduled for the following day. The first was to be an impromptu concert at the *Marienkirche* at 10 a.m., and the second was a full one-hour program following services at the *Kaiser-Wilhelm Church* on the Kurfurstendamm. Scheduling the churches for performances had been one of the most demanding features of Beth's assignment. Especially since one of the committee members had previously visited Berlin, and had made a specific request to have those two historic churches included in the concert docket. That they were among the most prestigious sites in which to perform in Berlin was undeniable, but it added greatly to the pressure of working out the logistics of the program for Beth. Fortunately everything ultimately worked out for the best as Anja's company was able to negotiate the arrangements to accommodate the choir's wishes.

Harry Briggs was counted among the number that would sing at the *Marienkirche* the next day. He looked frail and tired, but he was determined to participate in spite of the hidden demons that ravaged his body. Most of his hair was gone as a result of the chemo treatments. What remained were a few wispy white strands here and there, which would have looked much better if Harry had made the effort to shave them away. By that time however, Harry lacked the energy to bother with something he considered as merely an exercise in vanity. Besides, at this stage of the game, shaving his head was hardly a priority.

Once inside the church, choir director, Dr. David Peele, and his wife, Maria, promptly went about the business of aligning the singers amid the usual joking and organizational confusion. Peele had an Alfred E.

Neumann appearance about him, but the similarity stopped there. Like many people of inspired thinking and creativity, he had his eccentricities, along with his nerdy qualities, but his lifes work bordered on genius with hundreds of original compositions and countless honors both domestically and internationally. Only his devotion to his church, and the musical heritage he had so richly cultivated there for over four decades, kept him at his position. It certainly wasn't the money. A musician of his stature could easily have commanded three or four times the salary elsewhere. No, it was his dedication that made him remain where he was. A commitment to leave a legacy that would be the foundation for all future musical undertakings at the church.

The *Marienkirche*, or St. Mary's Church, is the second oldest in Berlin dating to the year 1240. It features Gothic and neoclassical architecture, and like so many ancient European churches the acoustics are phenomenal. Something about the stone added a texture of sweetness to the unified chorus of voices. A purity of tone where the music lingered in the air like the clear elegant ring of fine crystal, as if the walls themselves were absorbing every note. It was a musician's dream.

Impromptu concerts only lasted about 20 minutes so this particular performance didn't take its toll on Harry Briggs' stamina like a full program did. As a result, Harry was feeling unusually chipper following the morning program. The remainder of the day was allocated as free time with instructions to reunite for the evening concert at the *Kaiser Wilhelm Church* on the Ku'damm at 6 p.m. Except for a few adventuresome individuals who had their own agendas, nearly everyone, including Harry Briggs, elected to take an optional side excursion to Potsdam and the "Prussian Versailles" known as *Sans Souci Palace*. The outing proved to be a wise decision because it kept most of the group together at a leisurely pace, while also providing an opportunity to get out of Berlin for few hours. Scattered billowy white clouds created enough hiding places for the sun, which kept the mid-July temperatures at a comfortable level, as everyone dispersed throughout the massive palace acreage for self-guided exploration and picture taking. As the others familiarized themselves with the grounds of *Sans Souci*, Harry Briggs remained in the shade of an umbrella at the concession area, treating himself to a large German beer and a pair of knockwursts with mustard.

On the return trip to Berlin, the tour made a brief visit to the historic World War II site of the Potsdam Conference. After the war, the building had been turned into a romantic half-timbered inn nestled on the shores of a small lake with a lovely garden in between. It was a brief but popular side trip, which greatly appealed to the veterans in the group.

It was quarter till five when the motorcoach arrived at the *Kaiser Wilhelm*, which was ample time for shopping and browsing along the Ku'damm. A few people went in search of afternoon tea to take the edge off their hunger before singing. Meanwhile, Harry Briggs, who was now beginning to feel the effects of the prolonged day of touring, elected to take refuge inside the church, stretching out on one of the pews to conserve his waning energy. Since Beth had no singing obligations, she stayed with Harry in the event he needed anything prior to the concert, figuring that, if necessary, she could always get away during the program.

At one time the *Kaiser Wilhelm Church* was huge, but it was almost completely destroyed by Allied bombing during the war. Efforts to rebuild the 19th century neo-Romanesque structure were begun but never completed, though the old west tower, which once stood 207 feet tall, is now preserved in its ruined state. The once grand tower is clearly visible when arriving in Berlin by train, standing like a snaggled old tooth amid the skyline. The remains of the original building were made into a museum, while a new, octagonal shaped contemporary church was built next door. The *Kaiser Wilhelm* stands today as the symbol of the city, representing a bit of the past and a view of the future. It features something old and something new, a ruin, yet preserved as an ever present reminder of what was and what is to be, as if it was a string around Berlin's finger, forever pointing its ragged fang-like spire toward the sky.

The interior of the modern incarnation of the church features thousands of tiny blue windows, which unite into a massive tableau to create the illusion of the sky. The shades of blue change according to the amount of daylight outside, but whether the sanctuary is bathed in sky blue or Prussian blue or azurite blue or anything in between, the atmosphere is perpetually soothing. For Harry Briggs, in his present condition, the serenity of the ambient blue interior was a blessing.

Just before the choir assembled, Harry asked Beth to see if she could locate a restroom so that he could splash some water on his face to revitalize himself. The errand took longer than anticipated, but at last she was successful, and while Harry freshened up, Beth went in search of a soft drink to further revive her companion.

The concert went off perfectly, receiving appreciative applause from the sophisticated Berlin audience. If there was any flaw to the performance at all, it was with the church itself. Ironically, though it was the most contemporary structure of any of the venues in which the choir sang, it had the least satisfactory acoustics. There was no doubt however, that Dr. Peele was delighted with the end result, believing that each successive concert was having a cumulative effect on the overall quality of the program. The choir was now singing better than ever before. That fact especially pleased him with two concerts scheduled for Leipzig the next day. For Harry Briggs the extended period of standing, combined with the other festivities of the day, had weakened him considerably, so he gladly took advantage of the immediate bus ride back to the hotel in order to get a good night's sleep.

Europe has many cities with grand traditions of music. Vienna. Salzburg. Milan. Naples. St. Petersburg. And there is no question that Leipzig must be included among that number. As the city of Bach, it is impossible to ignore Leipzig's glorious musical heritage, and for a musician to have the honor of singing where the great master had written so many of his compositions was an emotional high of immense proportions.

For Harry Briggs and Dr. David Peele, Leipzig represented the musical equivalent of winning the Masters golf tournament or orbiting the earth or making the *New York Times* bestseller's list. Yet each man, in his own way, was inspired for different reasons.

For Peele, Leipzig reinforced his own musical roots. Perhaps it was Bach's longevity as choirmaster at the *Thomaskirche* that had subconsciously inspired Peele to choose a similar path in Charlotte. Or maybe it was a burning desire for continuity that drove him to follow the precedent established nearly three hundred years ago by another composer.

For Briggs, Leipzig had become a quest for survival. There was an all-consuming need to walk upon the same streets where Bach had walked. There was a passionate need to raise his voice in tribute to the master composer by singing his music in the very church in which it had been written. There was the personal joy of absorbing the purity and sweetness of each note through his pores, knowing full well that soon his soul, too, would reside with Bach's in that mysterious realm where angels sing at the hands of the Creator. Whatever the magnitude of the reasons for each man, Leipzig could not have been more meaningful or more poignant for either of them.

Leipzig lies about two hours southwest of Berlin. Following the wishes of one of the committee members, Beth and Jean had scheduled a short detour to the village of Halle, approximately 20 miles outside of Leipzig, to allow the choir to visit the lifelong home of George Frederic Handel. *Handel Haus* is now a museum featuring photographs, letters, compositions, posters and other memorabilia including several of the composer's contracts. Each room features an audiotape explaining various aspects of Handel's life, complete with brief interludes of opening and closing music. Though a direct drive would have offered more time in Leipzig, everyone felt the added benefit of the Handel excursion outweighed the need for extra time in the city of Bach.

Program number one was to be performed at the historic *Church of St. Thomas* where Bach worked for 27 years. The church has a rich and colorful history even without the considerable influence of Bach, though it is likely that it was Bach's reputation that made the church become an attraction for future historic musical events. It was at the *Thomaskirche* in May of 1539 that Martin Luther introduced the Reformation to Leipzig. Some 250 years later Mozart played the church organ there in 1789, and in the centuries that followed both Felix Mendelssohn and Richard Wagner also performed at the church. The church choir has been in existence since its founding in 1254. During Bach's time there were 54 singers in the chorale, but today it features the voices of 80 boys. The *Thomaschoir* is world famous, singing music particularly dedicated to Bach in weekly performances of motets and cantatas, as well as during regular Sunday services.

"Just imagine," said Dr. Peele trying to inspire his singers, who really didn't need any further inspiration, "First Bach, then Mozart, Wagner, Mendelssohn, the *Thomas Boys Choir* and now us. That's quite a history don't you think?"

Everyone laughed at Peele's little joke, but they all knew deep inside that this was a memory in the making for their choir director. That in itself was motivation enough to sing the performance of a lifetime, but on a personal level, each choir member felt the same inner desire for themselves as they did for their conductor.

To Beth's ear the choir sounded wonderful. Beyond that, she couldn't honestly say whether this occasion had been any better than the other performances. That opinion was not shared by the majority of the choir members, however. They were thoroughly convinced that one Mr. J. S. Bach had provided divine intervention of such significance that they would never again sing better than they did on that particular day. The important thing was that everyone was convinced that they had done an excellent job, and Beth was certainly in no position to argue the point.

On the way out of the church everyone stopped for a round of picture taking at the Bach statue at the side of the building. At the time it occurred everyone was certain that the performance at the *Thomas Church* would be the high spot of the tour to Leipzig. As it turned out, it was only the beginning, for the afternoon concert would have an even more profound effect upon the lives of each singer, especially Dr. Peele and Harry Briggs.

Lunch was held at the *Auerbach's Keller*, a favorite hangout for university students since the year 1530. Statues at the entrance to the subterranean restaurant, which was the setting for an episode in Goethe's *Faust*, commemorated the scene in which the bedeviled doctor engages Mephistopheles in lively debate. After a delicious meal, and an all too brief respite, it was time to move on to the site of the next concert at the *Church of St. Nicholas.*

St. Nicholas was only a few short blocks from the restaurant so the choir walked en masse to the church. After all the excitement of singing at the *Thomas Church*, followed by the exuberance of the lunch time atmosphere, most of the choir members anticipated a letdown as the afternoon session approached. To their surprise the matinee concert only reinforced the events of the morning by providing a majestic conclusion to an already significant experience. It was as if past and present had come together in a monumental collision that was magnified through the awesome power of music.

Though the *Church of St. Thomas* was Bach's primary venue in Leipzig, he was also choirmaster at *St. Nicholas* during the same period of 1723 to 1750. Oddly enough, *St. Nicholas* is nearly a hundred years older than *St. Thomas* dating to 1165. When it was built, the church was situated at the intersection of two important north-south, east-west trade routes which played an important role in its past, but it was the modern significance of *St. Nicholas* that brought history together and created the indelible impact upon Dr. Peele's choir.

One by one the singers filed through the front door of the *Church of St. Nicholas* past a small, almost insignificant sign with only three words written on it. The words simply read, "Open For All." Once inside, as Dr. Peele and Maria began organizing the choir, Anja spoke to the group.

"I would like to tell you just a little bit about this church as you get ready to sing. Perhaps it will make the music more meaningful for you. I hope so. You see the *Nicholas Church* was once located at an important crossroads in the city of Leipzig, so it has had a long and important history. I know that you already know about Bach so I will not explain that to you further, but you should also know what else happened here very recently,"

Anja continued to speak while pointing to a painting of an angel over the altar. "Perhaps you can see the painted angel above the altar. When the ancestors of this church painted it, they had no idea that such a simple idea would one day become so important. The angel represents peace. Each November in the early 80s, young people from all over the region would gather for ten days to pray for peace. There were huge demonstrations all over East Germany as people protested against the arms race, but the gatherings in Leipzig were little more than nonviolent prayer meetings. The only place where issues could be openly discussed was at meetings held at churches, and this church, the *Church of St. Nicholas* where you are now standing, where you will sing so beautifully in a few moments, was one of those churches."

"What happened?" interrupted a voice from the choir.

"Hush," said another, "Let Anja finish her story."

"Pretty soon a youth group from this church decided to increase the meetings by having prayer services every Monday evening. At first only a small number of people attended, but soon more and more people came to demand justice and respect for human rights. Many who came were non-Christians, but they had no other place to gather, and so they continued to come here. Through their discussions they studied the words of the *Old Testament* and the *Sermon on the Mount*, and they soon understood two things; that people should discuss urgent problems with each other, and that they also needed to meditate and pray to God for support and guidance. Slowly the movement became stronger. Each day this church was decorated with flowers, and each night it was filled with the light of hundreds of glowing candles. Soon the government became worried, and from May of 1989 all the access roads to the *Nicholas Church* were blocked and checked by police. The authorities exerted pressure to cancel the peace prayers, but they did not stop. Monday after Monday they continued even though many people were detained or arrested. Soon it was not possible for everyone to get into the church because the numbers were so great, yet still they came. At last, in October, the militia battered defenseless people in the streets, but the people remained passive. They refused to fight back. Hundreds were taken away in trucks. Many were locked up in stables. Yet the people still prayed. *St. Nicholas Church* was filled with more than 2,000 people inside where we are standing at this moment, and there were thousands more out in the streets. When the prayers for peace ended, the bishop gave his blessing and also an urgent call for nonviolence. When the people came out of the church, they found thousands of fellow East Germans standing in the square, waiting with candles in their hands. You see to carry a candle outdoors you must use two hands. One hand holds the candle, and the other keeps it from going out. In order to keep the candle lit, it was not possible to have a stick or a club or a stone. It was a miracle. The police came in and surrounded the crowd, but they didn't know what to do because they no longer had a desire to fight them. And the people did not wish to fight either, since it was a peace vigil and they were not armed. Soon the police began to talk with the people in the crowd, and eventually they withdrew. As one officer said when he left, "We were prepared for everything. Everything, except candlelight." The nonviolent movement lasted only a few weeks more before the dictatorship began to collapse. Not long after that you know the story of the wall coming down in Berlin. Here in Leipzig there was not even a single broken shop window. Not one. And this all happened exactly 450 years after Martin Luther introduced the Reformation to Leipzig. So your music has quite an important purpose when you sing in this place."

An all-encompassing silence fell over the choir as Anja concluded her story. Amid the hush, Beth gazed around the sanctuary, observing each reaction, trying to memorize each expression, searching her mind for words that would somehow convey the poignant message of the tale she had just heard. And then she spotted Harry Briggs standing alone, isolated at the rear of the group. He was crying. Soft, silent, quiet tears that made tiny glistening trails down his cheeks. This was what he had come for. To be a part of something powerful and significant in the fading hours of his life. To feel the strength of the music he so dearly loved. For Harry Briggs this was momentous.

Dr. Peele and Maria resumed the task of arranging the choir before donning their robes. The convivial attitude had subsided. It was all business now as solemnity pervaded the group. The happy-go-lucky atmosphere had become one of reverence and respect.

Emotion swept through each piece of music with mounting intensity, establishing a level of concentration among the choir that reverberated throughout the sanctuary with unparalleled unison. Through all the months of rehearsal and seven previous concerts, this was the first time the choir sang with their hearts as well as their voices. The program had become so familiar to each of them that they began to anticipate the pace and rhythms of the individual pieces which, on this day, added immensely to their sensibilities about the music. Suddenly the concert had taken on its own personality. It was different this time. There was a flow that had never existed during previous performances. On this occasion the music had a soul, and everyone felt it at precisely the same moment.

A collective sigh of satisfaction erupted at the conclusion of the program. The fervor of the singing had left everyone emotionally drained and uncharacteristically subdued, yet humbly proud of their accomplishment.

As the choir began to disperse, one of the singers emerged from the group, stepping forward to speak briefly with Dr. Peele. Mark Andrews wasn't a regular member of the choir. In fact, he didn't even belong to the church. Peele had requested that Andrews be included on the tour with the agreement that his expenses would be paid for in exchange for his participation. It wasn't unusual for Dr. Peele to use professionals from time to time in an effort to bolster a particular section of the choir. Especially for a tour of this caliber. During the normal church calendar, there were a few regular members of the choir who received small fees for their talents because they had a high level of training, and were therefore periodically utilized as soloists. When the choir went on tour however, Peele could only count on about half of his "specialists" being able to go along, and for that reason, he hired Mark Andrews to reinforce his ensemble. It was a win-win situation for everyone.

Peele nodded in agreement when he heard Andrews' suggestion. The young tenor moved to the center of the choir to prepare for a solo performance. He would sing his own accappella arrangement of *Amazing Grace*. After a momentary pause to ensure his concentration and to establish the proper mood, Andrews began to sing. The words were indeed those of *Amazing Grace*, but the tune was that of *Londonderry Aire*, also known by the more familiar title of *Danny Boy*. Andrews' pacing and timing couldn't have been better. He would not be rushed in his touchingly masterful rendition of the two familiar pieces of music that blended to perfection on day that had been filled with perfection. A hush fell over the sanctuary as Andrews concluded his number. Nothing more needed to be said. Nothing else needed to be added. The mood was moving, and electric, but it was also saturated with a sense of quiet gratification that had been intensified by the uplifting spirit of the music.

The performance was over. The glorious day of music and history had come to an end. Silently each member of the choir departed the *Church of St. Nicholas*. They were filled with hope and inspiration, not just from what they had learned and been a part of, but also from the awe-inspiring energy of the music. And as they each filed through the front door of the church, they once again passed the insignificant little sign. A sign with three little words written upon it. A sign that simply read, "Open For All".

When Beth and Jean had first begun to coordinate the logistics of the itinerary, they decided it would be best to have a free day between the two long excursions outside of Berlin. Two performances still remained which were planned for a pair of small towns two hours northwest of the city. The province of Mecklenburg-Vorpommern had long been isolated from much of the rest of the country during the decades under the Communist regime. It was therefore unfamiliar territory for excursions by even the most experienced local tour companies. Under normal circumstances, Sternberg and Mirow would not have been considered as part of the choir's tour program, but there were historic, as well as political reasons, for going there. Most important was the fact that Queen Charlotte of Mecklenburg, who married King George III of England during the latter part of the 18th century, was the monarch for whom the city of Charlotte had been named. Since the concert tour was a celebration of the 50th anniversary of the church, it seemed appropriate to trace the roots of the city to its origins. The political aspect of the project arose when the Bishop of Sternberg invited the choir to perform there first, in order to take advantage of their presence in the region. Dr. Peele could hardly say no, so an extra concert was added to the agenda.

Keeping all of that in mind, combined with the extended journey to Leipzig the previous day, Beth and Jean arranged for a day at leisure between the two long outings. Then they added another free day at the end of the itinerary to allow everyone to take care of last minute shopping or to do personal sightseeing.

The trip to Mecklenburg was an ambitious undertaking for a single day. Part of it was due to the amount of travel that was required, and another part was the result of the roads in the north being mostly of the two-lane country variety. A third reason was because the people of each village had planned grand welcoming receptions to greet their North American visitors. Over the years Beth had learned that such occasions were wonderfully festive and greatly appreciated, but they were also time consuming and tiring.

When the choir arrived at the tiny chapel in Sternberg, the church was already bulging to capacity for the 2 p.m. concert. Villagers had been waiting patiently for more than an hour, arriving at the church well ahead of time to ensure themselves of a seat. Throughout the former East Germany, especially in the smaller communities, many churches had deteriorated under Communism. Now there was a hunger for the return of traditional sacred music. Their music. At Sternberg many senior citizens brought their sons and daughters and grandchildren with them so that they could begin to familiarize them with the music that had enriched their own lives so long ago.

In preparing and organizing the music for the complete, hour-long program, Dr. Peele had taken several variables into consideration. First, he researched the cities, and the churches where the performances would be held. From that background he was able to determine which composers would have the greatest impact and the most pertinent message for the listeners. Then he considered the recent history of each region in an effort to decide whether it might be wise to incorporate other types of music into the repertoire. Next, he selected pieces of sufficient length to highlight the strengths of his choir, while at the same time choosing works that made logical transitions from one selection to another. This gave the music continuity by blending it into a cohesive, unified presentation. His final concept was to incorporate an outstanding mixture of music from the Old World in the first portion, with music of the New World in the second half. To begin there was Bach, Beethoven, Mozart and others, followed by New World pieces, which included a variety of American composers, as well as Negro spirituals. Between sections, Peele divided the program with a short transitional organ piece that he had written years before when he was a teenager. There were also four solos plus a duet in the program that, when everything came together, was truly a feast for the ears.

Promptly at 2 p.m. the bishop climbed into the pulpit to address his congregation. His brief comments were at first directed to the audience in

German. Then he turned toward the choir and translated his remarks into broken English. Though hardly perfect, the message was resoundingly clear.

"For all of my life I have been told of the evils of the Americans, and the peoples of the west. Our government told us of these things. I never really believed it, but how could we know for certain when that was the message that we heard every day," said the bishop. "Now today, you come to our village, and you sing for us. This is a great honor. It is a privilege for us. Today I know for certain that the politicians were not telling us the truth. I know that they were wrong, for you people are the best people. You bring us joy with your music."

Short and to the point. The English wasn't perfect, but the message was explicit, and it left an unalterable impression upon the minds and hearts of the choir as they prepared to sing. From the back row Harry Briggs reflected upon the irony of the bishop's words. Here he was, standing in an unknown little burg in northeastern Germany preparing to return traditional music to the people of its homeland. Music that for many had long been nothing more than a memory. Music that would now be fresh and alive once again, only this time for new generations born after the war. What a marvelous gift to present to these people.

It would be impossible to duplicate either of the performances in Leipzig, but the miniature size of the sanctuary and the enthusiastic response from the congregation gave the concert an interactive aura that had not been present during the other programs. It was easily the most appreciative audience of the tour.

After the concert, the congregation led the choir across the street to the bishop's back yard for coffee, lemonade and home made German cakes and pastries. Several hundred people mingled in the warm afternoon sun sharing handshakes, greetings and scrumptious desserts. Few of them spoke English. Even fewer of the Americans spoke any German. It didn't matter. Communications were frequently reduced to simple sign language, yet conversation and goodwill had been enhanced by the universality of great music, delicious food and a genuine desire to share personal encounters, no matter how brief.

Only one concert remained to be sung at 5 p.m. in the village of Mirow. When the motorcoach stopped at 4:30, the choir made a short tour of Queen Charlotte's palace and grounds. It would have been more appropriate to call it an estate than a palace, but the tour did put it into an historical context for the upcoming concert. Queen Charlotte was born in Mirow and spent the days of her youth there until her marriage to the English king. Due to renovations of the site, the tour was short-lived, leaving the group no alternative but to walk up the gradual incline to the church where Queen Charlotte had worshipped as a youngster. Like Sternberg, the sanctuary was already filled to capacity, but in this instance, the facility was about three times larger than the previous church.

Over the centuries the church had become dilapidated and run-down, but the state of disrepair in no way marginalized the enthusiasm for the music being sung by the visitors from so far away. Communism had obviously taken its toll on the lives of the people of Mirow, but for a little more than an hour at least, music would temporarily invigorate the quality of life of its residents. There within the landscape of the softly rolling countryside of northeastern Germany, music was about to transcend language, culture and politics once more.

Thunderous applause echoed throughout the room as several hundred citizens of Mirow responded to each piece of music. Occasionally there were tears of joy or sorrow when a particular composition had profound personal significance for an individual member of the audience. At the same time however, a potential problem was developing. As the program progressed, it was becoming increasingly difficult to sing. The building was musty, and the body heat generated from so many listeners combined with the energy required for the choir to sing for an hour was beginning to have a negative effect. Harry Briggs was sweating profusely in the back row, struggling to battle his way through this one final concert. It would probably be the last concert of his life, and he wanted to finish the program. But other choir members were having equal difficulty finishing the performance as well.

It was the final concert of a series of concerts that had frequently been filled with emotion. Now as the end was drawing near, the choir was beginning to collectively fight off the mental and physical fatigue that had been overcome for the past several days by sheer adrenaline. Rewarding as it had been, by the time the last note had been sung, everyone was thankful to finally, at long last, have the schedule behind them. To be sure they had been richly endowed. Their lives had been changed forever. Lifelong memories had been created that, over time, would far outlive any recollections of the fatigue. But at this moment, there was a universal sense of relief that the journey had mercifully come to an end.

Harry Briggs was ready to collapse. He had survived. Barely. But not without paying a heavy price to his stamina. What small amount of energy he had remaining was completely drained from his body. That mattered little to him now, for he was content, satisfied that he had achieved what he had set out to accomplish. Somehow he had mustered the fortitude to stave off the agonizing periods of prolonged standing so that one last time he could joyously sing to the greater glory of God. That pleased him. He had reached the end of his life in glorious triumph, and as far as he was concerned, he could not ask for anything more.

No one saw Harry during the remaining days of the tour until Beth rolled him to the bus in a wheelchair on the morning of the departure for home. He was smiling and happy, but weakened and devoid of energy. No longer was the anticipation of the trip driving him onward, and now the inevitable letdown had taken control of his ever-weakening body.

A month and a half after the choir had returned from Germany, Harry Briggs succumbed to his cancer and died. Jean Palmer called Beth on the phone in Winston-Salem to inform her of the passing.

For Beth there was no way of knowing how many days had been added to Harry's life because of the tour. Perhaps none. Maybe the tour hadn't made even the slightest iota of a difference. But Beth didn't believe that. In her heart she knew that Harry's life had been extended by that one final trip, and that his last days on earth had been enriched by the pure joy of singing the music he had come to love and know so well. There was one other thing Beth knew for certain. Harry Briggs had departed this world on his own terms, by singing his way into heaven. And now, he and J. S. Bach were savoring the music of the angels...together.

FAUX BASEL

Beth Jacobsen was feeling cocky. To her way of thinking, she had come of age. After years of travel writing, at long last she had finally turned the corner. For the first time in her career Beth was fully confident that her range of experience had brought her to a place about which she was more knowledgeable than her traveling companions. It was a pleasant, authoritative sensation, an aphrodisiac in an odd sort of way.

"Basel, Switzerland seems to me to have an inferiority complex," Beth said boldly one morning at breakfast. "Maybe that's the wrong term to use, but I sense a distinct undercurrent of snobbery here. There's definitely an attitude."

Lib Redman had just finished inhaling a large quantity of eggs when she asked, "How so? What makes you think that way?"

It was the exact question Beth wanted to hear because it opened the door for her to demonstrate her expertise about the destination. "Well for one thing, Basel is one of the best kept secrets in Europe. I mean how many times have you had friends tell you they were going to Switzerland to visit Basel. Never. They go to Zurich or Geneva, Lucerne or Bern or Interlaken. They ski in St. Moritz or Gstaad or Davos, but nobody makes a beeline for Basel."

"I suppose you're right," Lib mumbled between two more enormous bites, "but so what, and how does that prove your point?"

"It certainly goes to the idea of feeling inferior. Look, this town is quickly becoming one of the cultural hubs of the continent, but Americans pass it by in droves. And that's partly where the attitude comes in, because Baslers know they have something really special here, and they get uppity with pride whenever they get the chance to point it out."

Lib was too busy chomping down on a hard roll to comment further. She was an obese woman who appeared even larger because of her height. At nearly six feet, and well over two hundred pounds, she would have been an imposing figure had she been a man, much less a woman. While Lib concentrated on her grazing at the table, Paula Preston continued the conversation, "You mean Baslers think their cultural traditions go unrecognized by outsiders?"

"Absolutely. There's no question about it. Not by Europeans though. Europeans know about Basel. I'm talking about tourists outside of Europe. For Baslers it's deeper than just their cultural background. It's rooted in their history. It's part of their legacy, their evolution as a city. Yes, I really do think they feel unappreciated, so they have to keep telling themselves they're worthy of recognition.

Helmut Krueger had just walked into the breakfast room as Beth was completing her thought. As the only male member of the group, Helmut often found himself occupying his time alone, especially when conversations turned away from tourism and focused on girl-talk. If the truth were known Beth liked Helmut better than any of her female companions on the trip, so she was glad to see him come in. He'd been around long enough to be comfortable with anyone he was traveling with. He was flexible, and adaptable, and he had a casual ease in his demeanor that was particularly appealing. He was also gentle and compassionate while taking a genuine interest in the opinions of his fellow travelers. "Sounds like a pretty heavy discussion so early in the morning," he said with a big smile as he sat down with the trio of women at the table.

"Beth is giving us some insights into Basel," reported Lib prior to taking a swig of coffee to wash down her bread.

"Seems like a pretty good topic since we're in Basel. You must have been here before to have such strong opinions about the place," said Helmut joining in the dialogue.

"Several times. A few years ago I was involved in an extensive article about Swiss art and culture, and I did a good deal of research about this town, and it's role in Swiss history," Beth answered.

Lib excused herself momentarily to return to the breakfast bar while Helmut poured some milk into his coffee and leaned forward with interest. "And what did you discover?" he asked.

Beth finished spreading some honey on a croissant. She was delighted to offer a brief dissertation about her previous study. "Maybe it's because the research was in such depth that I found it so interesting, but I really believe it's more than that. You see, Basel is a crossroads. It's located on a bend in the Rhine where France, Germany and Switzerland all come together. I don't have to tell any of you how important the Rhine was in the past, or is today, for that matter, and that had a lot to do with what happened here."

"So what did happen?" asked Paula.

Lib returned with another plate of food and rejoined the conversation. "Well Basel was in the center of the transition from the Middle Ages to the Renaissance. The city was greatly influenced by the presence of Erasmus of Rotterdam, who lived here, and who professed a more humanistic approach to the world. To put it simply, the humanist movement was motivated by new concepts in painting, and by advances in printing. It was the advent of movable type that had such a significant impact on the printing of books. Remember that old story about Gutenberg that we studied in high school?"

Helmut nodded his head in agreement. "I suppose that would explain why we're going to the *Paper Mill Museum* later today,"

"Exactly," said Beth.

"But I still don't get it. What does that have to do with the personality of this town?" asked Paula with confusion in her voice.

Lib mumbled something through a mouthful of food, after which Beth answered. "That's a good question. You see Switzerland is one of the most democratic countries in the world. With all this happening around them, some of the great artists of the day made their way to this area. Of course, the art was nothing to compare with what was going on in Italy at the time, but that's another story. What took place here was that the Swiss decided that art should be made available to everyone. Remember, there were a lot of illiterate people in those days, and art was a primary way of communicating through pictures. In fact, many of those paintings often had hidden messages in them. Up until that time, all the really great art collections of the world were either in churches or in the hands of private collectors. Since the average citizen had no means of purchasing art, the Swiss came up with the idea of making art a public enterprise. At the same time, books were becoming more accessible with all the revolutionary changes in the mechanics of printing, and soon the metamorphosis to a more humanistic world was causing powerful changes all over Europe."

"So what was Basel's role in all of this?" asked Helmut.

"That's where the story starts to get interesting. Basel established the first university in Switzerland, and over time, as part of the university, they opened a museum of fine arts which was available to the public. It was the first public art museum in the world. That was the beginning of Basel's love affair with art, and eventually, with all the other cultural pursuits. The *Kunstmuseum* in Basel, which means "fine arts museum", is one of the best in Europe, though it's not nearly as well known as say the *Uffizi* or the *Prado* or the *Louvre*. We'll visit that museum this morning. Believe it or not, it was actually the birthplace of public art as we know it. I guess Basel has more quality museums for a city its size than just about anywhere else in Europe. They also have a world famous art fair here that is over twenty-five years old, and like I said before, they are becoming one of the artistic centers of the continent."

Lib poured another cup of coffee. "That's all well and good, but that should make them feel superior rather than inferior, shouldn't it?"

"Not really, and I'll tell you why," Beth answered. "People don't come to Switzerland for art. They go to Italy or France for that. They come here for scenery, chocolate, cheese, yodeling and quaint villages. So Basel sometimes feels misunderstood. Among their Swiss counterparts they have a tendency to look down upon the commercial aspects of tourism because they like to think they're above all that."

"That's understandable, I suppose," replied Paula.

"It is," said Beth, "But in my mind, I think maybe they've taken the process just a little too far."

"What do you mean?" Lib asked between bites.

"I think in some ways they've gotten to the point where they are afraid to admit that something might be of poor quality for fear that fifty years from now some so-called expert will decide that a certain volume of work, or a particular artist is nothing short of genius. For example, just imagine how they would feel today if they had rejected Picasso's early work. Can you see how a city that prides itself on its artistic legacy would be humiliated if it had failed to perceive Picasso's work as genius? In other words, they have become somewhat elitist, and in many ways apprehensive to state that something might be a sham or nothing more than artistic junk out of a deeply seeded fear that some obscure piece might one day be recognized as a masterpiece. You'll get a better idea of what I'm saying when we go to the *Contemporary Art Museum*."

"Well you've certainly given us something to think about before we begin," said Helmut. He was impressed by what he had learned from Beth in such a short period of time.

"The hotel provides us with food for the body, and you give us food for thought," commented Lib as she buttered another hard roll.

Beth still had something more to say. "If you don't believe what I'm saying, just look at the hotel we're staying in right now. It's an art hotel. What could be more telling than that?"

Beth was right. The group was staying at *Der Teufelhof Basel*, which means "Devil's House" when translated into English. Located amid the

back streets of downtown Basel, the purpose of the *Teufelhof* is to capital-
ize upon the rich cultural heritage of the city and to reinforce that attitude
by allowing patrons to experience art within the private space of their
individual rooms.

The hotel is the creation of its owners, Monica and Dominque
Thommy-Kneschaurek, who wanted to extend the artistic experience
beyond the theater and museums. It is their belief that food and wine are
as important to a total cultural atmosphere as the performing arts and the
fine arts. To Monica and Dominque culture is a way of life, and high gas-
tronomy is the link that awakens curiosity, and connects the various disciplines of the world of art.

It was impossible for the owners to deny their personal theatrical backgrounds, so they developed the property with two small theaters. The upper
facility features a fixed proscenium stage with seating for 96 people in chairs
purchased from the opera house in Zurich. The smaller lower theater is
designed primarily for dramatic readings and less ambitious productions,
and is intended to be more adaptable as individual performances require.

Monica and Dominque didn't stop there, however. It was also their
concept that art is always changing and that people should be allowed to
move around within that artistic environment for as long as they desired.
Though the hotel features only eight rooms, each is different, and each is
the interpretation of a different artist. The artists were commissioned by
the owners with only a limited set of guidelines for their work. Each artist
received a payment of 5,000 Swiss francs. They were given one month to
complete their projects with the freedom to design the room in whatever
fashion they desired with one stipulation; the bed must remain on the
floor. It was understood that the rooms would be changed every three
years, and that a new collection of artists would be commissioned to
design the renovated chambers so that there would always be new and different environments for patrons to experience.

Naturally Beth and her companions had already spent the better part of
an hour making their way from room to room to compare and contrast

the various offerings of the artists. Artists from all over the world had contacted the proprietors about a commission, but this edition of the hotel featured rooms designed by four Swiss, two Germans, an Austrian and an Australian. As might be expected, all the work was contemporary in design, and naturally, depending upon a client's taste, some rooms were more popular than others.

Beth had two favorites. The first featured a series of irregular white cutouts that seemed to hover in the air. It was a mobile of sorts but less mechanical looking than a mobile. It evoked a floating sensation that had a serenity about it that was difficult to describe, other than it had a subliminal quality that added a relaxing ambience to the room.

Beth's second choice was a room that had a series of old open suitcases climbing the walls and spreading across the ceiling. It wasn't the most artistic of the rooms by any means, but to Beth it showed great imagination, and it appealed to her wanderlust sensitivities.

There was one final aspect to the overall concept of *Der Teufelhof.* From the outset Monica and Dominique determined that they would offer all the amenities of a five-star property, while doing everything possible to keep the costs at a three-star level. In this manner, they would provide a unique artistic, cultural, gastronomic and accommodation experience at a price that is compatible for virtually any budget. Of course, with only eight rooms, availability is often at a premium, but the owners had already begun an addition to the property to create 24 new rooms in what would become the *Gallery Hotel.*

Beth looked at her watch. It was 8:15. Before leaving on the tour of Basel's museums she wanted to check with the reservation desk about the possibility of changing rooms. Her shower wasn't draining properly, and with the afternoon free, Beth figured she could make the switch then. Lib had already departed with a sweet roll in hand, while Helmut and Paula finished their last sips of coffee. Beth excused herself with a smile and said, "I'll see you in the lobby in about fifteen minutes."

By 8:25 everyone was assembled near the reception desk awaiting the arrival of the guide. Beth was already there, having made arrangements to move later in the day. As she glanced over at her female traveling mates, she came to a realization that had been bothering her since the trip began, but only now had come into focus. It was an odd sort of uneasiness that had been troubling her. Something she couldn't quite put her finger on. Now as she watched Lib, Paula and Marion Schwartz gabbing away in the center of the room, it became rather obvious. They all had the same "orangey" color of hair and virtually the same hairstyle. Except for the marked difference in their sizes, the three woman could have been triplets. For a moment Beth felt as though she was reliving a scene from the Sherlock Holmes story *The Red Headed League.*

Beth felt guilty for being so critical, but it really was an annoying color. A kind of peach-orange tint, or was it more like carotene or pumpkin? Whatever it was, when combined with the frizzy hairdos, they made Beth feel like she was at a "Ronald McDonald" convention. Of course, Beth had reddish hair too, though considerably deeper and richer in tone, not to mention being relatively straight and shoulder length. Looking at the three "Bozo's" almost made her want to change her own color to blonde or brunette, or something other than auburn. Maybe that was another reason she had become so fond of Helmut, because he was bald with fringes of gray around the sides and the back of his head.

In typical Swiss fashion the guide arrived promptly at 8:30. Beth sized her up quickly. She was a stern, humorless woman. Though dignified in her dress and poised in her manner, it took mere seconds for Beth to figure out that she was the personification of the uptight Basel attitude they had been discussing at breakfast. She was pleasant enough, but efficient and businesslike with little charm, absolutely no personality and definitely devoid of any charisma.

"Good morning to you all. My name is Beatrice. I'll be your guide for the tour, which I know you will enjoy. We have a great artistic heritage here in Basel, and I will explain as much as I can during our excursion. Of course there is just too much to see and to learn in a few hours, so it will not be possible to teach you everything, but I'll do my best. Do you have any questions before we go?"

Everyone looked at each other without comment. When Beatrice was certain no one had anything to say she motioned to the door, "Good, then we go. I think perhaps it is better to walk. The first stop is not so far and with so much traffic we can get there much more quickly on foot. Is this OK with everyone?"

Like many European towns, the system of one-way streets and traffic patterns in Basel often made it time consuming to go by public transportation or by taxi. There were usually short cuts that frequently made traveling on foot much more convenient. Still, Lib was not in what could be described as an Olympian state of physical condition, so while it was generally agreed that walking was the way to proceed, it was also clear that a trek of any length would quickly produce at least one defector.

Ask anyone in a small town in Europe how far it is to walk from point A to point B and they will almost always reply, "Oh ten minutes, I think. Not more." The walk to the *Kunstmuseum* was precisely that, ten minutes. By Lib's standards however, it might as well have been a twenty-mile forced march. Upon arriving at the courtyard leading to the entrance, which featured a magnificent sculpture by Rodin, Lib was gasping and wheezing for air, claiming that if there were any steps inside the museum she would simply have to forego that portion of the tour. There was little empathy at Lib's plight from anyone in the group, and Helmut even went so far as to say, "Look why don't you just get yourself a candy bar and wait for us in the coffee shop." That comment produced an indignant glare from Lib amid an undercurrent of snickering from the others.

There was no question that Beatrice knew her subject thoroughly, and that she had a passion for art and the role it had played in her city. She provided commentaries on Hans Holbein, the elder and the younger. There was an introduction into the work of Ferdinand Hodler, and special pride when she discussed native son, Paul Klee. She was informed about the mechanical sculptures of Jean Tinguely and the emaciated looking statues of Alberto Giacometti. She spoke of the unique brush strokes of Giovanni Segantini, and she was also well versed in the contemporary works of Joseph Beuys, Jasper Johns and Markus Raetz. There was reverence in her voice when Beatrice lectured about Marc Chagall, before bringing her tour to a conclusion by offering almost loving descriptions of several great masters including Van Gogh, Renoir, Monet and Matisse. All of which led the tiny group of writers to her final mini-seminar in the Picasso room.

Whatever Beth felt about Beatrice personally, she conceded back to her out of respect for the guide's insights concerning the world of art. Beatrice had an abiding love for every aspect of the creative process, and her passion did indeed make the information all the more poignant. Beth had always admired anyone who was the best at what they did, regardless of the endeavor, and this person was certainly the best in her chosen field. Even if she was a pill.

Beatrice brushed a wisp of her black hair away from her left eye, and then swelled with pride as she began to relate her story. "I have ended our visit in this room for a special reason, because there is a wonderful story which I must explain to you. It is about Mr. Pablo Picasso and our city. If you look on the far wall you will see two paintings. One is a harlequin and the other is a scene depicting two young brothers. These paintings were on exhibition here at the museum of fine arts many years ago, but at that time, they were only on loan from the artist himself. When the exhibition closed, they were supposed to be shipped to another museum for display. As I have explained to you, and as you have seen, Basel has a rich tradition in the world of art. The city did not wish to give up these treasures as we felt they were quite important to our artistic heritage. So the citizens of Basel took a vote, as we do with nearly everything here in Switzerland. The people of the city were asked if they would like to purchase these paintings so that we might be able to keep them in our museum forever."

"You mean the city of Basel actually voted to buy paintings for its museum? Isn't that unusual?" asked Lib.

"Most unusual. In fact, it was the first time in history that there was ever held a public referendum for the purchase of art. If you remember when we arrived here, I explained that our *Kunstmuseum of Basel* is the result of what was the first public art museum in the world. So is it not also reasonable that we should be the first city to purchase art for our facility by means of a democratic vote?"

"That's a wonderful story," said Marion.

"Yes, but it is only a part of the story," added Beatrice. "You see, Picasso heard of our desire to own his paintings for ourselves. Naturally, being in the world of art himself, he was very familiar with the reputation of our museum."

"Naturally," muttered Helmut sarcastically under his breath.

"So what did he do? Well I must say that Picasso was very touched by our efforts to save his works for Basel, and to keep them as our own. So he contacted our burgermeister, the mayor, and explained to him that he would donate yet a third painting of our choosing to the city in honor of our dedication and commitment to art."

"Whew," exclaimed Paula, "It must have been thrilling to have made such an impression on Picasso himself."

"Oh indeed it was. It was very exciting I must say, but please, let me finish. The mayor was not so knowledgeable of art as was his wife, so he allowed her to do the research in selecting the proper painting for the museum. Ahhh, but sadly she ran into a dilemma. The problem was that she could not decide which painting to choose between two of the canvases. She thought about it for a very long time, and finally she asked Picasso, since she could not make up her mind, if perhaps we could have both. Again Picasso's ego was inflated, and unbelievably he agreed. Suddenly, Basel was now blessed with four of the great artist's paintings."

"A hundred percent increase. Not bad," Helmut said.

"At the dedication ceremonies everyone gathered, including Picasso himself, who came personally to Basel for the occasion. All us were waiting eagerly for the unveiling of the new paintings that would soon be added to our collection. When the speeches were over, Picasso stepped to the microphone, and with tears in his eyes, he was quite emotional you know, he made a donation of two additional works as a personal tribute to our city. And so, as you can see in this presentation, Basel now has six wonderful paintings by Picasso on permanent exhibition."

Beth had to admit that it was a good story. She also knew it would be included in every article this bunch wrote because it went to the heart of what Basel stood for, and because everybody in the world had heard of Picasso.

The next stop was a tour of the *Paper Mill Museum*, which was located along the banks of the Rhine in a well-preserved historic district. Paula and Marion tried their hand at making paper, after which Beatrice went into an overly detailed filibuster about the significance of movable type on printing and the production of books. While it was easy to admire the guide's dedication, attention spans were beginning to wane. A little bit of Basel's city pride went a long way. After all, it wasn't as if they were in Florence or Venice. By now everyone agreed that Basel had more to offer than was visible at first glance, but the five writers were approaching information overload with yet another venue on their agenda.

It was at the *Contemporary Museum of Art* that Beatrice lost her audience, as well as some of her credibility. Her group of journalists had been pushed to the intellectual limits of their willingness to comprehend further philosophical elaboration about various schools of art. They were at a breaking point, and a contemporary exhibition was not a good place to challenge the sensibilities of five artistic novices. In addition, upon entering the facility, the first installation on view was not only graphic, it was pornographic.

The museum itself is located next door to the Paper Mill offering a nice contrast between the historic and modern points of view. Before taking the tour of the contemporary exhibit, Beatrice mustered her forces in the lobby to offer a brief background lecture about the museum and some of the artists on exhibition. But her choice of location could not have been worse. The sculpture behind her was a total distraction for every member of the group, thereby nullifying any comments she made.

The controversial artist in question was a sculptor whose chosen source of expression was neon. There were six of his works on display in the gallery, but it was the one immediately behind the reception desk that became the focal point. The sculpture featured a standing nude male figure outlined in glowing blue neon. At his feet sitting between his legs was a bright red neon woman who was also unclothed. The sculpture was designed in a series of sequential animations graphically portraying sexual interaction between the two figures. During stage one the red woman remained seated facing her masculine companion as his flaccid penis rose to a fully erect position. After achieving ultimate neon stiffness, the woman then moved forward to perform oral sex on her counterpart's member. The animation alone would have been distraction enough, but the concept itself gave it even greater impact.

At first everyone gazed at the colorful gaseous contraption in stunned disbelief which then quickly yielded to covert laughter. "Just a modern version of a blue plate special if you ask me," said Helmut thinking out loud, not realizing that anyone had heard him. The remark produced even higher squeals of suppressed merriment as each member of the group strained to force back their mirth and to retain their composure in deference to their guide's sincerity about contemporary art.

The neon display wasn't finished, however. Upon completion of her assigned duties, the red woman then laid down on her back while the man's penis returned to its previously limp starting position. That's when woman raised her legs to allow the neon man to move into a semi-prone position before electronically diving face forward into her crotch to perform oral sex upon her. It brought to mind the flickering of a neon sign in front of some dilapidated hotel where a couple of letters sporadically blink off and on because of a short circuit. In this case however, instead of the neon flashing, "HOTEL, OTE, HOTEL, OTE", the sculpture screamed, "Fellatio! Cunninglingus! Fellatio! Cunninglingus!" Needless to say, no one heard a single word that Beatrice said.

Though the remainder of the tour was far less exotic, it was no less controversial. Between Helmut's sarcasm and Lib's frankness there were several heated discussions regarding the boldness of some artists to insult their viewers by trying to make them believe that some sort of statement was being made. Beatrice stood her ground, but it was a losing battle. She was simply outnumbered. Before the session was over it was obvious that both sides considered the other to have an ignorant, unenlightened point of view.

Several installations had triggered debate. After a long morning of detailed lecturing, each successive encounter became proportionally more intense, fueled by the fact that everyone was getting tired and hungry.

The exhibit that ignited the initial negative response was in a large white square room, which featured eight so-called sculptures. Like the neon exhibit, the space appeared to be larger than necessary for displaying the work. The artist's medium was iron rods placed in various positions along the walls and the floor. As far as anyone could tell they were not connected in any way. Rather, they were strategically placed to form whatever message the artist was trying to convey. When Lib saw a single iron rod leaning against a wall at a 45-degree angle with another rod of similar length extending along the floor from the tip of the leaning rod, she went ballistic. "What kind of crap is this?" she demanded in an angry tone. "Are you really trying to tell us this person is a serious artist?"

Beatrice didn't hesitate with an explanation. Plausible as it may have sounded, it was still not enough to convince any of the writers. Beth nudged Helmut, "See what I mean? These people cannot acknowledge that this stuff might be worthless because somebody said it was good, and they're afraid to admit that they might not know something about art."

"I don't care what you say, I call this stuff garbage," ranted Lib.

"Ahhh, but you see it arouses your anger. It makes you react. That's exactly what the artist wants you to do. He wants you to react. He doesn't care if you like it or if you don't like it. The main thing is that you respond. Don't you see?" asked Beatrice.

"I sure do," said Lib fuming that she was being duped. "I see that this is a lot of hooey. Have you ever played 'Kick the Wicket'? Why don't I show you how far I can boot that rod across the room? Maybe it'll make a hole in the wall, and we can call that art too!"

Another room featured an artist who was working with felt. One sculpture displayed three sticks protruding under several felt pads, which were piled on top of the sticks. At the point where the sticks extended from under the pad, the artist had created a small lump in the first mat. With each successive piece of felt the lump became increasingly larger until it was incrementally huge at the top layer.

Beatrice explained that the artist was a university professor in Germany who had become well respected for his philosophical concepts as well as his innovative ideas using felt as his medium. Unlike Lib, Helmut was less boisterous when he spoke. "Wouldn't you say that perhaps this man has convinced someone that he is doing something worthwhile, and by virtue of the fact that you believe he has something to say, he therefore creates controversy. It seems that controversy by its very nature draws attention to itself. It stirs awareness which magnifies its significance and which may well be unjustified. This looks like a big hoax to me," said Helmut firmly.

"But do you not see his message? Do you not see the increasing size in the layers of the bump? It is like a cancer. It begins small and then it grows mathematically until it becomes impossible to control," replied Beatrice.

"I'll tell you exactly what I see," answered Helmut. "I see three sticks under eight pieces of felt. That's what I see."

The coup de grace came in the final room where an immense circle comprised of nothing more than bits of charred wood took up approximately 2/3rds of the floor space. Beatrice was not long into her explanation before she was once again interrupted. "You see the artist sent this installation in more than 50 boxes along with a detailed drawing of the exact position of each piece of wood."

"Wait a minute, wait a minute," screamed Lib, "You mean to tell us that all the artist did was to send you a drawing of what this thing is supposed to look like and then you put it on the floor according to his specifications?"

"That is correct. Many artists do so. This is not new."

"But this is just a bunch of burnt sticks in a circle. It's a jigsaw puzzle. Nothing more. How can someone make a circle out of burned up wood and call it art? I'm sorry, I don't buy it. This tour is over for me."

With that Lib left the room. Beatrice continued her attempts at clarification, but what little enthusiasm that had remained was now completely gone. An air of uneasiness pervaded the room. It had been a tedious morning. For the most part it had been significantly rewarding, and after a few days of reflection, when much of the background information was either discarded or absorbed, Beth was certain that everyone would feel it had been a tremendously useful outing and learning experience. Unfortunately, in her enthusiasm, Beatrice had simply pushed her audience to the limit without knowing when to quit.

Lunch was served in a tiny restaurant beside the *Paper Mill Museum*. Beatrice escorted her group into the dining area and thanked everyone for their attentiveness. "I must tell you how much I appreciate your coming to our city. I hope I have shown you something of the wonderful things we have here in Basel. Perhaps you cannot understand it all as we who live here do, but I hope you now have a better feeling about the cultural history of our town."

Even after the humbling events of the previous few minutes, Beatrice could not bring herself to concede the idea that perhaps her dedication to the subject matter may have made her personality not only tedious, but overbearing as well. The writers thanked her for her efficiency and congratulated her on the depth of her knowledge. Though the excursion through the *Contemporary Museum* had been intense at times, it was understood that the disagreements were not personal, but stemmed from varying points of view about artistic interpretations.

Beatrice said goodbye, then walked out of the restaurant to the tree-lined riverbank promenade and headed toward the cathedral in the center of town. The remainder of the day was free for the writers to indulge in personal exploration or shopping in Basel, but for the next hour they settled down to a welcome respite and a light lunch before embarking on their own.

After lunch Beth went immediately back to the hotel to undertake the task of changing rooms. She wanted to do it right away in order to take full advantage of the afternoon at leisure.

The new room appeared to be one of the least creative of the artistic series. The walls were slate gray with matching sheets and pillowcases. In fact, the entire room was done in shades of gray, except for a continuous design of yellowish-green tape that stretched in odd patterns along the walls, up to, and across the ceiling. As near as Beth could tell, there was nothing especially unique about the design. To her untrained eye it seemed that the whole idea could have been executed in a single day, much less a month. To her way of thinking the artist, who was from Zurich, had taken full advantage of the commission, with the added benefit of having the least distance to travel.

Because the itinerary called for an evening at the theater, dinner was scheduled for 6 o'clock. The group was met at an intimate downtown restaurant by the head of the local tourist office, Greta Schellenburg. Though Greta was infinitely more ebullient than Beatrice, there was still a stern Germanic edge to her personality that occasionally surfaced during the evening. She was extremely outgoing, personable and friendly, though it wasn't long before the now recognizable Basel attitude crept into the conversation.

"I am sorry that we must dine so early this evening, but otherwise we could not get you to the theater in time for the performance. It is just a short walk away. Five minutes perhaps. It was very difficult for us to obtain the tickets for this program. Even with our contacts at the tourist office we had difficulty, so I hope you will enjoy it. You must enjoy all of the cultural activities while you are here, I think. Yes?"

"What are we seeing tonight?" asked Marion.

"The program is called *Carmina Burana*. It has been most popular. Tomorrow night is the final performance, so you are very fortunate to see it, I think."

"Can you tell something about it?" inquired Paula.

"Well I must say that I have not seen it myself because the tickets are so difficult to obtain, but I can tell you a little bit perhaps," said Greta.

Lib prided herself on her intellect, believing in her own mind that she was a prime candidate for the Mensa Society. There was music in her background however, so she felt compelled to speak up before Greta could complete her response. "It's a collage of several of the performing arts," Lib explained. "It's a ballet with a full symphony orchestra and a chorus, written by Carl Orff. In fact, you probably don't realize it now, but you'll recognize some of the music once the program starts. It's a stunning production. I've never seen it, but I've heard that it's simply magnificent."

Greta continued the thought. "It is quite pagan. That's always appealing, no? The story takes place in a monastery during the Middle Ages. It is very powerful. Quite dramatic, I think."

"Sounds exciting," said Paula.

"Yes, but now we must eat. We cannot allow you to miss the curtain," answered Greta with apprehension in her voice.

Mealtime in Europe is normally relaxing. People do no rush through a dining experience in order to get on with the next activity as is so typical in the States. That presented a problem for Greta. She could have planned the dinner for 5:30, but she assumed that would be too early. By making the reservation for six, it put her in the uncomfortable position of trying to maintain the calm atmosphere of an elegant dinner while keeping a watchful eye on the clock to ensure that her group of writers did not miss the concert.

Despite the time constraints dinner was pleasant, highlighted by an ongoing discussion of the events of the morning outing with Beatrice. By now, tempers had cooled and the conversation was significantly more genteel than earlier in the day. By 7:45 everyone had nearly finished dessert and was waiting for coffee and after-dinner drinks. Greta was beginning to get edgy. She could tell just by looking at Lib that this was not going to be an easy group to move rapidly.

After a couple more minutes Greta was forced to speak, "Please, I do not wish to rush you, but I think we must leave now so that you are not late for the theater."

Everyone wolfed down the remains of their meal in a less than casual manner and followed Greta out into the night.

"We will walk. It is much faster that way. The theater is just two blocks," she said with urgency.

It was five minutes until the curtain. Halfway to the theater a steady rain began to fall. Not a downpour, but neither was it a sprinkle. It was just soaking enough to force everyone to run the final block in order to protect their clothing and hairdos. Upon arrival at the theater, the mood became chaotic as Greta led the writers into the lobby. People were still in the process of filing into the auditorium, so the primary fear of missing the curtain was now nullified.

Greta reached into her purse and extracted five tickets for the performance. "Your seats are not together. It was not possible because of the sellout. I hope you don't mind if you are sitting alone," she explained as she randomly passed out the tickets to each member of the party.

"Now you must go in. Please. I will meet you here in the lobby after the performance is concluded."

There was no time to look around because everything had been so hectic during the past ten minutes. Rushed or not, in the process of moving through the theater, Beth realized that it didn't resemble a theatrical lobby at all. Far from it. It actually looked like an airport ticketing facility complete with electronic departure boards, computerized reservations counters, ticketing windows and information booths. Because of the last minute dash, there was little opportunity for Beth to orient herself, but she knew Switzerland well enough to understand that there had to be a logical reason for this odd combination of venues.

The luck of the draw placed Beth and Helmut beside each other for the concert, while the others were scattered throughout the auditorium. There was time enough before the overture for Beth to ask Helmut if he had noticed the unusual configuration of the theater lobby, which doubled as an airline terminal.

"You know I saw that," said Helmut. "Leave it to the Swiss to come up with a clever idea like that to maximize the use of the space. I suppose it saves people from having to go all the way to the airport. They can just take care of all their airline needs right here in the city, and they can make arrangements for theater tickets too."

"They really are efficient aren't they?"

Suddenly Helmut had an idea. "You know this is perfect for me. I have to reschedule my return plane ticket anyway, and I was wondering when I'd have the chance. I can do it during intermission! This is wonderful!"

The house lights dimmed and the orchestra began to play the overture. For the next hour and a quarter the audience sat spellbound by the combination of symphony, chorale music and dance. Beth had no preconceived notion of what to expect, but *Carmina Burana* proved to be a spectacular evening of theater. Though she hated to admit it, Lib was absolutely correct, some of the music was very familiar, which made it all the more inviting to listen to. When the curtain came down for the interval, electricity permeated the audience.

"Did you like it, Helmut?" asked Beth.

"Fantastic. Just fantastic. I don't know much about this kind of thing, but I know what I like, and I liked this very much."

"Should we go to the lobby? I need to use the restroom. Then we can meet the others, and you can take care of your plane ticket."

"Good idea," Helmut answered. "It really will be nice to have that out of the way."

The lobby was elbow to elbow with people buzzing about *Carmina Burana*. Helmut worked his way over to the ticket counter while Beth made her way upstairs to the powder room. "I'll wait for you right there at the counter," said Helmut before Beth left.

"Sounds good. I'll be right back."

In the process of making a serpentine path through the room, Beth had a chance to get a better perspective of the combination lobby/airline terminal. She climbed the stairs and found the ladies room in the far corner of the upper level.

It wasn't until Beth came out of the restroom and surveyed the lobby from above that she came to a startling conclusion. Beth looked for the three "clown-women" but couldn't locate any of them in the amoeba-like mass of humanity down below.

When Beth reached Helmut at the ticket counter, the intermission was nearly over. It was time to return to their seats. Beth plowed her way through the myriad of people who were re-entering the auditorium. Finally she reached Helmut. Grabbing him by the arm she said, "Helmut, the curtain is getting ready to go up for the second act. We need to get back to our seats."

Helmut was flustered. "But, but, I didn't get anything done. Nobody would wait on me. The Swiss aren't usually like that. They're always so efficient. Do you think they're closed?"

Beth guided Helmut away from the congestion of the lobby into the theater. When they finally reached their seats Beth looked at him and said, "I've got something to tell you. You're not going to believe this, but the lobby isn't an airline terminal at all."

"It isn't?" questioned Helmut. "But it looks like one.

"I know it does, but guess what? It's an art exhibit! The whole thing is a phony. It's a mock-up. Fake!"

Helmut was shocked. His head turned abruptly toward Beth in stunned disbelief. "No! I don't believe you!" he exclaimed. "You're kidding. I saw it. It's real. Everything works. You can't be serious."

After witnessing Helmut's reaction Beth could no longer contain herself. The expression on his face when he heard her explanation was priceless. Beth roared with laughter so loud that everyone in the vicinity took notice. Even the other writers heard the outburst above the din of conversation preceding the curtain. Beth stood up and looked around for Marion, Lib and Paula. When she caught their eyes she pointed at Helmut all the while convulsing in hysterical glee. Now Helmut was laughing too. Reality had set in. He was still amazed that he had been so easily fooled, but the humor of what he had done was undeniable. The other women were too far away to understand Beth's hand gestures, having no choice but to take their seats in a state of bewilderment. In the meantime, Beth and Helmut had regained most of their composure by the time the symphony began to play the music for the opening of the second act.

The second half of the program was as electrifying as the first. The conclusion produced a standing ovation and numerous curtain calls before the overflow crowd filed out into the darkness of the Basel night. Greta was waiting for her band of writers at the door eager to hear their reaction to the program. One by one each journalist filtered through the crowd until at last everyone had reconvened.

"So did you like it? Was it worthwhile?" asked Greta.

The vote was unanimous. Everyone had nothing but accolades for the strength, power and dynamics of every aspect of the show.

"Maybe the run through the rain was not so bad after all," smiled Greta.

"Well at the time it was pretty severe, but it was worth it. I'd run twenty blocks to see that again," said Lib enthusiastically.

"Don't exaggerate now," Marion said. Then she turned to Beth with curiosity in her eyes and said, "I've got a question. Just what were you and Helmut so tickled about during the intermission?"

Beth detailed the story of Helmut trying to exchange his plane ticket with frequent interruptions by outbursts of spontaneous laughter as she told the tale. "It was just hilarious. You should have seen the expression on Helmut's face when I told him that this lobby isn't an airline terminal at all. It's an art exhibit!"

"You mean this really isn't a terminal?" asked Paula with surprise.

"This is all a fake?" questioned Marion.

Lib's mouth dropped. "You're kidding," she gasped in disbelief.

For the first time since they had arrived everyone took a long look around the lobby giving it a thorough inspection. Beth was right. It was indeed nothing more than an artistic exhibition.

Now everyone was laughing. Beth's sides were beginning to hurt from the prolonged hilarity. She was certain that only she and Helmut had been fooled by the terminal display, surmising that the others had probably figured it out just as she did during the intermission. When Beth and Helmut saw the responses of their three traveling companions they knew that everyone had been hoodwinked by the clever installation.

Even Greta was laughing uncontrollably at the mistaken interpretation of the room. Each person in their own way was now reflecting upon the activities of the day, especially the scenes at the *Contemporary Museum*, which had been so contentious. And now, in the end, they had all been duped.

The stroll back to the hotel was filled with constant laughter and comments about all that had occurred during the day. There was no rush now. There was no place anyone had to be, and in that relaxed atmosphere, everyone continued to be amused by their glaring naivete about art.

Beth was still giggling to herself when she entered her room. After wiping away a few remaining tears from the prolonged jubilation of the walk back to the hotel, she undressed and climbed into bed. Then she pulled the covers under her chin and turned out the light. Staring into the blackness of her surroundings she saw a glow from the yellow-green pattern on the walls and ceiling. The tape was fluorescent! In the infinite void of the darkness the luminescent shape gave off an eerie sensation of freedom and space. What had seemed to be nothing more than an interesting series of lines and curves by day was transformed at night into the flowing outline of a golden bird in flight. Once again Beth had fallen victim to an artistic illusion.

Beth smiled to herself as she rolled over and fell into a deep, restful sleep. She was content, joyful in the valuable lessons she had learned during her delightful day in Basel. Lessons that reinforced what she already knew, and which dramatically reminded her that one should never be too critical, for art isn't always what it seems.

EPILOGUE

When the well-journeyed author Paul Theroux wrote in *Riding the Iron Rooster* that "travel writing is a minor form of autobiography," Beth Jacobsen had no idea what he meant. Fourteen years later she knew exactly what he was saying. In the beginning Beth had no concept of the adventures that lay before her. Now she often felt frustration at her inability to get to them all. There was no way that she could do it in a single lifetime, or ten. Each of her journeys had, in its own way, served as a catalyst to generate bold new directions for future exploration, yet each had also provided her with a personal unity that frequently brought past and present together.

Travel for Beth had evolved tremendously. It had become a quest far more substantial than merely getting a view of the Eiffel Tower from the window of a motorcoach, or a hearing a lecture about the Parthenon from a guide who could hardly speak English well enough to convey the proper information. Travel was richer and more poignant than that. It was deeper now. More intimate and personal. Travel was all encompassing. Beth didn't always like every place that she went, but throughout her career, never once did she find a destination that had not stimulated her in some way or aroused her curiosity about the world.

After spreading her wings for a few years as a travel journalist, Beth had gradually begun reading the works of other writers. It became her passion to learn of their personal travel philosophies and perspectives of the world she was just beginning to know. One particularly eloquent quote by James Boswell in his biography of Samuel Johnson seemed to summarize it all. "When giving me advice as to my travels, Dr. Johnson did not dwell upon cities, and palaces, and pictures, and shows, and Arcadian scenes. He was of Lord Essex's opinion that "I had rather to go an hundred miles to speak with one wise man, than five miles to see a fair town."

Edith Wharton expressed similar feelings when she observed, "The foreground is the property of the guidebook and of its product, the mechanical sightseer; the background, that of the dawdler, the dreamer and the serious student. Dawdle."

In recent years the musings of others who had romanticized about travel began to infatuate Beth more and more. She remembered a statement by a fellow travel writer, Betty Langley, who once said in the course of conversation one afternoon that "almost every story you read is a travel story, whether it's the news or fiction or biography, it's still a travel story." Beth had never perceived travel in quite that way before, but over time, she came to realize that Betty was correct. After all, wasn't life itself, by definition, a journey?

Travel had truly been a source of discovery for Beth. It was a collage of many things. People. Places. Events. Architecture. Art. History. Cuisine. Literature. Personalities. It was the escape from her daily rituals that added character and knowledge and tolerance and understanding to the person she was at the moment, and the person she would become. And since the journey was never-ending, so too was the perpetual evolution of her soul. Travel had become a process of continual metamorphosis.

Every traveler has his or her own favorite destinations. Ask ten journalists to name the best place in the world to visit and likely you'll get ten different answers. Beth had her favorites too, for a variety of reasons. Experience had taught her to disregard the early philosophy of Doris Blackstone who had said long ago that, "I want to see every place once before I see any place twice." Beth had come to realize that there was joy, as well as comfort, in returning to places again and again, and that joy in no way minimized her quest for new destinations.

As the years progressed, Beth found herself drawn more and more to Europe, especially Switzerland, Italy and Sweden with an honorable mention to England. She didn't know why really, but for some reason Europe spoke to her in ways that other parts of the world didn't. Each of her favorite countries beckoned to her for different reasons. But Beth also knew, only too well, that it was a fragile alliance that could easily change with the shifting of the winds.

There was an odd phenomenon about travel writers that Beth had come to discover as she had matured as a journalist. Those eccentric people who roamed the world, and who periodically came and went through her life, sharing a week or two now and then before vanishing into another brochure, often had unusual gaps in their resumes. For whatever reasons, there was frequently a void here and there, where veteran writers somehow missed even the most basic of destinations. Beth had hers too. She had never been to San Francisco or Hawaii or Hong Kong, for example. Each were traditional stops in a travel writers dossier that had somehow eluded her. She had a good friend who had been to the likes of Jakarta, Dubai and Ephesus but had never been to London. She had met writers who knew nothing of Paris, yet who could write volumes on Argentina and Brazil. Beth's personal aspirations for new destinations included Portugal, Norway, Luxembourg and South Africa among others, yet she had no desire to visit Hawaii. She didn't know why exactly. Hawaii just didn't have the allure of other places that called out to her more.

Quite often it had been people or events that dictated Beth's wanderlust desires. There were even a few traveler's goals which had escaped her, and which could never again be fulfilled. Moments in time that had passed and would never return. Beth regretted that she had not yet been to Hong Kong, but more than that, she was disappointed that she had not seen it before it was returned to the Chinese. The same was true of Berlin. For Beth, Berlin was a perfect example of why Doris Blackstone's philosophy was no longer valid. Though Beth felt that she now knew the city quite well, it saddened her that she had failed to experience its atmosphere when the ugly, menacing wall separated its people.

On the other hand, there had been victories too. She had been fortunate enough to view the *Sistine Chapel* before, during and after its restoration.

She had flown on one of the famed Concordes before the aging fleet was grounded by a horrible accident. She had felt the oppression of Russia and Romania under their Communist regimes, and she had visited the former Yugoslavia before it was ravaged by war. She had toured the new *Globe Theater* in London while it was still under construction, and she was lucky enough to have been in Stockholm one winter for the presentation of the Nobel Prizes. There was a dugout canoe trip on the Orinoco River in Venezuela searching for fresh water dolphins while fishermen stood along the shore catching piranhas in their nets. Another time Beth found herself sitting sidesaddle between the humps of a camel in Lawrence of Arabia's desert, and on another she had toured Petra on horseback. There was also the sublime, such as Tchaikovsky's *Nutcracker Suite* gloriously synchronized with a fabulous fireworks display along the shores of Lake Geneva during the annual *Fete de Geneve*.

And then there were the people. Beth could never forget Hans Erni or Angela Rosengart. Carl Jan Granqvist. Hans Odermatt. Harry Briggs. Or even, the ogre-man.

Travel had broadened her knowledge of art. It had given her insights into the lives of Michelangelo and Picasso that she otherwise would never have known. She had learned something of music and visited the apartment where Mozart once lived in Vienna, which surprisingly functions even today as it did centuries ago. There was the exquisite *Abbey Library* in St. Gallen, Switzerland and there had been whitewater rafting above the Arctic Circle in Sweden.

Like Julie Andrews in the *Sound of Music*, travel had provided Beth with her own list of "favorite things." She had developed a fondness for Sherlock Holmes, hotel balconies and sidewalk cafes. She had discovered the liberation of standing naked to the world on a secluded beach and a luxurious patio high above a city. She had dined on meals of risotto, rosti and maloons and capoons, savored the sinful pleasures of gelato and bananas foster and cherries flambe. There had been trains too, wonderful trains. Panoramic trains. High speed trains. Luxury trains. Overnight trains. Narrow gauge trains. Funiculars. Cogwheels. And rack railroads.

There were also numerous stories Beth had discovered along the way that she longed to one day detail in depth. She wanted to research the exotic tale of Jimmie Angel, who while flying through a canyon in search of hidden gold in the jungles of Venezuela, unsuspectingly discovered the world's highest waterfall. To Beth's way of thinking, the saga of Jimmie Angel was a real-life Indiana Jones adventure just waiting to be told.

She wanted to write about the silk industry of Thailand, which was perfected by an American named Jim Thompson. Thompson was an art collector, and his priceless collection remains to this day on display in his former house that nestles along one of the klongs of Bangkok. During World War II Thompson became involved in espionage activities that eventually led to his mysterious disappearance. To this day no one knows for sure what happened to him, but no less than three theories exist surrounding the strange and sinister riddle of how he vanished. Beth yearned to investigate more about each of those theories.

In addition, Beth had also developed a fascination with the lives of the German brothers Grimm who wrote down so many of the fairy tales that have become familiar to each of us. The brothers were linguists who cleverly disguised political messages in their stories, and Beth wanted to explore their lives on two levels. First, she wanted to study the stories from a child's perspective, and then later retell those same stories from the point of view of an adult.

Those were but a few of the subjects that Beth ached to explore more closely. She knew of at least a dozen more. If only she had the time, and more importantly, the financial resources to do them.

Early in her career Beth had learned of a unique, mythical group that travel writers called "The Century Club." At any given time, there are roughly 230 countries in the world. Wars or natural disasters and the like can alter borders and change names, but generally the number remains somewhere in the range of 230. "The Century Club" represents a particular

landmark for a travel writer when they are able to claim that they have journeyed to 100 countries, or about 40% of the world's destinations. In reality,
the club doesn't exist, but it is a goal to which many writers aspire.
Individual writers have different sets of specifications to qualify for mem-
bership. Some writers believe that the only requirement is to have stepped
on the soil of a particular country for it to count on the list. For Beth, her
official total was now up to 65, but by using the "touchdown rule" she could
have added six or seven more to her list. Beth's personal criteria did not allow
those countries to count however. Her philosophy was that a writer had to
spend at least one night in a country in order to qualify. There are other
nuances to the club as well. For instance, Alaska and Hawaii, though actually part of the United States, are regarded as separate destinations.
Therefore, they are given special consideration in a writer's overall tally.

At the outset, Beth had been able to click off the numbers rather quickly,
but now, as she was growing older and more experienced, it was becoming
increasingly difficult to add to her total. Time was taking its toll, and new
ports of call were becoming more and more challenging to obtain.

Travel had become the greatest single aspect of Beth's life. So much
influence did travel have on her that she even began to understand how
certain times of day affected her attitude. She came to adore the serene,
soothing freshness of a new day. Barbara Grizzuti Harrison described an
Italian dawn as arriving "with theatrical brush strokes," and early morning
for Beth had indeed become a time of renewal. She cherished those precious golden moments when the veil of night lifted to reveal the dewiness
of daybreak. When the world was cleansed with moisture, beckoning
through a scrim of earth-clinging clouds that whispered to the flowers and
trees, gently nourishing them in clear, tiny droplets of life, while caressing
them in a cool misty shroud. That time when a peach-colored sun was but
a formless shape in the sky, innocent and subdued, dispersing its grada-
tions of light across the horizon. When birds were little more than hushed
silhouettes with wings, made all the more distinct by the backlit palette of
a delicate pastel sky. A sky that would swiftly yield to the graceless turmoil

of commerce and enterprise. Morning became that fleeting portion of the day when tranquility prevailed with muffled sounds that introduced a sunrise, all unified into a single uplifting serenade. Daybreak was a symphony for Beth's soul.

On the other hand, late afternoon had always had a death-like sensation for Beth. Cary Grant expressed it best in one of his old movies with the line, "Days die like people die, fighting for every ray of light before giving up to the darkness." Beth didn't know why, but for some reason Grant's description was an accurate summation of her feelings about that time of the day.

Beth Jacobsen sat in front of the computer on her desk trying to write something prolific. She was engrossed in her thoughts. Deep in concentration. She was now just over 50. A decade and a half of travel had been good to her. Todd Harper was a fading memory among her vivid recollections of worldly encounters, which had now become the primary focus of her life. Now and then she thought about Todd, and whether his life had been as fulfilling as hers. Down deep she just knew that it hadn't, and that was satisfying to her for. Sometimes it left Beth wishing that she could spend a few hours with him so that she could see his face when she told him of the things she had seen, the places she had been, the people she had met. She wanted him to know that she had not been defeated by their parting of the ways. Anything but. She had accomplished all that she had wanted to achieve, and more.

Physically Beth hadn't changed that much. Traveling had kept her young, in spirit and in body. Her weight had remained reasonably constant over the years. Maybe she was five pounds heavier. Maybe seven. The auburn hair was a good deal shorter now, trimmed closely at the back of her neck with bangs in the front. It still had the perkiness of youth, highlighting the magnetism of her sparkling personality, but gone forever was the naivete. That had been replaced by an air of confidence and quiet wisdom. The symmetrical contour of her breasts had not yielded to the passage of time. She was

proud of that. True, they were fuller now, but all things considered, they were still well proportioned for her body, and best of all, they had somehow retained much of their firmness. And she still had those killer legs. Even at 51, she could still see men contemplating their source. Once or twice she had even overheard supposedly private discussions about them. The nice thing was that they seemed to appeal to males of all ages, and that, too, kept her feeling youthful.

From one day to the next Beth never knew if her most recent journey would be her last, or if others would follow. She had been blessed with years of blissful globe-trotting, and she had rationalized in her mind that if she never traveled again, she would be thankful for the granted wishes that already filled a treasure chest of memories. She carried them permanently and deeply within her heart. They were memories that could never be taken away. Never. Not for any reason.

Travel was still intoxicating. It was Beth's passion, and she could not escape it. Sometimes she felt guilty for selfishly wanting her explorations to continue forever. As she sat at her desk, she reflected upon another quote by Barbara Grizzuti Harrison. "My unconscious mind reached a deep intuitive understanding of the past (my past), only to see more levels, deeper levels, hidden pasts. It meanders sinuously among artifacts lost and found, unknown but known. It travels many ways to arrive in the same place."

"How true," thought Beth out loud, "How true." She opened the drawer to her desk and began searching through a file folder of quotes for the perfect statement to summarize how she felt at the moment. She was melancholy. The scope of all that she had seen and all she had done was dwarfed by all that she knew existed, and all that remained undiscovered. There was so much to see, so much yet to learn, so much that seemed unattainable that it often left her feeling blue. She realized it was impossible to discover everything, regardless of how often she traveled, but still she wanted to try.

She opened the thick manila folder full of writings that she had been gathering for years. Ironically the most relevant quote was the first one she read. She glanced down and focused upon the words of Daniel Boorstin. "A traveler goes in search of people, of adventure, of experience. A tourist goes for sightseeing. Just like the question is more interesting than a statement, and a road more intriguing than a map, I aspired to be a traveler. Be brave. Go through open gates."

Beth put the folder down on the desk, and prayed for more open gates.

www.ingramcontent.com/pod-product-compliance
Lightning Source LLC
Chambersburg PA
CBHW061334280526
45784CB00001B/9